D1095883

Cq
979.441
Yohalem, Betty
"I remember..."

c.13

EL DORADO COUNTY FREE LIBRARY
345 FAIR LANE
PLACERVILLE, CALIFORNIA 95667

CQ 979.441 Y   SO
"I REMEMBER ... " :   YOHALEM, B
EL DORADO COUNTY CHA C19   MN 1ST

3 1738 00177834 7

"I remember..."

The spirit of endurance and the timelessness of the Mother Lode country is captured in this photograph by John Winning of an old homestead at Indian Diggings. Baked by the hot sun in the summer, buried by snow in the winter, many times under drifts five and six feet deep, lashed by winds and rain, this barn defies the elements that challenged the pioneers of El Dorado County.

"I remember..."

Stories and pictures of El Dorado County pioneer families

Researched and written by Betty Yohalem
Design and graphics by Wm. A. Steward
Photography by John Winning

Published by the El Dorado County Chamber of Commerce

EL DORADO COUNTY FREE LIBRARY
345 FAIR LANE
PLACERVILLE, CALIFORNIA 95667

C9
979.441

Photograph from Cora Myer Collection

For Lanita + Warren
Best Wishes
Betty Yohalem — 1978

This book is dedicated to

the El Dorado County Pioneers and their Families

Copyright © 1977
by the El Dorado County
Chamber of Commerce
Placerville, California

First Edition
All Rights Reserved
Printed in the United States of America
Library of Congress Catalog Card Number 76-14124

c. 13

Publication of this book was made possible by the
El Dorado County Chamber of Commerce and the El Dorado County Board of Supervisors

Foreword

It's been more than 20 years since Betty Yohalem moved to the quiet life of El Dorado County, far away from the excitement of the theatrical world that she knew as Betty Mack, a talented personality who had starred in road companies of such well-known musical comedies as "Irene", "No, No Nanette" and "Little Jessie James". On the Orpheum-Keith circuit she appeared on the same bill with such performers as Bert Lahr, Kitty Doner, Julian Elting, Sandy Lang, Bob Hope, Burns and Allen, and others of that era. Her career progressed from vaudeville and musical comedy to drama and the legitimate theatre. When Francis X. Bushman appeared opposite her in a play titled "Thin Ice" in Chicago, he encouraged her to go to Hollywood.

Her first picture was a western with Harry Carey Sr. made at the Trem Carr Studio in Hollywood. She continued to be cast in westerns, appearing with Hoot Gibson, Tom Tyler, Bob Steel at Columbia Studios. Once established in westerns she found herself typed. She changed agents. Then she began to appear in comedies. She co-starred with Charley Chase in more than 20 comedies at the Hal Roach Studio in Culver City, where she also worked with the "Our Gang" and "Laurel and Hardy" companies.

On May 3, 1941, she married George Yohalem, then a writer and production manager at MGM Studios. She appeared in only three films after her marriage, one with Ann Harding at RKO, one with Paul Muni, and another with Fredric March, both at Warner Brothers. In December of that year came Pearl Harbor and she turned her energy to volunteer work.

During World War II she was a leader in the Women's Ambulance and Defense Corps, served on the Army Control Board in Los Angeles. She directed the sales of more than $3,000,000 in War Bonds in Hollywood, and prevailed upon her friend Sid Grauman to let her convert basement dressing rooms and the orchestra green room into a first aid station in Grauman's Chinese Theater. She organized volunteers to pick the tomato crops when farmers could get no pickers, and spearheaded the Victory Garden idea in Hollywood.

In 1956, the Yohalems moved to El Dorado County to a parcel of land on the Omo Ranch road. In 1957 they opened The Pioneer Book Shop in Placerville. Mrs. Yohalem continued her charitable work in El Dorado County, where she is well known and respected and loved by those who have had the privilege of knowing her.

Betty Yohalem's life itself is full of colorful history and maybe that's why she has taken such a keen interest in compiling the data for this historical book.

Richard W. Stanfield
Sacramento Bee Staff Writer
Placerville, California

7

Preface

This book is the result of an idea of El Dorado County Chamber of Commerce Manager, Jacqueline Branch. She suggested that some of the stories of El Dorado County's pioneer descendants be preserved before the recollections were lost to memory. The Chamber Board and the El Dorado County Board of Supervisors accepted and endorsed the idea and the task fell to Betty Yohalem. Because of Betty's knowledge and background in El Dorado County and the news media the choice proved to be a wise one. The project was launched on July 3, 1974 by Betty, who interviewed second and third generation descendants of pioneer settlers in El Dorado County. The wealth of material presented a challenge to her and to Wm. Steward, who combined Betty's written material with photographs by John Winning into this book.

You will find many quotations because of Betty's desire to relate these stories as they were told to her. These remembrances are the stories of pioneer descendants who heard them either from their parents or their grandparents who pioneered here. These accounts provide embellishment to recorded histories in the form of family tales either directly experienced or handed down. You will find a vividness and immediacy in these interviews.

It is hoped that the impact of this work will be twofold. First, the reader will be able to share these tales with those persons closest to the people who experienced them. And second, that the telling of these tales will stimulate other remembrances that might otherwise be lost for not asking. We have to thank Betty Yohalem for getting us started on this adventure into the past.

Noble Sprunger, County Counsel
EL DORADO COUNTY

Contents

Contents

How safe was it in 1862?

Ruth Caroline Ward Corker, one of many descendants of El Dorado County early day settlers, was born in Georgetown on September 23, 1891. Her mother, Caroline Smith Ward, was also born in Georgetown, in 1867. Her father, Henry Ward, was born in Dayton, Nevada, while Nevada was still a territory. Her grandparents, Jonathan and Mary Ann Smith, crossed the plains by wagon train in 1862, an experience documented in a news story in the *San Francisco Chronicle* on November 1, 1908. It is a story that reveals the courage and daring of the people who settled the West.

The news story carried the headline, "An Unwritten Page of Early Emigrant History". It was written by Grace Birdsall Gates, a *Chronicle* reporter who traveled into the Sierra foothills to interview Mrs. Smith.

Mrs. Corker, when interviewed, was at first reluctant to answer questions about her grandparents. Yes, she knew they had crossed the plains to come to California, but she would rather not talk about it . . . "It was too horrible".

The following is a slightly condensed version of the Grace Gates interview with Mary Ann Smith and probably tells us much that Ruth Corker did not want to talk about.

MARY ANN SMITH was 82 years old when this picture was taken in Georgetown in 1908. That she and others in the Smith wagon train party survived the wounds suffered when attacked by Indians and the hardships of walking nine days on the plains without food or water is a story of courage and faith. Mrs. Smith is the grandmother of Mrs. Ruth Corker, a native of Georgetown now living in Placerville. Pictured with Mrs. Smith are her daughter-in-law and a grandson.

"In 1862 James P. Smith, husband of Mary Ann Smith, formed a company of which he was elected Captain. It was the intention of the party to cross the plains and establish themselves in a new country to which so many of their friends and relatives had safely journeyed, and of whose wonders they wrote continually.

"The danger of attack from Indians was considered practically a thing of the past, and on the 12th day of May, 1862, they left Warren County, Iowa, with Captain Smith in command.

"The train was comprised of several families, mostly relatives of Captain and Mrs. Smith. There were 42 persons in all, 16 small children, five nursing babies, and the remainder men and women.

Note: In the above article, Grace Gates refers to James P. Smith. According to Mrs. Corker and other records, this should be Jonathan P. Smith.

JAMES M. SMITH AT THE AGE OF 19

An Unwritten Page OF EARLY EMIGRANT HISTORY

"THEY FOUND THEM MILES BACK ON THE TRAIL"

By GRACE BIRDSALL GATES.

THAT the spirit of adventure does not lessen with age was forcibly illustrated to me when in a beautiful meadow far up in the Sierra, nestling in a grove of yellow pine and cedar, I came upon the camp of Mary Ann Smith, her daughter-in-law, and little grandson. As we sat in the shade, Mrs. Smith, who is a dear, pleasant-faced old lady now in her eighty-second year, recounted to me the story of her trip to California.

In 1862 James P. Smith, husband of Mary Ann Smith, formed a company of which he was elected captain. It was the intention of the party to cross the plains and establish themselves in the new country to which so many of their friends and relatives had safely journeyed, and of whose wonders they wrote continually. The danger of attack from the Indians was considered practically a thing of the past, and on the 12th day of May, 1862, they left Warren county, Iowa, with Captain Smith in command. Captain Smith's family comprised, besides himself and wife, four children—a girl of 9, a boy of 6, a girl of 3, and a nursing baby eight months old. The train was composed of several families, mostly relatives of Captain and Mrs. Smith, there being forty-two persons in all. Sixteen were small children, five nursing babies, and the remainder men and women. The train was fitted out in the most approved fashion. The families were well-to-do, having droves of cattle and splendid ox teams, with provisions and outfit sufficient for several months. They had started by what was known as the Oregon route, as part of the train were intending to locate in Oregon and the remainder in California. On the way they met some Mormon campers, who informed them that they could not get over the Oregon route. On hearing this, Captain Smith decided to take the cut-off to the California route.

All went well; there had been little sickness in the party, and it was a grand frolic for old and young. In the evenings around the camp fire they built their "castles in the air," picturing in the glowing embers their future homes in the land of promise, the land whose rivers flowed over sands of gold. No Indians had molested them, and all were well and happy. One day, beside the road, they came upon several freshly made mounds; the headboards with the grewsome words, "Killed by Indians," gave mute testimony to the deadly nature of the attack which those preceding them had encountered. On the third day's travel on the cut-off they came upon the wreck of an emigrant train. A fearsome sight for this small train to meet. There were several bodies only partially covered, as though their friends had been forced to seek safety in flight before they could complete the burials. These they gave decent interment, although fearful that each moment might bring a return of the enemy. A short distance away they came upon half burned wagons. The little handful of people was becoming each moment more apprehensive, fearing that the Mormon campers whom they had met, and who had directed them to take this route were decoys: for, as they afterward found, the Oregon route was the regular stage route and was well guarded. Several days passed without further signs of Indians, and confidence was being restored. The children ceased to be fearful of every sound; mothers relaxed their vigilance and let the little ones run about unrestrained; the stern features of the men became more placid; jocose remarks once more passed from lip to lip. How brief was to be their respite from anxiety.

Attacked by Indians.

On the 2?th day of August, very early in the morning, they were attacked by a band of Indians, who shot at the guards who were protecting the stock, stampeded the cattle and succeeded in capturing their outfit and provisions and drove off all their stock with the exception of four head of oxen, which, being fagged out with the journey, were lying down in some willows and were overlooked by the Indians. No one was killed during the early morning skirmish, but several had very narrow escapes—one man having the toe of his boot shot away as he was dressing. One surprising feature of the attack was the apparent wish of the Indians to capture the stock and outfit rather than to kill the members of the party. Thankful to have escaped with their lives, the now thoroughly frightened emigrants waited until the Indians had disappeared in the distance, then Captain Smith ordered the four oxen yoked to one wagon and again they started on their way, traveling until evening, when they stopped beside a stream to rest, intending to travel all night, for they knew there was a train a few days' travel ahead of them, and it was their wish to overtake this party. The cattle were fagged out, and there was little to eat even for the hungry little children, who had pulled off their shoes and stockings and were wading in the shallow stream.

Suddenly the pickets saw the willows on the bank moving, and again they were at the mercy of the Indians. They fled for their lives to the nearest timber, which consisted of a bunch of willows farther up the stream. This they were prevented from reaching by a band of Indians about 100 strong, who, mounted on ponies, surrounded them. Cut off from reaching this retreat, they were forced to seek shelter in the sage brush, which grew waist high. There was no time to get the children's shoes and stockings; mothers with their babes at their breasts sought shelter in the bushes. A fierce battle ensued during which several Indians were killed and wounded. The emigrants had plenty of guns and ammunition, but with such scanty shelter were practically at the mercy of the enemy. Of the unfortunate Smith party four were killed and five wounded, among them Captain Smith, who was seriously injured, being shot through the arm and both legs. Mary Ann Smith, the Captain's wife, was also seriously wounded, being shot through the back as she sat nursing her little baby, the bullet dropping into the bosom of her dress. Another bullet passed through her right hand, crippling it for life. The baby nestling in its mother's arms was uninjured. Their little three-year-old girl was not so fortunate, being shot through the back. The little one lingered for six days, mercifully relieved of suffering by the nature of the wound, which produced paralysis. Of the three Ball brothers two were killed, one being shot over the right eye and one over the left, the wound in both instances being the same distance from the eye. Captain Smith's father and brother were also severely wounded.

The plight of the emigrants was now desperate indeed. Robbed of the four oxen which had been overlooked by the Indians on the previous day, without food, with five members of the party seriously, perhaps fatally wounded, and three dead, the demoralized party took counsel among themselves. Captain Smith now proved to the little band his courage and unselfishness. Although seriously wounded, he directed all to keep as quiet as possible, hoping that the Indians might think the entire party was slain and leave them. Darkness was now coming on. The Indians fired a few desultory shots in the direction of their hiding place, and receiving no answering fire they dashed away in the gathering darkness. Fred Heiman was not killed outright, but told them he was dying and asked them to leave him and save themselves. Under cover of darkness they fled, carrying their wounded with them, without food, conveyances or clothing, other than what they wore.

Captain Smith now ordered the stronger members of the party to go on and if possible overtake the train ahead. If this was impossible they were to try and reach Salt Lake City and procure food and conveyances. Heartless as it seemed for the strong ones to leave behind them this party of helpless humanity, it proved, nevertheless, to have been a wise precaution. Had they been hampered with the injured and the small children and without food they would soon have become exhausted, and the entire party agreed with their captain that if help were to come it must come through the efforts of those strong enough to go for aid. Severely wounded as she was, the captain's wife, with Spartan fortitude, carried her little eight-months-old baby nearly all the time for seven days—days of intense misery—without food, nothing with which to dress their frightful wounds, nothing for the hungry children, who begged for bread. It was often the subject of much speculation how those little ones came so soon to a realizing sense of the futility of asking for food.

CAMP OF MRS MARY ANN SMITH

Goes Back to Die With Mother.

On the sixth day Mrs. Smith's little girl was relieved of suffering. They buried the little one on the plains, digging her grave with a short piece of iron which they picked up on the way. They piled immense rocks in a pyramid to mark her grave. Broken hearted at the loss of her little girl, and suffering untold agony from her wounds, Mrs. Smith gave her baby into the keeping of another, and telling them not to let her husband know that she had dropped out, besought them to go on without her. When he found it out he sent back and they found her seated beside the road with her one little six-year-old boy beside her. Missing his mother from the train, the little fellow had shrewdly surmised that she was too weak to travel farther and without a word to any one he had slipped quietly away and returned to bear her company on the vast and lonely plains. They could trace him for miles by the blood from his poor, lacerated little feet. What wonder that her smile is without malice as she recounts this tale. Dearer than all else in life to her must be the memory of that child's devotion.

For nine days they traveled without food of any kind except the seed of the wild rose which grew in great profusion on the plains. This they broke open and fed to the children. Sometimes they found a few late berries and the root of the fern, which was sweet and palatable. Often they were without water, for they had nothing in which to carry it, and thus they suffered more from thirst than from hunger, especially the injured whose wounds caused intense fever. Added to their misery were the mirages. Clear running water with willows dipping into the stream was constantly before their eyes.

Captain Smith encouraged the disheartened ones with the hope of being overtaken by some emigrant train. This seemed a forlorn hope, as day after day passed and no help came; but the strong ones ahead were rejoicing. On the ninth day they had come upon a train of emigrants with 100 wagons who were also headed for California. When they heard the sad story of the Smith party they camped where they were, while a party was sent back with food and conveyances. They came upon the straggling little group upon the banks of the Bear river. Fortunately for the injured there was a good doctor in this train who dressed their wounds and advised the injured to go to Salt Lake City and remain until they recovered. They, however, gladly welcomed all members of the Smith party who were able to travel to join them. They accepted the hospitality of their new-found friends, and all who were able to travel without being a burden to them went with them to California.

In the meantime word had been sent to Salt Lake City and some men came out with teams to meet them; charging the poor, crippled wayfarers $2 per head to be taken to Salt Lake City. Many of them had no money; they were forced to part with their guns and watches, all that they had left in the world. When they reached Salt Lake City they were forced to pay for all their food and clothing; nothing was donated by the residents.

What was to become of these forlorn people now? Destitute, sick, with only the clothing they wore and in a community obnoxious to them and from whom they could expect no help, unless they accepted the doctrines of their faith, they kept to themselves as much as possible during the five months they were forced to remain there. Those of the party who had money generously shared it with their more unfortunate companions. Mrs. Smith now faced a new and serious problem. Her right hand was entirely useless; her children, as well as herself and husband, were without clothes. The little boy was sent to bed while his uncle volunteered to try and make him a pair of trousers, using the only pair which the child possessed for a pattern. It was a long, tedious task, but at last they were completed. This was the first sewing the uncle had ever attempted. The little boy, with characteristic patience, remained in bed until the trousers were finished.

During the long, hard journey the little hero was never known to complain but once. They had been some time without water and the child had nearly perished with thirst; when it seemed that he must surely die they came to a beautiful brook of clear, cool water; the old grandfather, who was carrying the child, dropped a few sprinkles on his swollen tongue. Worn out with suffering, he rebelled at this seeming injustice. There was a whole brook running to waste and he could have but a few drops.

After remaining in Salt Lake City for five months the party went by stage to Carson, where they remained four months; from Carson they went to Georgetown, El Dorado county, where, with the exception of seven years spent in the neighborhood of Salinas, they have made their home; it having been in Georgetown that Mrs. Smith's brother, Milton Woodside, had located.

Mrs. Smith's daughter, who is now living, will never speak of her experience, saying, when asked to do so: "It is too horrible! I want to forget it."

It is interesting to note that Mrs. Smith is now living with the son who, as a little boy of 6, went back, perhaps to die beside his mother.

Monks Who Live Amid Snow

AMID the dreary, sterile scenery of the Alps, ?00 feet above the level of the sea, all near to the region of eternal snow, ?? year in and year out, a band of devoted men, who spend their youth and strength in the service of those whose business obliges them to traverse the dangerous pass between Italy and Switzerland during the nine-months winter.

They are the monks of the world-famous Great St. Bernard Hospice, which for nearly a thousand years has ministered to the wants of travelers. The provost of the hospice is ? Bourgeois.

"It is, perhaps, a healthy life," he says, "to those of strong constit... And it has its interests, though some might think them narrow. But we are never idle; we always find plenty to do. Seldom a day passes, when the weather is fine, even in the winter, but we have travelers to entertain, and, perhaps, to succor.

"The conditions of our work at the hospice have changed within my own memory. Modern science, which has touched everything, has not left even the great pass undisturbed. For twenty years and more the hospice has been connected with the valley by telephone. So we always know when travelers are setting out, and we are able to meet them with the dogs.

"We have fifteen dogs just now. We train them ourselves, but they do not require much training; they seem to find their way through the snow, however thick it may be, by instinct, and they never fail to discover a traveler whatever depth of snow may cover him.

"The winter is long and very trying at first to those who come to us from the plains. Summer, as we call it, begins in July and ends before September is far advanced. But perhaps you would not call it summer at all, because frequently we have snowstorms in July, though the snow melts, except in the hollows of the pass, where it seems to be always. Sometimes a party of tourists will start from the valley in great heat, the ladies wearing muslin dresses, and when they have climbed to the hospice the snow has been so blinding they could scarcely find their way. Even in the summer we have garments ready for travelers, for one never knows what the weather may be in the pass, though it is smiling summer in the valley.

"From September onward we are surrounded by snow. Around the building there is often seven or eight feet, and the drifts sometimes accumulate to the height of forty feet. And it is very cold, generally below zero, in the early part of the year.

"Many tourists come to us. This year I think we have welcomed about 5000. We do our best to entertain them, and some of the monks play and sing to them.

"Of poor travelers we have perhaps 15,000 in the year. Many of them are workmen crossing the Alps in search of work. They are most numerous in the spring, for in the autumn, when they return to their own country, they have plenty of money and they are able to take the train. We have many beds in the hospice. Eighty travelers would not incommode us, and we could give shelter to three times as many.

"You can imagine that when perhaps 100 are making their way over the pass during the day, as often happens in February and March, we have plenty to do.

"And always," added the provost, "we have the dead with us to remind us of our duty to the living. Those who have perished in attempting the pass are placed in the morgue just as they died until their friends claim their remains. But some are never claimed, and there are perhaps twenty still in the morgue, which is their only tomb."

SAW THE ROYAL ACADEMY.

Recently a little girl was taken to London by her parents. On her return she was describing all the places she had seen to some young friends. One of them, of a somewhat morbid disposition, asked: "Did you see the Old Bailey, where they hang the murderers?"

"No," replied the girl, "I don't think so; but I saw the Royal Academy, where they hang the artists."

The British Admiralty began experimenting with submarine boats in Plymouth harbor in 1771.

"77"

Humphreys' Seventy-Seven breaks up Grip and

COLDS

We do not respond to requests for free samples because a few doses of "Seventy-seven" is apt to break up the most serious Cold, and we think that a quarter of a Dollar is not much of a risk for assured health—for that's what freedom from Colds means in this climate.

All Druggists sell, most Druggists recommend "77."

Humphreys' Homeo. Medicine Co., cor. William and Ann Streets, New York.

CARTER'S LITTLE LIVER PILLS.
Genuine Must Bear Fac-Simile Signature
Brent Good
REFUSE SUBSTITUTES.

SICK HEADACHE

CARTER'S LITTLE LIVER PILLS.
Positively cured by these Little Pills.
They also relieve Distress from Dyspepsia, Indigestion and Too Hearty Eating. A perfect remedy for Dizziness, Nausea, Drowsiness, Bad Taste in the Mouth, Coated Tongue, Pain in the Side, TORPID LIVER. They regulate the Bowels. Purely Vegetable.

SMALL PILL. SMALL DOSE. SMALL PRICE.

CARTER'S LITTLE LIVER PILLS.
Genuine Must Bear Fac-Simile Signature
Brent Good
REFUSE SUBSTITUTES.

Attacked by Indians!

"With Mr. and Mrs. Smith were their four children, Harriett Matilda, age nine, James, six, Mary Josephine, three, and Lora Ellen, a nursing baby eight months old.

"The families were all considered well-to-do, having droves of cattle and many ox teams, with provisions and outfit sufficient for several months.

"They started by what was known as the Oregon Route, as part of the train planned to locate in Oregon. On the way they met some Mormon campers who informed them that they could not get over the Oregon Route.

"On hearing this, Captain Smith had to change his plans and take the cut-off to the California Route.

"All went well, according to Mrs. Smith, then one day they came upon several freshly made mounds with improvised headboards marked 'Killed By Indians'.

"On the third day they came upon the wreck of an emigrant train. There were several bodies only partially covered as though the survivors had been forced to seek safety before they could complete the burials.

"Although fearful that each moment spent at the scene might bring a return of the attackers, members of the Smith train remained to give decent burial to the victims.

"Traveling a short distance farther, they came upon half-burned wagons. At this time the small handful of people became apprehensive, fearing that the Mormon campers they had met, and who had directed them to take this route, were decoys; for as they afterward learned, the Oregon Route was the regular stage route and was well-guarded.

"Several days passed without incident. Then on the 26th day of August, very early in the morning, they were attacked by a band of Indians. They shot at the men guarding the stock, stampeded the cattle and succeeded in capturing their outfit and provisions.

"They drove off all stock with the exception of four oxen. Worn out from the journey, they were lying down in some willows and were overlooked by the Indians.

"No one was killed in the early morning skirmish but several had narrow escapes. It seemed apparent that the Indians wanted only to capture the stock and outfit rather than kill members of the party.

A reproduction of the page from the San Francisco Chronicle of November 1, 1908 that carried the story of the Smith wagon train.

JAMES M. SMITH, son of Jonathan P. and Mary Ann Smith, and his wife Minnie, nee Gilbert. James Smith was six years old when the family migrated to California. He witnessed three Indian attacks on the family while crossing the plains. He saw his three year old sister, Mary Josephine, shot through the back during one attack. She lingered six days before dying and was buried under a large pile of rock.

JONATHAN P. SMITH led 42 people across the plains. An Indian attack on August 26, 1862, left four members of the party dead and five wounded. Captain Smith was shot through one arm and both legs. This picture was taken by Monaco, Excelsior Art Gallery in Stockton, years after the Smiths had settled in Georgetown.

LORA ELLEN SMITH is the baby Mrs. Smith was holding when she was shot in an Indian attack upon the Smith wagon train. She lived to marry George J. Wilton, a miner and farmer in the Georgetown area.

HARRIETT MATILDA SMITH was nine years old, the oldest of the Smith children to survive the ordeal of the 1862 migration to California. She is pictured with her husband Stephen Pendelton.

Photos from Corker Collection

MARY ANN SMITH, the wife of Captain Smith, was the sister of Milton A. Woodside, who was living in Georgetown at the time of the Marshall gold discovery. The story of her courage during the Indian attack on the Smith wagon train was published in 1908, 46 years after the event. She died in Georgetown at the age of 87.

JOHN ADAM SMITH, brother of Captain Smith, and his wife survived the Indian attack and the hardships of the 1862 emigration to California. They settled near Chico. Born May 2, 1800, John Smith died in Chico on July 5, 1889.

"Thankful to have escaped with their lives, the now thoroughly frightened emigrants waited until the Indians disappeared, then Captain Smith ordered the oxen yoked to a remaining wagon. They traveled until evening when they stopped beside a stream to rest, intending to travel all night.

"The children had pulled off their shoes and stockings and were wading in the stream when the Indians attacked the second time. About 100 in number, mounted on ponies, the Indians surrounded them.

"They were cut off from their attempt to reach some willows upstream and were forced to take cover in the sagebrush, which was about waist-high.

"Several Indians were killed and wounded. Of the Smith party, four were killed and five wounded. Captain Smith was seriously injured, shot through the arm and both legs.

"Mrs. Smith was seriously wounded, shot through the back. At the time of the attack she was nursing the infant Lora Ellen. The bullet dropped in the bosom of her dress; another bullet passed through her right hand, crippling her for life. The baby was uninjured.

"Three-year-old Mary Josephine was not so fortunate. She was shot through the back and lingered, completely paralyzed for six days until she died. They buried her on the plains and piled rocks in a pyramid to mark her grave.

"Robbed of the last four oxen, without food and five members of the party suffering severe wounds, the demoralized party took council. Captain Smith ordered the stronger members to go on and if possible overtake a train they knew to be traveling ahead.

"If this was impossible they were to try to reach Salt Lake City and procure food and conveyances. It was agreed that if help were to come it must come through the efforts of the strong.

"Severely wounded as she was, Mrs. Smith carried her baby in her arms nearly all the time for seven days. Broken-hearted at the loss of her young daughter, and suffering from her wounds, she gave the infant to a member of the party and asked them not to tell her husband that she had dropped out.

"When Captain Smith learned what she had done he sent members searching for her. They found her seated beside the road with her six-year-old son James who, missing his mother from the train, had quietly slipped away to find and be with her. They traced him for miles by the blood from his lacerated feet.

John Winning Photo

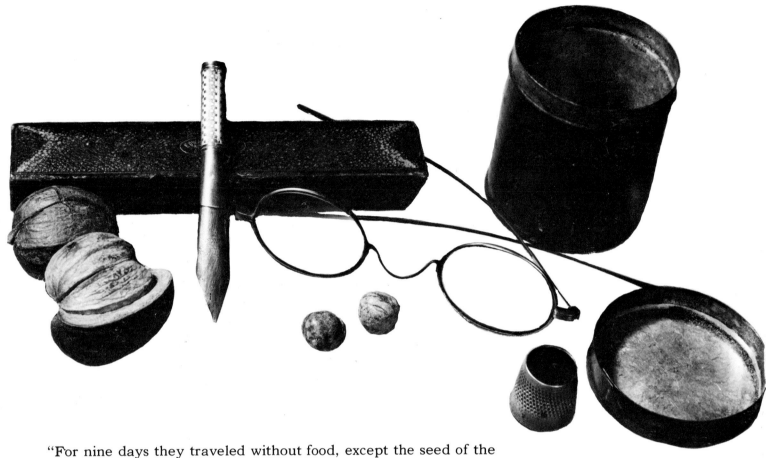

"For nine days they traveled without food, except the seed of the wild roses which grew in great profusion on the plains. These they broke open and fed the children. Sometimes they found a few late berries and the root of the fern, which was sweet and palatable.

"Often they were without water, for they had nothing in which to carry it. They suffered more from thirst than from hunger, especially the injured whose wounds caused intense fever.

"On the ninth day they came upon a train of emigrants with a hundred wagons who were headed for California. When they heard the story of the Smith party they camped where they were and sent a party back with food and conveyances.

"They came upon the straggling group on the banks of the Bear River. Fortunately for the injured, there was a doctor with the train who dressed their wounds and advised the injured to go to Salt Lake City and remain there until they recovered.

"Members of the Smith party who were able to travel were invited to join the train. All who could travel without being a burden went with them to California.

"Word of the wounded travelers reached Salt Lake City, carried by others heading east, and soon some men with a team met the party. They charged them two dollars per head to take them to Salt Lake City.

AMONG MRS. CORKER'S KEEPSAKES are two hickory nuts her grandmother carried in the pocket of her apron when they crossed the plains in 1862, her eyeglasses, her thimble, and two balls from an Indian musket. Her grandmother almost lost her life when one musket ball passed completely through her body, the other one through her arm. The pen was given to Mrs. Corker's husband, Jack Corker, by his father J. Fred Corker, who was Chief Deputy United States Marshall of Utah Territory.

"Mrs. Smith remembered that those who did not have money had to give up their guns and watches. When they reached Salt Lake City they had to pay for the food and clothing they needed so badly. Members of the Smith party who still had some money shared it with their companions. No one in the Utah community contributed or offered to aid the now-dispirited group.

"After remaining in Salt Lake City for five months, the party went by stage to Carson. They remained there for four months and then went on to Georgetown, El Dorado County, where, with the exception of seven years spent in the neighborhood of Salinas, they have made their home; it having been in Georgetown that Mrs. Smith's brother Milton Woodside had settled."

It is interesting to note that when interviewed by Grace Gates of *The Chronicle* in 1908, Mrs. Smith was living with her son James, the boy who left the train to find his mother.

With the exception of the one child, Mary Josephine, who died of her wounds and was buried on the plains, the Smith family started their new life on a farm just out of Georgetown.

In 1867 a daughter, Caroline, was born. On April 2, 1885 she married Henry Herman Ward, a carpenter and blacksmith in the area. Ward was a native of Nevada, having been born in Dayton, Nevada, while it was a territory.

Of this union a daughter was born on September 23, 1891. They named her Ruth Caroline and she attended the Georgetown grammar school.

On December 20, 1911 Ruth Ward married Jack Corker, in her words, ". . . a young engineering chap who came to town in 1910 with the Stone and Webster engineering firm of San Francisco. They were surveying on the Rubicon River, the first surveys that were made up there."

Of her school days Mrs. Corker says, "I don't remember too much . . . I think I remember best the winter days, plowing through the snow the two miles to school."

Teachers at the Georgetown school she remembered to be "Ellen Stanton, one of the original teachers, Suzie Weidman and Margaret Kelley. All grades were taught in the one room and usually numbered around 60 pupils."

As a child, she recalls, "folks" talked about Grandmother's brother, Milton Woodside, living in Georgetown at the time Marshall discovered gold at Coloma. President Ulysses S. Grant often visited her brother-in-law who lived in Georgetown and President Herbert Hoover and his family spent the summers in Georgetown. It was said that he spent most of his time fishing. "I think it is quite important to Georgetown to have had two Presidents visiting up here, and while they were in office," said Mrs. Corker.

The Corkers

RUTH CORKER, granddaughter of Jonathan and Mary Ann Smith, was born in Georgetown, September 23, 1891. She has lived a life of devotion to her family, her community, and El Dorado County.

That El Dorado County developed into a civilized community following the lawlessness that permeated every camp and town during the Gold Rush era must be attributed to the hundreds of families such as the Woodsides, the Smiths, the Wards, and the Corkers.

Ruth and Jack Corker had six children, five girls and one boy. Only two are alive today: Jackie Barrett, who lives in Camino, and Winifred Ward, now living in Las Vegas, Nevada.

Jack Corker died in 1957. But the evidence of his work in El Dorado County is everlasting. One can hardly find a recorded survey of important developments in the county that does not bear his signature.

He surveyed the railroads from Folsom to Pino Grande and the new road at Riverton after the cable burned at Pino Grande. He surveyed for Michigan-California Lumber company for many years. Outstanding pictures of the lumber industry, property of Corker, can be found in Dr. Polkinghorn's book *Pino Grande*.

Corker Street in Placerville was named for Jack, and his name is on the Marshall Hospital Plaque, dedicating the new wing of the hospital in 1975. He was a director at the time the hospital was founded.

The name of Ruth Corker is found over the door of the Senior Citizens Craft Room on Pacific Street.

Mrs. Corker not only raised her family of six, she also devoted 30 years to Scouting. She was the director of the Girl Scout Camp in the county for 20 years. She served six years on the County Fair board of directors, five years on the Recreation Commission, worked for the school lunch program, belonged to the Jeep Herders, the Rod and Gun Club and the Mineral and Gem Society.

Her contribution to the community did not go unnoticed. She was awarded the high honor of the Girl Scouts, "The Scout Statuette"; she was made an honorary member of the Soroptimist International Federation of the Americas, Inc. by the Placerville club, which has granted only two such honors in its 37-year existence. In 1964 she was the first woman in the county to be named "Woman of Achievement".

JACK CORKER surveying on the Rubicon in early 1910.

20

Photos from Corker Collection

THE FARM in Georgetown where the Smith family settled and lived out their life free of fear. Ruth Corker who related the Smith family story was born here.

HULDA was the first child born to the Smiths after they settled in Georgetown. She married Harley McDade of Georgetown.

MR. AND MRS. HENRY WARD
Mrs. Ward was Caroline Smith before her marriage in 1885. Daughter of Jonathan and Mary Ann Smith, she was born after the Smiths settled on a farm in Georgetown.

21

John Winning Pho

MONUMENTS OF WHITE MARBLE stand like sentries overlooking the ghost town of Indian Diggings. Ruins of a few homes, several barns, and long spans of weatherbeaten rail fence are all that remain of a once-thriving mining camp.

22

John Winning Photo

JINKERSON

MOTHER
ELECTA
MAY 30, 1842
DEC. 9, 1908

FATHER
AUGUSTUS H.
APR. 23, 1846
AUG. 15, 1920

Indian Diggings – Ghost Town

How many people lost their lives while attempting to reach the California gold fields and the number of men killed in mining accidents will probably never be known.

Riley Bruner was born in Indian Diggings in 1900. His mother Minnie was the daughter of Electa and Augustus Jinkerson of Indian Diggings.

Indian Diggings, one of the most thriving mining camps in the county during the 1850's and '60's is now a ghost town. A few ruins of homes, a barn or two, long spans of weatherbeaten rail fence . . . and on a hill overlooking it all is the Indian Diggings cemetery.

Monuments of white marble stand like sentries guarding the remains of a chapter in the history of El Dorado county. One grave, that of Thomas J. Holston, touches the life of Riley Bruner and his family.

Thomas Holston was killed at the Little Big Claim mine, a hydraulic mining operation, just two months and 11 days after he married Electa Hardy, who later became Bruner's grandmother. To this day, Riley Bruner refers to Holston as his grandfather, although in reality he was not.

Electa Hardy and Thomas Holston were married June 24, 1862 in ceremonies performed at midnight in the Masonic Lodge hall in Indian Diggings, according to an entry in a diary written by Holston. The diary contains entries from January 1, 1862 thru September 4, 1862, the day he was killed.

In 1864 the young widow married Augustus H. Jinkerson. That Holston's diary was cherished by Mrs. Jinkerson must be assumed because of the fact that when she reached old age she entrusted it to her daughter, Bruner's mother, who before her death placed it in the hands of her son Riley for safekeeping, where it remains today.

No record could be found of how or when Holston arrived in California nor where he had been prior to his arrival in Indian Diggings. However, his diary does tell us something of the man.

WAS IT COINCIDENCE that the grave of Electa Jinkerson is located less than 20 feet from that of Thomas Holston, her first husband of less than three months? After the accidental death of Holston in a mining accident at the Little Big Claim, in Indian Diggings, the young widow married Augustus Jinkerson in 1864. The tombstone at the left is that of Holston.

"Grandfather wrote a fine hand," said Bruner, and chuckled as he drew attention to the shaky, uncertain penmanship following an entry in the diary that read, 'Going to Indian to do the town.' "He must have had a high old time," added Bruner.

Entries in the Holston diary, though brief, record the weather condition of each day, where he went, what work he did and mentioned the names of people he saw during the day. Unfortunately, he referred to most of them by their last name only.

That he was a hard working young man is evident by his recordings of days spent ploughing, planting, butchering, hauling supplies, wood and pitch, cutting posts and making fences. Many of these activities were carried out in severe weather conditions.

How much land Holston owned is unknown but it must have been considerable . . . for during the month of June he wrote of bringing in and planting cabbage — a total of more than 2000 plants, beside planting other crops of wheat, oats, beets, turnips, oyster plants, corn, carrots, potatoes, squash, pumpkin, onions and melons. This would lead one to believe he was planning to go into the produce business, perhaps selling to other camps and towns in the area.

"It makes you sad to read Grandfather's diary," said Mrs. Bruner. "He worked so hard . . . through all the bad times . . . then one day it was all gone. He didn't write anything about being in any trouble but he lost it all . . . and just 13 days after he married." She then drew attention to the July 7th entry in the diary that read: 'Give up Ranch and Crop, horses and wagon to Tedi and Humphreys for note held by them against me for $2240.00 I kept chickens, house, furniture.' "It looks like they waited until all the hard work was done and the crops ready to sell before they took his farm," said Bruner.

Other diary entries of interest referred to were: "*Thursday*, February 13, fine weather today. Dock White killed Sweeny and McGee and shot twice at Delory for trying to tear his dam out at Clear Creek."*

Then in a seemingly jovial spirit, he wrote — "*Thursday*, March 20, Fine warm day. Bicknell went home in the afternoon. Humphreys went to Cedarville, Margaret went to Summers, and I went to Splitting Posts. "*Tuesday*, June 24, I went to Loveless Ranch with wagon and taken Miss Hardy up to Indian. Come home and taken a load of passengers over to the hall. Miss Hardy and I was married at midnight. "*Saturday*, June 28, Humphreys went to Indian in forenoon, come back and cut barley and irrigated in the afternoon. Bailey stayed all night. Simpson killed himself at Indian."

ACCIDENTAL DEATH.--On Friday last, T. J. Holstin was killed at Indian Diggings, El Dorado county, by the caving of a bank upon him in hydraulic diggings. He was from Tennessee, aged about 25 years, and had been married about two months.

THE LITTLE BIG CLAIM, at Indian Diggings, claimed the life of Thomas Holston in 1862, when the side of the mountain gave way under the force of water applied in the hydraulic mining operation.

24

-Sioli's History reports this incident as having occurred in 1860.

June, SATURDAY 21, 1862

June, TUESDAY 24, 1862

I went to Lovelep Ranch with wagon and taken Miss Hardy up to Indian come home and taken a load of passengers afer to Ball, Miss Hardy and I was married at midnight

WEDNESDAY 25.

Come to Brownsville with load of passengers, then went back to Indian, and then to Lovelep Ranch, Stayed all night

THURSDAY 26.

Fixed and come home at 1 Oclock P. M. and then fixed up Bed and so on. Bailey come over and stayed all night. Humphreys did not work

February, WEDNESDAY 12, 1862

Clear and warm this morning.

THURSDAY 13.

Fine weather to day. Dock Site killed Sway and Lee and Shot three at Coloy for trying to tear his Ranch out of Cedar Creek

FRIDAY 14.

Fine weather to day. Went to Cerarville. Will went to Indian in the evening and stayed all night

July, SUNDAY 6, 1862

Remick wife and Mrs Clover was up on a visit. I taken them to Indian in wagon come home at Sundown Fode and Seth was over

MONDAY 7.

Gave up Ranch and crop Horse and Wagon to Fode and Humphreys, for Notes held by them against me for $22,40.00, I kept chickens, House furniture &C.

TUESDAY 8.

Doing nothing to day Seth and I went down to Ranch. I bought House from Robison Bill for $5.00

A WIDOW AT AGE 20 - *Electa Hardy came to California in the late 1850's. She was 20 years old when she married Thomas J. Holston, 24, in ceremonies performed in the Indian Diggings Lodge, F. & A.M. No. 38, at midnight June 24, 1862. On September 5th, two months and eleven days later, Holston was killed in a mining accident.*

Photos from Bruner Collection

THE STREET OF PAINTED LADIES
When Justice Jinkerson took action to rid Indian Diggings of the source of its acquired name, "Whore House Gulch," he ordered the burning of a row of cabins that lined the creek just out of town. The rubble and ashes, visible between the trees in the foreground of this picture, were all that remained of the dwellings.

INDIAN DIGGINGS - This picture is a reproduction of a ferrotype photo now on display in the Sutter Museum in Sacramento. It is the property of Riley Bruner, who said the flume carrying water to the mines was built in 1852. Water from the Indianville and Cedarville ditches was carried from hilltop to hilltop through this and other flumes like it, supplying the mines at Brownsville, Cedarville, and Fairplay.

"I guess Indian Diggings was no better or no worse than any other mining camp in those days," said Bruner. The town, once reported to be a boisterous, booming camp with nine stores, five hotels, several saloons, a livery stable with two stages a day running to Sacramento, had a population of more than 2000.

"It was much smaller in 1900; you remember the old town burned . . . all of it in 1857 . . . and another fire in 1860 took most everything," said Bruner. "When we lived there it was still quite a town. Mining was still the big thing . . . I can remember the mining . . . ground sluicing, tunnels, placer mining and the hydraulic mines and hydraulic nozzles . . . they stick in my memory. When I was a kid I used to put a stick on the column of water that shot out of the nozzles and watch it fly away. Yes, it was quite a town."

Reminiscing, Bruner continued, "There was a hotel, a store, a couple of saloons operating . . . I remember the saloon, it was run by a fellow by the name of Kulich . . . they played poker and drank and sold groceries there. I remember one time I went in there and they was playing poker with $20 gold pieces . . . $20 gold pieces all over the table.

"Guess there's nothing left down there now," he continued sadly, "just the old two-story house that was Grandfather Jinkerson's home, then the old Dhallin place, and our home . . . that's where we run the post office . . . the old blacksmith shop is gone and that row of shacks along the Creek." Mrs. Bruner quietly added, "They called that the 'Street of Painted Ladies' ".

"My uncle Jinkerson was the Justice of the Peace then, and when he heard that folks was calling Indian Diggings 'Whore House Gulch'* he ordered all the houses burned down." Bruner continued. "And another thing..he named the creek where they were 'Onit Creek' and to this day it's still Onit Creek . . . right on the maps. Guess he was joking."

As a child, Bruner attended and graduated from the Indian Diggings school, one of the first school districts in El Dorado County in 1856. The school was located in the canyon halfway between Indian Diggings and Omo Ranch according to Bruner, who had to walk three miles to school from Indian Diggings.

Of the teachers, he recalled a Mrs. Stickell and Don Barnett.

*-Edwin G. Gudde-California Gold Camps, Univ. of Calif. Press.

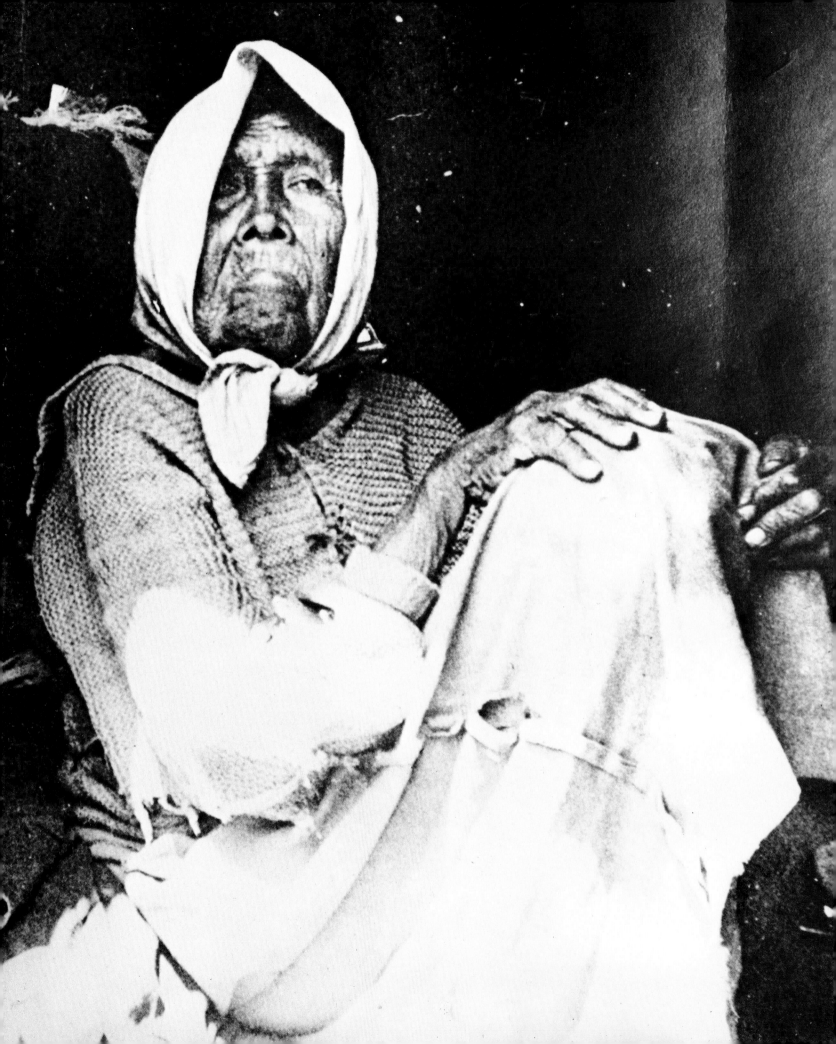

About the Indians ?

"Well, when I was a kid," said Bruner, "there was quite a few Indians living around here, but they gradually moved away. I remember the last Indian living up here, 'Cone Jennie' they called her . . . folks said she was over 100 years old.

"When the Indians left the area," Bruner said, "she refused to go and continued to live alone in a small hut where, one day, they found her dead in front of the fireplace. That was in 1937. She's buried up here somewhere. I'm not sure just where. It could be in the Indian Burial Ground or in the cemetery, I never did know."

The town got its name after a party of white men on a prospecting trip in 1850 discovered some Indians panning in the bed of a creek. Mining journals report that Indian Diggings Creek was among the richest surface or creek diggings in this part of the state.

It did not take the white man long to move in. Word spread through the countryside and soon another mining town, "Indian Diggings" was added to the fast growing county of El Dorado.

About the Chinese ?

"There was quite a lot of Chinese here when I was a kid. They had a Chinese boarding house down there; my Dad used to take me there and I can remember eating rice . . . funny how a little thing like that sticks in your mind.

"Another thing . . . there were no doctors up here in those days . . . all doctors were in Placerville . . . but there was an old Chinaman by the name of Quat, and he used to treat the people with herbs and stuff. I remember one time when Dad hurt his foot and blood poisoning set in, Quat walked up to PiPi and got some ginseng root. He took his knife and cut Dad's foot open . . . right to the bone . . . he scraped it real clean and put the ginseng root on it and he got well."

CONE JENNIE, the last Indian to live in the town of Indian Diggings, is believed to have been more than 100 years old when she died in 1937. She continued to live there long after all other Indians had moved from the area.

Yohalem Collection

THE INDIAN DIGGINGS SCHOOL comprised one of the first school districts formed in El Dorado County in 1856. Riley Bruner was one of several hundred children to graduate from the school. This picture is believed to have been taken about 1906.

After the Legislature passed a law restricting hydraulic mining, miners and families started leaving the town. The hotel closed, then the one remaining store, and eventually the school. A new school house was built on the ridge out of the canyon, retaining its district status and the name Indian Diggings School.

It was not long until most families had moved away. Among those who were in no hurry to leave were the Bruners; they stayed on until 1946 when they sold their livestock and moved to their present home on the Omo Ranch road, bringing many of the mining-day relics and artifacts with them. The town site and adjoining lands around Indian Diggings are today posted private property.

In recent years the Bruners operated a roadside grocery store and gas pump adjacent to their home, accommodating their neighbors and the tourists who learned of the shorter route out of Plymouth, Amador County, to Highway 88 and the high country. Because of Mr. Bruner's ill health, this was discontinued in 1974.

It was in January, 1975, that Riley and Ida Bruner were interviewed for this publication. Mr. Bruner had been in poor health for some years. However, his wife Ida, who had cared for him through the years of his illness, died in her sleep on November 9, 1975. Mr. Bruner followed her in death on February 28, 1976.

THE BRUNER HOME - In the shade of a giant walnut tree is the former home of Riley and Ida Bruner, who functioned as postmasters of Indian Diggings. Across the street from their home was the town's blacksmith shop. Although the fence has long since fallen, the gate still stands.

30

Alice Dillinger Remembers

Mrs. Alice Dillinger was born in Placerville on January 15, 1893. She was nearing her 84th birthday when she was interviewed at the home of her daughter, Mrs. Howard Wentworth, overlooking the city from Sacramento Hill, a short distance from where she was born. Mr. Simon Altar, Mrs. Dillinger's grandfather, came to El Dorado County during the Gold Rush. Her grandmother, Sara Jean Altar, arrived later, via the Isthmus of Panama, from Massachusetts. They made their first home in Chili Bar and later moved to Placerville. Simon Altar became a ditch tender, a man of considerable importance at that time as he controlled the distribution of water in the area. Mrs. Altar started a private grammar school and gave music lessons in their home on Sacramento Street.

Mrs. Dillinger was born in her grandmother's home and lived there until she was ten years old, when her mother remarried and they moved to a home downtown. That home still stands on Reservoir Street, facing the City Hall on Main Street.

Her grandmother's home burned in 1919, resulting in the loss of priceless articles that had been in the family for years. Mrs. Dillinger said that her grandmother's father, who was a sea captain, always brought home furniture and art objects from the European ports where he stopped in his travels. The collection included many marble pieces from Italy, Spain, and other countries. When her mother died, Mrs. Altar went to Massachusetts and shipped the collection around the Horn to Placerville to furnish her home on Sacramento Street.

Because their home was so close to town, Mrs. Dillinger knew many of the early-day places of business and remembers their location. She said, "There were three millinery shops in town; Phoebe Hicks had a nice one, where the Randolph Jewelry Store is now. In that same block was Max Baer's Clothing Store, Al and Hal Simons Dry Goods, Tom Patton, and the Runkles Bakery.

"Grandmother would send me and my sister Alma to the bakery for bread . . . it was 5¢ a loaf and cookies were 10¢ a dozen. I remember on the way home we used to tear open the paper wrapper on the bread and we'd each take an end piece and eat it on the way up Sacramento Street. We liked the crust.

CLARKE HOWARD, husband of Marion Altar Johnstone and step-father of Alice Dillinger, was born in Latrobe. He was a prominent Placerville attorney in 1883, Justice of the Peace in 1888. He later appointed Superior Court Judge of Alpine County. His marriage to Mrs. Johnstone took place in 1903.

Photos from Dillinger Collection

Photos from Dillinger Collection

RNITURE & UNDERTAKING with a
of political campaigning on the side
med to be in order at the C. P. Winchell
re on Main Street in Placerville in 1900.
te the campaign poster in the window
l the bulletin board on the store front
posting funeral notices. The gentlemen
bered for the occasion of having their
ture taken are, from left, George E.
kes, W.D. Rantz, S. Euer, Joseph Joeger,
ck Holdridge, Frank Wright, C.P. Winchell
l Philip Cram. On August 16, 1916,
A. Dillinger bought the store and business.
e Dillinger Furniture Store celebrated its
th anniversary in 1976.

NATOR H. A. DILLINGER was a native of
va. He came to California in 1910 and to
Dorado County in 1911. He married Miss
ce Johnstone of Placerville in 1913. He
ired from the State Legislature in 1951
er serving eight years in the Assembly and
elve years in the Senate. After retirement
devoted his time to writing and publishing
struction in Esperanto," a beginner's
mmar on the Universal Language. In 1959
retired from the furniture store business
t he had established in 1916. This picture
s taken on the day of his retirement from
State Senate.

"Every other door on Main Street was a saloon in those days. They all had swinging doors. Alma and I used to walk down the street, and if a man went into a saloon we'd hurry before the door stopped swinging and glance in to see what we could see. We thought that was great sport."

She said she remembered the dusty streets in Placerville, ". . . dust in the summer and all mud in the winter. The sidewalks were made of boards. They had iron shutters on the doors and kerosene lamps for light at night.

"I remember the barber shop. When I was about four years old Mother used to take me to Doc Johnson to get my hair cut. He was the black barber in town. We didn't have many black people here then. Perly Monroe and the Burgess boys used to come over from Coloma once in awhile. We had a lot of Chinese though. They were all mixed in with the 'fast ladies' on Benham Street."

When asked about the 'fast ladies', she said, "My sister Alma and I always called the women on Benham Street who wore bright red kimonos 'fast ladies'. Of course it was forbidden, but sometimes when we were going to town, if Mother or Grandmother wasn't looking, we'd sneak down Fisk Street. It led right to the houses where they lived and worked on Benham Street. The Old Star Saloon down there always left their back door open. We'd walk by and see them drinking and dancing with the men. We thought we were real naughty because we liked to see their pretty red kimonos."

33

El Dorado County Historical Museum Collection

A CHINESE STORE located on Sacramento and Pacific Streets in the mid-1800's.

The Chinese – The Chinese people lived in the general area of the present Post Office site on Sacramento and Pacific Streets. The Chinatown quarters extended into Benham Street and Quartz Alley, according to Mrs. Dillinger, who talked about her little playmate, the daughter of the Wings, who had the Chinese restaurant on Main Street. "We were six or seven years old. She had a dog named Nero. We hitched him up to a cart we made from a box and rode up and down the street." She said the restaurant was in the same location as that of the present day Chinese restaurant. "There has always been a Chinese restaurant there," she added. She also remembered Sadie Hing Tye and her brother George who lived with their mother in Chinatown.

"I was about 10 years old when my mother married Judge Clarke Howard," said Mrs. Dillinger. "He was her second husband. When she married, we moved from Grandmother's house to our own home downtown. It is that white house that stands on the hill at the end of the alley street that passes Carpenter's Typewriter Shop on Main Street. It faces the City Hall. We lived there when the Court House burned . . . we saw it all. Mother had the house enlarged when we moved there. She added a bedroom with a bay window and a dining room. I always liked the stone room. There was a room made all of stone . . . it's still there."

Placerville, according to Mrs. Dillinger, always had a big celebration on the 4th of July. The whole county would turn out. At dawn someone would shoot off the cannon on Cannon Hill and the celebration would start. Crowds filled the Sigwart Opera House to hear the

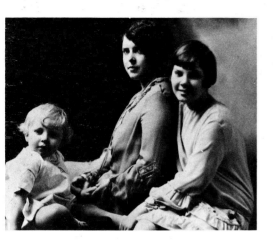

MRS. ALICE DILLINGER and her two children, Marion Alice and William Clarke Dillinger. Marion married Howard Wentworth, who now manages the Dillinger Furniture Store. William and Carol have five children, Ellen, William, Ranius, Annie, and Carl Dillinger. They live now in Sacramento.

Photos from Dillinger Collection

THE CLARKE HOWARD HOME still stands on the hill on Reservoir Street facing the City Hall on Main Street, Placerville. When Alice Dillinger was ten years old her parents moved to this house where she lived until she married Mr. Dillinger in 1913. In later years the house was sold to a Mrs. Yaeger, and still later to Mrs. Cox.

speakers. "I remember they used to hold the county fair in the Opera House. It would be filled with beautiful fruit and flowers and smell so good when you opened the door. That's where they held Saturday night dances too. I met 'Dill' at a dance there. Mr. and Mrs. Sigwart were my godparents when I was born."

"Dill" was Mr. Harley Alvyn Dillinger. She said he hated his name and always used the initials H.A. "He never would tell anyone what his name was. In all the years I was married to him I never called him anything other than 'Dill'."

Mr. Dillinger came to El Dorado County in 1910 and practiced law in Placerville for several years. In 1913 he married Alice Johnstone. The wedding was held in her grandmother's home on Sacramento Street. In 1916 Mr. Dillinger bought the furniture store and undertaking business from Charlie Winchell. "This year, 1976, we will have been in business 60 years," said Mrs. Dillinger.

When the conversation returned to Placerville and earlier days, she mentioned the old Earl Fruit House "that shipped all over the country." She remembered the Giebenhain Brewery, Morey's Foundry, and the Southern Pacific Depot, located in the area where Denny's restaurant is today.

"There were lots of livery stables then. Of course, that was the only means of transportation for years. Tuck Holdridge had a big stable. He had one beautiful black horse called "Annie". Everybody wanted to hire Annie. I remember one Sunday I invited 'Dill' to dinner. He arrived in his overcoat and gloves . . . just so. After dinner he hired Annie and the rig and we went for a ride up to Camino. I thought that was so exciting.

"I had a wonderful childhood," said Mrs. Dillinger, "and I enjoy thinking about all the old places and times . . . Mr. Quigley's store, where Orr's flower shop is now. Mr. Mason had a store there earlier, when the Post Office was where the bakery is now at the Tower. The O'Donnell home was across from the Masonic Temple. They had a store here for years. It was later run by Mr. Murray. We used to go upstairs and pick out the toys for Christmas. Then there was Alec Forni's butcher shop, McQuen's Second Hand Store, Shelly Inch where George Duffy has been so long, the Placerville Hardware Store, and the Mountain Democrat. Grandpa had his office in that building at one time.

"There are so many memories — the time the prisoners escaped . . . I can see the militia marching down the street in their uniforms . . . the time Alma and her friend were hurrying home to get out of the storm and lightning struck a telephone pole right by her and knocked her down . . . the pretty girls who were chosen to be Miss Liberty on the 4th of July . . . and all the other celebrations. Yes, I have wonderful memories of Placerville."

AMY HORN AGE 3

GEO

H. W. Hulbert, Publisher. }
Established April 9, 1880. }

GETOWN GAZETTE
SHED EVERY THURSDAY BY
W. HULBERT.

SCRIPTION RATES!
in advance $1 5
s 1 0

VERTISING RATES;

vertising, for one square (eleven line
, or one inch), first insertion, $1.00
quent insertion, fifty cents,

S. PRICE & SON

SSAY OFFICE
.........AND.........
CAL LABORATORY
SACRAMENTO STREET,
ANFRANCISCO.

AMERICAN FEED AND
ERY STABLE

E AMERICAN HOTEL, George
El Dorado Co., Cal.

R Bros.,--- Proprietors

LAR ATTENTION Paid to Transient

L. CRAWFORD,

TORNEY-AT-LAW
&
OTARY PUBLIC.

attend to all business befo
ce Courts of the Divide.
Collections made.
ncing promptly attended t
nd Business a Speciality.

--71 Church St. Georgetown.

Lodge. No. 37. I. O. O.
its regular meeting in Odd Fello
getown, every Saturday evening.
W. A. HEUSER, N. G.
NGLEY, Secretary.

S. HICKMAN, M. D.

YSICIAN AND SURGEON.

Pioneer Building, up stair

L. CRAWFORD,

ESTATE Agent, Georgetow

WM. BURTON.

Deputy Surveyor, Civil E
and Notary Public. Land Pa
red, Conveyancing done.
O., GARDEN VALLEY, Cal.

RGETOWN GAZETTE.

GEORGETOWN. EL DORADO CO., CAL., MAY 29, 1890.　　NO. 9, VOL. 11

Everybody Crazy

1a$b2$c3

What is home without one of those fine suits of clothes just received by Shepherd, and which he is selling way down for cash.

Having an overstock of straw hats I am selling Men's Straw Hats from 15 cts up. Boys Straw Hats for 20 cts. Girls Straw Hats, trimmed, 20 cts. Gents Celluoid Collars 5 cts. Gents Celluoid Cuffs, 50 cts. pair.

Gilt Wall Paper, 25 cts to $1 per double roll.　　House Lining 5 cts per yd.　　Paints and Oils of all kinds.

Ladies Hose, solid black, 15 cts.　　Corsets 50 cts per pair (A 1).　　Gents Summer Coat and Vest only $1.50. Sateen Parasols, 24 inch, only 75 cts., selling fast. Boys 2-piece Suits only $2.25.　　Boys knee Pants 40 cts Boys knee Pants, corduroy, 90 cts—extra.

Autograph Albums, something nice,
Hair Ornaments 15 cts.　　I sack Tolo,
Extra heavy Matting 25 cts per yd.

Give us a trial in the Boot & Shoe a large stock of the very best.
Goat shoes, $1.75.　　Ladies Fine C
Ladies fine low cut shoes, $1.50.　　Gents shoes, $4.00.　　Gents tap sole Buckingha ining boot, $5.　　Boys button Shoes only 50 cts.
Toilet Soap, 12 inches long, 10 cts Whips 6 foot long, 25 cts.　　Young M hirts, all the rage, from $1.50 to $4. Cal

Give us a trial for anything yo ooth-pick to a saw-mill, and we owest prices and best goods.
B. F. S

J. SCHERF

Manufacturer of and De

BOOTS & SI

Main St., Watson Building, GE

I HAVE Alwa

MAKE T

Gents' Boots & Shoes from $2 to $12
Boys' " & " " $1.50 to $6
Ladies Shoes, Ties and Slippers of all styles and at prices to suit the times. Misses', Childrens' and Infants Shoes at rates to defy competi

TRAVELER'S GUIDE.

GEORGETOWN

VIA.

PLACERVILLE & SACRAMENTO.

Stages Leave Georgetown for Garden Valley, Kelsey and Placerville daily (Sundays excepted) at 6:30 A. M.　Returning, leaves Placerville at 1 P.M
Passenger trains leave for Sacramento at 11:30 P.M
Leave Sacramento for Placerville at 7:15 A. M
Arrive at Sacramento at .... 2:40 P. M.
Arrive in Placerville at .... 10:30 A. M

GEORGETOWN

VIA

AUBURN & SACRAMENTO.

Stages leave Georgetown for Auburn daily (Sundays excepted) at 6:30 A. M.　Leave Auburn Station for Georgetown & Placerville at 4 P. M. Central Pacific Railroad trains leave Auburn as follows :

GOING EAST.

Train No. 1 .... 10:35 P. M
Train No. 3 .... 2:00 A. M
Train No. 25 (Local) .... 1:55 P. M
GOING WEST.
Train No. 2 .... 4:45 P. M
Train No. 4 .... 4:40 A. M
Train No. 26 (Local) .... 8:50 A. M

Bucklen's Arnica Salve,
THE BEST SALVE in the world for Cuts, Bruises, Sores, Ulcers, Salt Rheum, Fever Sores, Tetter, Chapped Hands, Chilblains, Corns, and all Skin Eruptions, and positively cure Piles, or no pay required.　It is guaranteed to give perfect satisfaction, or money refunded.　Price 25 cents per box.
For sale by B. F. Shepherd.

The Placerville home-made cigar is growing in popularity.
Call for Clark's white labor cigars.
Good Nickel Watch for $5 at Sheps
For a tasty and substantial article in foot wear go to Scherrer's.
Fire arms of all descriptions, ordered and laid down here at 10% profits, at Shepherd's.
Fine stock of fresh candy and nuts at Shep's.
Beef for boiling very cheap at Dobbas' City Market.

Pioneer Newspaper

To transport a Washington Hand Press, a small job press, and many fonts of type from Auburn, Placer County, to Georgetown, El Dorado County, in 1880 was not an easy matter. It meant a 20 mile haul by horse-drawn wagons over a narrow dirt road that was cut out of the side of a mountain, winding down more than 600 feet to the bed of the American River.

After crossing the river, the road up the grade on the opposite side hugged the mountainside, winding up 1000 feet before reaching the top and the town of Cool. (Today that road is on Highway 49.) From Cool the road on to Georgetown was not so hazardous.

Amy Horn Drysdale whose grandfather, Horace Hulbert, made the above mentioned trip with his family, told of the incident in a tape recorded interview on March 5, 1975. She also told of her grandparents' and her great-grandparents' migration to California.

Fourth District—FRANK MILLER.
Fifth District—A. T. LEACHMAN.

QUICK TIME AND CHEAP FARES

to EASTERN AND EUROPEAN CITIES

MAIN STREET, GEORGETOWN.

I am also the proprietor of THE GREENWOOD MARKET. At both shops will be kept the best of Beef, Pork, Mutton and Veal; Sausage and

Photos from Drysdale Collection

The Hulberts

CELIA WELLEFORD was 20 years old when she married Horace Hulbert in Yuba City on July 4, 1874. When the young journalist became the publisher of several country newspapers prior to 1880, she worked with him and learned the printing and newspaper business. When he lost interest in the Georgetown Gazette and turned to mining, she continued to publish the paper with the help of her teenage daughter Maude.

It was early spring in 1861 when Joseph Warren Hulbert, his wife Betsy, and their four children, three boys and a girl, left Council Bluffs, Iowa, with a wagon train headed for California. The train was comprised of 50 wagons and led by a man named Richardson.

A research made by the California Society, Daughters of the American Revolution, reports that the train traveled the Northern route. Taking the Sublett's cut-off via Fort Laramie, they passed Independence Rock, Sweetwater, Green River, Fort Hall, American Falls, Snake River, Granite Creek, through Humboldt Basin to Deep Hole Springs to Susanville, then to Magalia and the Buttes.

They arrived in Sacramento in September of 1861, according to Mrs. Drysdale, who recalled hearing about the family's early days from her grandparents and her mother.

Shortly after their arrival Joseph Hulbert purchased a 360-acre farm from a man named Perkins. It was located on the Sacramento River between Colusa and Meridian. He is reported to have planted the first orchard in that area.

Horace Hulbert, Mrs. Drysdale's grandfather, was 17 years old when the family reached California. After three years on the farm he decided his interests and future lay elsewhere. He left home and learned the printing trade.

In 1864, at the age of 20, he started his career in journalism with the *Ukiah Herald*. He bought an interest in the *Sutter Banner* and later published the *Colusa Independent*.

On July 4, 1874, he married Miss Celia Welleford in Yuba City. She was a native of Texas and came to California with her parents (year unknown). On April 10, 1875, their first child, a girl, was born. They named her Maude.

"It was in the fall of that year that the family moved to Auburn," said Mrs. Drysdale, "where grandfather started the *Auburn Advance*. And it was about that time the 'mining bug' got Grandpa. In 1880 he packed up the presses and moved to Georgetown. I remember Mother telling me...clothes and furniture were immaterial...getting the press there was all that interested Grandfather.

"On April 9, 1880, the first *Georgetown Gazette* was printed and continued publication by the family until 1925. However, once the paper was established, Grandfather spent most of his time at a mine he had acquired, The Bridal, located two miles north of town. This left Grandmother with the responsibility of getting the paper out.

"The Bridal? Mother said Grandpa mined all year and when the rains came and they could sluice out the little dab of hard rock they had, why, he'd come home cheering...'We made $90 today!' or, 'We made $100 today!' But he never figured out that what he made in three or four days had taken all year to mine."

HOME OF GEORGETOWN GAZETTE In 1882 Horace Hulbert moved his family and his printing press into this building on Church Street in Georgetown. The newspaper, founded by Hulbert in 1880, continued to be published from this location until 1924. Standing on the porch are, left to right, Horace Hulbert, John C. Horn and Maude Horn. The infant in the buggy is Amy Horn and on the right is Amy's aunt, Celia Hulbert.

The Hulbert Women

That the newspaper continued publication must be attributed to the women in the family. First it was Mrs. Drysdale's grandmother, Celia Hulbert, who had to take over when her husband turned to mining. Her mother, Maude, had to quit school at the age of 14 to help her mother at the paper.

When her mother, Celia Hulbert, died in 1896, Maude Hulbert carried on alone until 1898, when she married John C. Horn. Three children were born of this union, Amy, Doris, and John.

In 1921 Maude Horn was again left with the newspaper to run following the tragic death of her husband in the Ohio House Hotel fire in Placerville. She continued publishing the paper until 1925, when she sold it and, said Mrs. Drysdale, "took a much needed vacation."

"Mother had been held down by that paper since she was 14 years old. She and Josephine Forni Swift sailed for Hawaii in 1926 and stayed three months. In 1930 mother was appointed Justice of the Peace in Georgetown. She served only one term because of ill health. She learned she had cancer. She died in 1935.

"Looking back . . . I really believe our family newspaper was a real service to Georgetown. At a time when there was no radio the small town papers were as necessary for the development of a community as the merchant, the farmer, the lawyer, or doctor. Grandfather, and Mother and Father for that matter, weren't afraid to take a stand.

"In the back files of the *Gazette* . . . which, incidentally, I have donated to the Bancroft Library, you will find one editorial of Grandpa's that was quite daring at the time. It was during a controversy over a new school house.

"In August of 1889 the people of Georgetown decided to build a new school. A $4000 bond issue passed 53 to 13. The problem was where to build it.

"In September of 1889 a meeting was held at the Post Office. Three sites were discussed. 1-The site of the first school with its deep gullies, ditches and small area of flat land. 2-A lot on Main and El Dorado Streets that could be purchased for $1200 with a stone building to be torn down for an extra $300. 3-Railroad Hill site, which the Central Pacific railroad offered as a gift to the district. It comprised five acres.

JOHN C. HORN taught the young people of San Francisco the niceties of ballroom dancing by night and worked as a printer at the San Francisco Chronicle during the day. Among the names of the Professor's references is that of Mrs. Dora Gray Duncan, the mother of the famed Isadora Duncan. References were required to obtain a license to teach dancing at the time (1887). Horn left the Chronicle to work for Miss Maude Hulbert at the Georgetown Gazette.

40

MAUDE HULBERT at age 18. When she was 14 she had to quit school to help her mother at the newspaper. This experience prepared her for her life as a newspaper woman. When she was 18, her father, founder of the paper, made her editor and manager. She was also a telegraph operator, receiving and sending messages from Georgetown on the Coloma, Georgetown, Bottle Hill line. The company call letters were M-A-U-D-E. She studied court reporting and passed the examination to become a reporter at the State Legislature. This career was denied her when her mother died and she had to remain in Georgetown to run the paper and look after her younger brother and sister. In later years she was appointed Justice of the Peace in the Georgetown district. She was active in all community affairs.

DRESSED FOR A GEORGETOWN PICNIC in 1903 are (from left) Maude Horn, her sister, Celia Hulbert, and Mrs. Elizabeth Murdock. The child is Amy Horn.

ON JULY 31, 1898 MAUDE HULBERT AND JOHN C. HORN were married in Yuba City. He was an experienced newspaper man who worked at the San Francisco Chronicle by day and taught dancing at night. She was the editor and manager of the Georgetown Gazette. On June 1, 1899 their first child, a girl named Amy, was born. A boy, John Hulbert, and a girl, Doris, completed the Horn family.

PROF. J. C. HORN,
(OF SAN FRANCISCO)
→ TEACHER OF →

...ncing, Deportment and Physical Culture,

SAMOSET HALL,
VALLEJO, CAL.

→ → ※ ← ←

...ll the Very Latest as Well as Fancy Dances Taught.

→ → ※ ← ←

Parties wishing a personal conference in reference to arranging for instructions, in class or otherwise, will confer a favor by communicating by letter, in order that a satisfactory appointment may be made for an interview.

→ → ※ ← ←

THE WALTZ.

Many persons despair after taking one or two lessons in Dancing, with the thought that they could not learn to WALTZ, but under my instructions all are successful, as my course is thorough and in every case gives satisfaction where others have failed.

PROF. J. C. HORN.

(OVER)

41

Photos from Drysdale Collection

"The controversy over the site mounted," continued Mrs. Drysdale, "and April 5, 1890 was set for the selection of the site by vote. Well . . . women couldn't vote then but Grandfather in his editorial wrote:

" 'In all justice, the women should vote on this proposition, for we believe, as a whole, they are possessed of more good common sense and discretion regarding a school site than the self-assumed lords of creation. Wake up fellow citizens, discuss this situation with an eye single to the best interests of the public and for the generations to come.' "

A news story in the *Gazette* following the election read: "Of a total vote of 151, the Railroad Hill site got 121. As the results were tallied and Railroad Hill totals forged ahead the bells were rung and there was a great celebration. The boys kept up an incessant jubilee, building bonfires on Railroad Hill, marching around town with the drum band, singing, firing giant powder and just whooping it up, they celebrated their victory over the opposition that had opposed on a variety of issues.

"There were bugaboos about mineral rights, water, insurance, roads, clearing land, distance to town, rights of way, etc., all emanating from the fertile brains of the chronic fault-finders, magnifying difficulties."

Mrs. Drysdale's life followed much the same pattern as that of her mother. She attended the Georgetown Grammar School, and learned the newspaper business from her parents, graduating from "printer's-devil" and hand setting obituaries, to writer and reporter. At one time she wrote for several papers, namely *The Mountain Democrat, Placerville Times, Sacramento Bee, Sacramento Union* and the *Auburn Journal*. In 1938, she was elected Justice of the Peace, an office held by her mother before her.

Mrs. Drysdale is an authority on the early day history of Georgetown, and she will be the first to concede that much of her knowledge was acquired from the files of her family's newspaper.

THE FIRST SCHOOL HOUSE
In 1854, when Georgetown's population grew, public subscription raised $653.00 to build a school. It was built on Lot 1, block 22, on the town plans drawn up following the 1852 fire. The site was selected because it was far enough away from the saloons and business part of town that the pupils would not hear the rough talk. A story printed in the Georgetown Gazette told of the difficulties little girls encountered when they climbed trees....the hoop skirts and petticoats often left them stuck in the branches.

EDWIN MARKHAM was a teacher at this Georgetown school until 1882, when he became Superintendent of Schools. He is pictured here with a group believed to be the 1880 class. The first formal graduation held in El Dorado County took place here on May 15, 1885, with Superintendent Charles E. Markham presenting the diplomas. He was later to be more widely known as Edwin Markham, famous California poet.

Photo William (Mike) DeNatly Collection

WHEN FIRE DESTROYED the Ohio House Hotel in Placerville in 1921 it took the life of John C. Horn. His body was found on the third floor where, according to reports, he had gone from room to room to make sure all guests were out. Apparently overcome by smoke he was unable to make his way out. He was the husband of Maude Hulbert Horn and the father of Amy Drysdale.

The Mines

"I can't tell you much about the early day mining that hasn't already been written in any number of books . . . but I can tell you that when the Depression hit in 1929 the gold mines opened and Georgetown boomed again. The mines closed down, you know, before World War I and didn't open until the Depression.

"Electricity was brought in in 1928 just before the crash, making modern mining possible.

"There was one incident I want to tell you about. A Russell Wilson and his partner Ed Wilson bought four acres in Garden Valley. People there thought it was one big joke . . . those "City Slickers" would never get anything on four acres. Well, that was the Black Oak Mine. They took out a couple million dollars.

"That four acres was good, deep loam and there had been a nugget taken out there worth a couple hundred dollars, so the old timers thought that was the end. The Wilsons weren't related. I don't know where Ed was from, but Russell Wilson was from San Francisco. His father was with the Government in the Philippines.

"All this mining brought up groups of Los Angeles promoters, and they were going to make fortunes.

"One such group came up in which there were four 'Chiefs' and two 'Indians'. The 'Chiefs' of course held all the stock and they gave the 'Indians' a share or two apiece for their money.

"A man by the name of Walter Drysdale was with that group. He was later to become my husband. I remember him telling me the pay then was $4.00 a day for under-ground mining. Walter soon got out of being an 'Indian' and went to work as a miner. They worked thirty days a month, or thirty-one, depending on how many days were in the month. During the Depression that was considered pretty good pay.

"Drysdale was a writer and public relations man for the group that he was with, but after they arrived there wasn't much in the way of profit for him so that's why he went into the mine. That's really how we got acquainted . . . our mutual interest in writing and newspapers.

"In 1935 we were married and worked together. I refused to marry him until he got out of mining. I'd seen too much money go into empty holes in the ground. In 1936 he joined the staff of the *Placerville Times*. That was when George Burris and Wesley Davis and Walter became partners."

Mrs. Drysdale spoke of her husband's service during the war and showed many of his paintings and writings. And during the interview she expressed great admiration for one early day settler who wrote 'Recollections' for her grandfather during the 1880's and 90's.

DR. W. S. HICKMAN, *who moved to Georgetown in the early 1800s, is said to have compounded his own prescriptions. He administered to the physical and mental needs of the community and was present at most of the births. He remained a bachelor, and died of the flu in 1918.*

44

Photos from Drysdale Collection

DEFYING SUPERSTITION - If it is bad luck for women to enter a mine, as most miners believe, the ladies of the Shakespeare Club no doubt never heard of it or didn't believe it.   For on November 4, 1911, the Placerville Shakespeare Club entertained visiting dignitaries from the State and Northern California clubs by taking them into the Pacific Mine in Placerville. Those identified are, from left, Mrs. Abe Darlington, President of the American Club; Mrs. G. W. McCoy, President of the Northern District, Placerville; Mrs. A. W. Francisco, Secretary, State Federation. The two gentlemen in back are Frank Goyan, mine foreman, W. D. Kirk, Editor of the Nugget. Miss Anna Gilbert, Sacramento; Mrs. Edgar Beeson, President, Sacramento Shakespeare Club; Mrs. F. H. Sargent, Fair Oaks; Mrs. E. B. Stanwood, Marysville; Miss Gertrude Kirk, Placerville; Mrs. C. E. Thompson, Dunsmuir; Mrs. M. A. Horn, Georgetown (Mrs. Drysdale's mother); Mrs. George Armstrong, Woodland; Mrs. Stingers of the Pacific Mines.   Seated center are Mrs. R. H. Hargrove, Madera, and Mrs. M. A. Sayler, Orland.   The ladies dressed in appropriate clothing for the visit.

FATHER O'KANE held services and lived in this store building. Mrs. Drysdale said that old-timers remember him sitting in front of the "Church," soaking his tired feet, and commenting on the weather to all passersby.

William T. Gibbs

"I wish I could have known him," said Mrs. Drysdale. "He was such an interesting man. He came to Georgetown with the first wave of miners in 1850. He mined down in Oregon Canyon and over in the Georgia Slide area.

"In 1851 he married a widow, Mrs. Cynthia A. Turner. Theirs was the first marriage performed in Georgetown. He was the first post-master, the first mining recorder, and the first merchant in the town.

"I remember one article Mr. Gibbs did about the exaggerated reports, coming out of Washington D.C., about the population in the mining towns.

"You see, it happened this way. Mr. Gibbs started this business of recording the mines, and in those days the mines were 15 feet wide and across a creek-bed, or a river bed. Whether it was 20 or 30 feet across, that didn't matter but it couldn't be more than 15 feet wide.

"Of course it was placer mining, and if a man didn't find it in a hurry he'd move on and stake another claim. Many men had as many as 10 and 15 claims in a year. They were all recorded as mines though they were only 15 feet wide. Well, you can see what that was doing back in Washington . . . hundreds and hundreds of mines were recorded.

"Then there was another thing. Mr. Gibbs claimed that Georgetown was one of the few towns that had the voting population correct. When California first got the vote many places were voting steamer lists; there are records of this actually happening. They even voted laundry lists, any old kind of list.

"But in Georgetown, according to Mr. Gibbs, 'they always vote the man.' That is, a boy was a man when he could stand up to a whiskey barrel and drink his shot, go in and stamp his ballot, go out the window and get in line again. So 600 men could easily vote 5000 times.

"Then when that 5000 got back to Washington D.C. and they started figuring the population, they figured that one vote represented a man, his wife and two children. So you multiply 5000 by four and you get 20,000 people in Georgetown, which actually had a population of 600."

Today Mrs. Drysdale makes her home in Placerville. She drives her car, visits old friends in Georgetown, takes several trips each year to Mexico, and in general takes interest in what happens in the county. Her primary project is arranging publication of a sequel she has written to *The Tommy Knockers*, a story by her late husband Walter Drysdale.

WILLIAM T. GIBBS was one of the original pioneers and prominent citizens of Georgetown. Mr. Gibbs had the distinction of being the first in several fields: the first to marry, the first mining recorder, and the proprietor of the first stationery store in Georgetown. He was instrumental in getting the telegraph line from Coloma to Georgetown to Bottle Hill. He was also on the committee that laid out the wide streets in Georgetown after the fire of 1852.

Judge Drysdale

BEING A JUDGE in a community where she was born and raised presented no problems for Amy Drysdale. She said one reason for this was that she followed the advice given her by her mother, who was a judge before her. She announced, in court and out, "You all know me as Amy. You're all friends, but when you come into this courtroom you're all strangers to me. Now, if you want to come in and expect me to judge you as a friend, you will embarrass me, but I will hear your case and decide as I believe is right. And if you are guilty I will fine you double the amount the fine would be to anyone else."

She continued, "In all my years on the bench I only had two who insisted that I treat them as friends. I don't know why. I guess they thought I wouldn't go through with it, but I did."

When Mrs. Drysdale retired as judge in 1964, the State Assembly presented her with a resolution commending her for her years of service. It read in part..."due to her ability and the confidence placed in her, she averaged only one jury trial every two years, and had only four cases appealed, none of which were reversed by the higher court."

Photos from Drysdale Collection

C. M. FITZGERALD, a prominent citizen of Georgetown, was Superintendent of Mines and the Water Company.

Georgetown Native Daughters

The names of the Native Daughters pictured at this gathering of El Dorado Parlor No. 186 N.D.G.W. of Georgetown in 1910 will provide the reader with additional names of some of the county's pioneer families. Identified, 1st row-Elizabeth Ruchler Irish, Mary Norris, Clara (Sipp) Bauer, Lena Caprara, Hattie Heindel, Emma Lou Humphrey (Grand President), Mary Thorson, Ida Bailey, Ethel Francis and Irene Irish.   In the 2nd row-(one not identified) are Mrs. J. Kelley, Della (Kelley) Stanley, Edith Hume, Ida Childress, Annie (Thorson) Heindel, Maggie Smith, Maude Horn, Dora Wood, Lena Buchler and Elizabeth Murdock.   3rd row-Metta Buchler, Addie Vernon, Maggie Roberts and Clara Rupley.

Georgia Slide Band

Photos from Drysdale Collection

Ladies Aid Georgetown

The Methodist - Episcopal Church in Georgetown had an active Ladies Aid. Members pictured in 1911, at a meeting in the home of Mrs. Lane are, back row left to right: Mrs. Henry (Kate) Ward, next three young ladies not identified, Mrs. J. C. Horn, Mrs. Whitney, Mrs. Robert (Margaret) Murdock. Seated left to right: Mrs. Richard ("Tish") Buchler, Mrs. Lane, Mrs. Brede, Mrs. William Wurish, Mrs. Philo Hotchkiss. Children: the minister's daughter and Doris Horn.

E 49'ers - Alex Connell, Thomas B. Patton, n Paul Davidson, Ben C. Currier, Soloman ry. These prominent gentlemen were onsible for the laying out and the building Georgetown, including the water supply the telegraph.

Upper Left: *THE VAN MINE, located between Georgetown and Georgia Slide, was visited in 1891 by Horace Hulbert, publisher of the Georgetown Gazette. Hulbert, standing center with hand in pocket, was getting a story about the mine.*

GEORGETOWN 1912 - *An eight horse team hauling mining equipment for a Georgia Slide stamp mill on Blue Rock. Home shown in photo is owned by Mr. and Mrs. Victor Forni.*

Left: MEN OF THE EUREKA IN 1908
The Eureka Slate Quarry is located north of the American River six miles from Placerville on Route 193. In 1907 the El Dorado County Board of Trade reported that the Eureka was the only slate mine in California that contained a sedimentary slate deposit large enough and pure enough to make the production of roofing slate a commercial success. The mine property at that time consisted of 600 acres. A report written by Edwin C. Eckel of the United States Geological Department states, "The mass of the Eureka quarry product is a dense, deep black slate splitting very finely and regularly with a smooth glistening surface much like that of the Bangor and Lehigh slates of Pennsylvania."

$1800.00 NUGGET - *Mr. G. F. Barklage displays what was said to be the largest nugget found in the Georgia Slide area. The gold, taken from the Beattie mine, weighed 60 ounces.*

51

THE GEORGETOWN CALABOOSE *was facetiously named by early-day settlers. This Old Justice Court, built on the site of the Old Union Church, served as the jail and Justice Court, with two cells in the rear and the Court Room in front. A bell in the belfrey was rung to signal fire. The young people in the foreground are - John Hulbert Horn, Doris Horn (Amy Drysdale's brother and sister), and friend Clinton Murdock. Picture taken about 1908.*

Photos from Drysdale Collection

A FREIGHTER LEAVES GEORGETOWN - A shipment of potatoes and one passenger, Walter Grover, are on their way to Sacramento. The driver and others on the porch of the hotel could not be identified.

THE SOUND OF BELLS could be heard for miles, echoing through the mountains and canyons, warning oncoming travelers and other freighters that teams were on the road. The bells, attached to the horse collars, are called Hames Bells. Usually they are on the lead horse only, but in this case we see that they are on each horse. This load of sawed sugar pine and red fir was being freighted from the Barklage Mill, located above Blodgett Forest on the Wentworth Springs road.

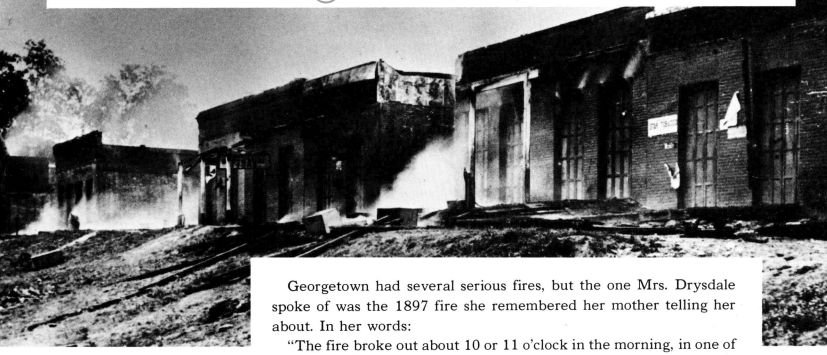

**GEORGETOWN
BUSINESS BLOCK IN 1910**
*All the wooden buildings shown in this
picture were destroyed in the Georgetown
fire of 1934. Only the brick buildings
survived this, and earlier fires. The brick
building on the corner, left, was built in
1860. In 1960, Amy and Walter Drysdale
restored the old building. After the death
of her husband in 1969, Mrs. Drysdale
sold the building, and today the ground
floor is occupied by The Georgetown
Pharmacy, a realty firm, and the
Georgetown Justice Court.*

Georgetown had several serious fires, but the one Mrs. Drysdale spoke of was the 1897 fire she remembered her mother telling her about. In her words:

"The fire broke out about 10 or 11 o'clock in the morning, in one of the stores on Main Street. Most of the buildings were brick and had big iron doors; the doors were to keep the fire out. Mother said the mines were operating at that time, and most of the stores had giant powder stored in the basement. Now they weren't supposed to, but they did.

"Sometimes the powder would just burn, and again, it would blow. Well, everyone was waiting to see what it was going to do. Well, about 2 o'clock, it did. The powder blew, and iron doors flew through the air . . . 100 feet or more. In fact, there is a cedar tree in Georgetown now that you can see where it was sheared off with one of those doors. I know where it is.

"This was before my mother was married . . . but Mother said she waited, just like everyone else. The print shop was in the home, some 400 or 500 feet from the blast. When they heard it, she said she ran outside and the concussion from it hit her in her stomach and almost knocked her down. She said she looked up in the sky and saw bolts of cloth and things unwinding flying through the air. Parts of the debris were found a half mile out of town.

"There were two people killed in it. And they had no business being there. There was an elderly man and an elderly woman and between them was my uncle, a 16 year old, who had no business being there, either. Everyone had been warned, but you see . . . the longer they waited, the more they had to go see if it was going to blow. These two that were killed, they had kegs of nails blown through them and something hit my uncle and broke both legs."

55

Meyers Station at Lake Tahoe

Mrs. Hilda Meyers, nee Tappan, was born March 31, 1897, in the Tappan family home on Sweeney Road near Coles Station, El Dorado county. When she was 18, she married George Elmer Meyers, a grandson of George D. H. Meyers, who owned Meyers Station, at Lake Tahoe.

When interviewed at her home on Grizzly Flat Road in March of 1975, she spoke of her childhood, her ancestors, and recalled names of friends and families who had also settled in the Somerset-Grizzly Flat district.

When a child, she attended the Willow School, a one-room school on the Grizzly Flat road. She said, "I remember our teacher was Miss Mabel Wiltz. She most always had 40 or 50 kids in a class. The school was about two and a half miles from our home so I rode my horse to school. Most kids had to walk to school then.

"I remember one day, I had my horse all saddled and was going to Juckes ranch to get some vegetables, and I saw this smoke . . . a fire was burning down on the Middle Fork of the Cosumnes. It was all greasewood and burning fast. It only took 10 minutes for it to burn right to the top of the hill here. Our house was just two miles up the road. I rode over to Juckes, and the men were all there . . . eating. They had been fighting fire for two days and nights at the Cole place.

"They didn't even finish their food, they grabbed their shovels and went to the fire. Our house caught fire two or three times, but they got it out and saved our home.

Photo William (Mike) DeNatly Collection

"We didn't have a fire crew then ... everybody just got in and helped whenever anything happened. I remember when my folks moved up here, Father wanted a log house. Well, Joe Juckes, a neighbor, told father he could have the timber from his place. He even loaned Dad a team to haul the logs. Then some other neighbors came and helped, and that's the way our house was built. We had a real good community then ... there was no stealing, like now. Everyone respected the other man's property."

As she recalled the names of other families that had settled in the area she mentioned Columbus and Americo Sciaroni, the Odlin family, the Leonis, the Coles, the Juckes, Campinis, Smiths, McAfees, and Tom Murphy. "Everyone knew Tom," she said. "He grew the finest strawberries in the county and he owned the Crystal Caves down on the Cosumnes ... it used to be called the Copper Mine. I remember Indian Betsie too. She lived across the Cosumnes down by the DeForce place, beyond the Happy Valley Road."

About the Mines? — Mrs. Meyers said, "There was the Eagle King, the Last Chance, a placer mine over where Clear Creek and Steely Creek meet. Then there's the Gray Eagle, the Black Hawk ... I can't remember them all. You see, the Mother Lode vein runs through Placerville and the East Lode goes through Grizzly Flat and on over to Hazel Creek.

"Mr. Meyers, George H.D. that is, was working at the Mt. Pleasant at Grizzly when he met Sarah Newell, my husband's mother. She was working at the Somerset House, waiting table when they met. When they married, his father, George D.H. Meyers, made them a wedding present of 40 acres of land in Camino. That's where my husband, George Elmer Meyers, was born. And that's where the Michigan California Lumber Company is now ... on that 40 acres.

"I guess you've heard of the Somerset House? That's where the Bullion Bend holdup men killed deputy sheriff Joseph Staples, and wounded constable George Ranney. I think someone by the name of Reynolds owned it at that time, at least that's what I've been told. Later Mr. Domique La Robardier and his wife bought it.

"He was a real 49er. He was crossing the plains back in 1851 when his oxen drank the alkaline water in Nevada and died. So he loaded what he could in his wheelbarrow and went on to Indian Diggings, which was a booming mining town then. 'Robardier' ... that's what everyone called him ... said he saved half of every dime he made. No matter what he earned, he always saved half. No one knew how much he had, but it was a lot. He lived to be almost 100 years old. He's buried over in the Indian Diggings cemetery.

58

"ROBARDIER" at age 90

IN 1851 young Domique La Robardier of New York crossed the plains with a generous supply of provisions and stock. On reaching Nevada the last of his ox team died after drinking the alkaline water. He continued on foot to the mining camp of Indian Diggings, carrying his remaining possessions in a wheelbarrow. Many years later this yoke, bearing his name, was found at Luther Pass. Some enterprising innkeepers at Lake Tahoe had it on display as a tourist attraction for years.

Photos from Meyers Collection

SOMERSET HOUSE, where law enforcement officers trailed the men who held up the stage bringing silver bullion from Virginia City on June 30, 1864. The robbery took place at Bullion Bend above Sportsman's Hall, 14 miles east of Placerville. In an exchange of shots, one deputy sheriff was killed and a constable wounded. The robbery gained notoriety because the robbers confessed the money was stolen to aid the Confederate Army and gave the stage driver a written receipt to that effect. At the time the picture was taken, about 1889, Mr. Domique La Robardier (right) and his wife (standing near the window) owned Somerset House.

THE HIGHCLIMBER - considered the most dangerous work in the woods. The pay was high, but the chance of a 'top' whipping around and hitting the tree and the man was even higher. Men were injured, never to climb again, some were killed outright. There are reports of a climber being decapitated. A slight wind, one miscalculation on the part of the climber and he was in trouble. This picture was taken in the PiPi area between Grizzly Flat and Ham's Station by Mrs. Mattie Flower, who was the cook at the Caldor Lumber Camp.

RIGGING THE SPAR POLE - Once the tree was topped the surrounding area was cleared. The tree was stripped and the climber set blocks and ran lines (cables) that would go to the steam-operated donkey engine to pull the logs into position for stacking and hauling.

"They knew his story was true because, years later, they found his ox yoke out in the desert...it had his name on it. After Mr. Meyers sold Meyers Station to the Celios they had the yoke hanging up there as a tourist attraction."

When the conversation drifted to lumber, Mrs. Meyers said, "I liked to watch the high climbers. They would top a tree, then attach the blocks and run lines down to the donkey engine to load the logs. Logging was hard work . . . they didn't have chain saws then.

"I remember when Caldor Lumber Company built a railroad line up here. We used to go down and they'd pick us up when they saw us on the railroad tracks. We'd ride the 13 miles and then walk back. The train had a caboose, and if you wanted to ride to Diamond Springs it cost a dollar and a half."

When asked about her parents, Mrs. Meyers said, "My mother and father came to California from Nebraska. Their first stop was in Old Mexico, then they went to Lodi, where my father's parents and grandparents had settled. My father was a Tappan, George Tappan. He was from a long line of Tappans."

Then from several documents referring to the Tappans of England, she pointed out the following:

"May 10, 1637 — The examination of Abraham Tappan of Yarmouth, aged 31 years, and Susan, his wife, aged 30 years, with two children, Peter and Elizabeth, and one mayde (sic) servant, Anna Goodwin, aged 18 years, are desirous to pass to New England to inhabit."

A second document read: "Old Newberry, Essex County, Massachusetts. — Abraham Tappan, being licensed by John Endicott, Esq. (Governor of Massachusetts Colony) to live in the jurisdiction thereof, and hath here promised under his hand to be subject to any lawful order that shall be made by the town." It was signed by Abraham Tappan.

Apparently the descendants of Abraham did not feel bound to honor his pledge to the Crown, because the name of John Tappan, son of Asher and a brother of James Tappan, Mrs. Meyers' grandfather, is inscribed on a bronze monument erected by the Syracuse Chapter of Sons of the American Revolution, honoring the men who fought in the War for Independence against Great Britain.

That the Tappans did "inhabit" is borne out by the fact that in Boston, Massachusetts, there is a "Tappan Lane". On the Hudson River in New York you will find a "Tappan Bay" and "Tappan Village". There is also a "Tappan Street" in Baldwinsville, New York, named after Col. Gabriel Tappan.

60

INDIAN BETSIE was well known to the residents of Pleasant Valley and Somerset. She made weekly visits to the homes of people in the area to ask for and receive some token of food or clothing.
Mrs. Meyers remembered, "Mother said she would always have a bag filled with some food stuffs and things she thought she could use. But each time Betsie would look through the bag, then say 'No I flour No I needle?' It seemed there was always something Mother would forget."

HAYING TIME ON THE JUCKES' FARM. Pictured in the foreground, from left, Guy Wentz, Johnny and Joe Juckes, seated on right are Dora and her mother Tillie Juckes. Standing on the hay wagon, right, Herman Leoni, cousin of Abeona Juckes, seated left, who was named after the sailing vessel ABEONA on which her grandfather, Mark Wood Juckes sailed to America from England as skipper in the early 1800's.

THE PICNIC - In 1905 a popular recreation was the gathering of friends for a picnic. This group was headed for the Crystal Caves near Fairplay on the Cosumnes. Hilda Tappan was then about eight years old. She is in a white dress, about center of picture, in front of the man dressed in black with the white hat. She identified the man and woman on the left as Mr. and Mrs. Albert Cole, with infant daughter Elinor. She recognized others as being Cora, Dora, and Ed Juckes, Beatrice Beebe, daughter of Mr. Beebe, center, who operated the Grand Victory Mine, Arthur Taylor, teacher Harriet McCory, Mr. Funk, who owned a butcher shop in Placerville, Ben Taylor, and George McGee.

US MAIL DELIVERY from Grizzly Flat to Placerville was always on time when Henry Cole of Cole's Station had the contract. Cole is shown standing by his team and rig at the family home. In an emergency he was known to take a passenger for a fee of $1.00. This picture was taken in 1906.

100-YEAR OLD JUCKES HOME burned down when lightning passed down a telephone wire, setting fire to the house. Pictured, from left, are: Mrs. Joe Juckes, whose maiden name was Tillie Bacherer, her daughter Abeona; husband Joe at gate; Mrs. Juckes' mother, Mrs. Bacherer, seated; and young daughter, Dora.

Photos from Meyers Collection

"My father, George Tappan, was Editor of a newspaper in Broken Bow, Nebraska, when he married Mother. My mother was a Burdick," said Mrs. Meyers. "Her name was Ida." Again Mrs. Meyers referred to records showing that her grandfather, Joshua P. Burdick, was a descendant of the Burdicks of Scotland.

"Seven Burdick brothers emigrated to America in 1700," said Mrs. Meyers, then reading from the article: "They purchased a whole township of land in New York State. From them sprang the Burdicks of America. Abel fought in the War of 1812. Albertus enlisted and served under General McClellan. He died in Richmond, Virginia in 1862. Joshua enlisted, furnished his own horses and served in Company E, 2d, Nebraska Cavalry.

"After the war, and his marriage to Jane Gray, Joshua settled on his 640-acre farm in Cass County, Nebraska, and became one of the state's foremost citizens and cattlemen."

"In his stock operations Mr. Burdick ships annually about eleven cars of cattle and swine, and keeps about 30 head of graded Percheron horses." (Taken from a Cass county, Nebraska biographical book on Nebraska's prominent citizens.)

Today, Hilda Meyers, now 79 years old, is also in the cattle business. Since the death of her husband in 1953, she has continued to live in the home that once was that of Sara Newell Meyers, her husband's mother. "Sarah's father was William Newell, an early day settler," said Mrs. Meyers. "He was in the Gold Hill area first, then came over here and homesteaded this place."

About the Cattle? — "I have about 100 head now . . . that's calves and all. You know cattlemen, they count how many cows you have. I have about 45 or 50 cows usually. I feed a lot of hay . . . about half a ton a day. I have a Jeep pickup . . . Columbus Sciaroni, my neighbor on the hill, he helps me. We load the hay on my truck, take it out to the pasture and put it on the ground. I feed 11 or 12 bales every morning."

An incident that occurred at the time this interview was to be arranged may be of interest to the reader and give an example of this little lady's determination and stamina. Efforts had been made to reach Mrs. Meyers by telephone. There was no answer for several days so inquiries were made at the Somerset post office, and of a neighbor. "Oh," said the neighbor, "don't worry about her. She's all right. She didn't like the price of hay in El Dorado County and got in her Jeep and went to Nevada to buy some hay. She'll be back in a day or two."

HILDA TAPPAN AGE 6

HILDA with schoolmate and friend Ed Juckes

Thelma Lewis Photo

A MECCA FOR PHOTOGRAPHERS AND ARTISTS today is this old barn on Mrs. Meyers' ranch. When the mines operated at Grizzly Flat this was one of two stops where a driver had to change horses, taking a fresh team to continue the haul into Placerville.

John Winning Photo

HILDA with neighbor Columbus Sciaroni

THE BURDICKS OF AMERICA - Pictured are members of the sixth and seventh generation of the Burdick family. (Seated - from left) Albertus, James (grandson of Abel), Lucy Hadsell Burdick, and her husband Abel Burdick. (Back row from left) Barbara, Sarah, Euphemia, and Abel II. Hilda Meyers of Somerset is of the eighth generation.

Days of Human Bondage

Would Andrew and Sara Ellen Monroe have left Missouri to face an unknown future in California if Andrew's mother had not encouraged them?

Ninety-year-old James Monroe could not say. When interviewed at his home in Sacramento on January 14, 1976, he recalled the following:

"My grandmother came out first, in 1850. She was a slave and came with the people that owned her. They crossed the plains in a wagon train and freed her after they got here. Some of the slaves took their names from the slave owners. Her name was Gooch, Nancy Gooch, and Grandfather's name was Peter."

Mr. Monroe said his grandmother was a good cook and cooked for the miners in the Garden Valley area. She saved her money and sent for her son Andrew, his wife, Sara Ellen, and their two sons Perly and Grant. They came from Missouri by train in 1870. "There were nine in our family," said Monroe, "eight boys and one girl. Two died when they were but infants. They are buried in the Coloma cemetery."

In a tape recording made by the County Friends of the Library in 1961, Mrs. Dorcas Hooper Papini of Coloma spoke of the Monroe family and said Nancy Gooch paid $700 to the owners of her son Andrew, freeing him to come to California.

James Monroe was born in Coloma in 1886, one year after the death of James W. Marshall, who had discovered gold at Sutter's Mill. He was four years old when a monument honoring Marshall was dedicated. "My father and brother Perly, who was then 17 years old, helped that day. You see . . . our homestead land cornered right there on that side of the hill where they put the monument. It wasn't on our land but we cornered there . . . next to it.

"We had 80 acres and raised fruit. Our house was down there close to where that drive-in is now, on the main road through the park. Our land was all along there. You know where the caretaker's shop is, after you pass the drive-in? There's two houses above there . . . well, we took in those houses and all. Yes, we had a good homestead."

The Monroe children attended the Coloma school. When the school burned, they went to the Slatington school, near the slate quarry.

"I'd get up at five o'clock in the morning, start the fire, feed the hogs, milk the cow, clean the barn, and then get ready for school by eight-thirty. Then after school, do the same chores all over again."

FARMERS IN COLOMA - Andrew Monroe and his wife Sara Ellen (center) raised their family on land homesteaded by his mother who was brought to California as a slave in 1850. Pictured with Mr. and Mrs. Monroe are (from left) their only daughter, Cordelia, William, James (in white dress), Garfield, Grant (on wagon), Perly, and Andrew Jr. The house in background was just being built. Their original home was destroyed by fire. James is the only living member of the family.

Coloma Gold Discovery State Park Collection

Monroe Collection

STELLA AND JAMES MONROE
at home in Sacramento.

HINESE WING DAM - The ditch in the fore-
ound is one of hundreds dug by the Chinese
hen they mined in Coloma. This one was on
e main street. Ditches were dug when the
ter was low. But when the rains came and
e water was high it was turned through these
ches leaving the original river bed to be
orked for gold.

The Monroes did no mining, but Mr. Monroe remembers: "The Chinese were mining the river. They came in and put in wing dams and turned the river. There was generally about 50 of them in a camp. They'd dig a big trench, generally in the summer when the water was low. They'd dig this canal and then they'd put a bunch of logs together and sacks of dirt and turn the river through the canal. Then they'd mine the river bed.

"Down by Bacchi's place, Michigan Flat, there would be about 200 Chinese . . . there'd be one bunch right there in Coloma and another one down on the beach at Lotus. They'd turn the river there below the bridge. Not the one that's there now but the old one, practically right there in front of the church in Lotus. Yes . . . they put those wing dams all along."

Documents? "No, I don't have anything like that now. They were all done away with when we moved." He smiled as he thought back and said, "I did have one book or ledger thing. You see, Claybirth used to be a barber at Lotus and it was from his place. They used to get a haircut and a shave for a quarter." Then, chuckling, "Some of them were on credit."

When asked if he could recall the cost of any other things during that period, he replied, "I think we used to get flour for about . . . less than two dollars for a 50-pound sack. Sugar never varied much in price from what it is now. It used to be when Shafsky had a store in Placerville, Albert Shafsky, we used to get it there in 100-pound sacks for $10. We did most of our buying at the local stores, but for sugar and flour and the like we went to Placerville. It took about two hours by horse and wagon."

Mr. Monroe spoke of the kerosene lamps and candles used before electricity was brought to Coloma in 1930. "Oh, some of them had these generators for electricity. Like the hotels, the Vineyard House and the Sierra Nevada House. It burned down, but they built it up again.

"The Vineyard House was built before my time. They were the Allhoffs . . . the boys, Mart and Joe, and their mother. She was a . widow . . . her name was Chalmers. I knew Louise Chalmers.

"Then there was the Wellers. He had a store there where it's mined out next to the Kane place. Mrs. Kane used to bake and sell bread. She lived where Mrs. Edwards is now."

In 1915 James Monroe left Coloma and worked out of Oakland on the Pullmans. When his father died in 1920 he returned and lived in Coloma until 1949, when he went to Sacramento to work at the State Capitol. His older brother, Perly Monroe, did not leave Coloma until later . . . about 1964.

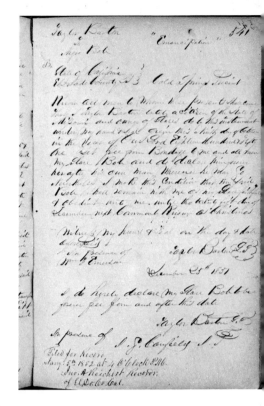

Taylor Barton
    To   **"Emancipation"**
Negro Bob

State of California
El Dorado County   **Cold Springs Precinct**

Know all men to whom these presents shall com
that I Taylor Barton lately a citizen of the State
Missouri and owner of slaves do by this instrum
under my hand & seal given this Ninth day of O
in the Year of Our Lord Eighteen Hundred & Fi
One set free from Bondage to me and all men
my slave Bob and do declare him forever
hereafter his own man wherever he may go.
Nevertheless I make this condition that my slave
Bob shall remain with me as my slave faithful
& obedient unto me until the twenty fifth day c
December next Commonly Known as Christmas

   Witness my hand & Seal on the day & date
   aforesaid
     In presence of   *Taylor Barton*
     Wm. L. Emerson

                      December 25th 18
I do hereby declare my slave Bob to be
forever free from and after this date

In presence of   *Taylor Barton*
    I. G. Canfield I. T.

Filed for Record
Jany 5th 1852 at 4 O'Clock P.M.
  Jno. A Reichert Recordr.
  of El. Do. Co. Cal.

The above document is from records in the
El Dorado County Recorder's Office through
courtesy of James Sweeney, County Recorder.

Yohalem Collection

*OLLOWING THE DEDICATION of the
*arshall Monument on May 3, 1890,
*ndrew Monroe (front row right) joined
* group gathered in Coloma on the road
*ading to the monument (circled left).
*ouis Steffani of Garden Valley carried
*he Swiss flag to honor John Sutter, who
*as of Swiss descent, who had built the
awmill where Marshall discovered gold.

In 1890 the state purchased land for the Marshall Monument site. In 1927 additional land was acquired and Coloma was designated the Marshall Gold Discovery State Park.

However, the actual discovery site where Sutter's Mill stood was on Perly Monroe's portion of the Monroe homestead left him by his father, Andrew Monroe. In 1964 the state acquired that land, expanding the park. Perly Monroe is said to have moved from Coloma about that time. He has since died. Records show that Andrew Monroe suffered a heart attack on November 1, 1919. He died while walking across the Coloma bridge.

James and his wife, the former Stella Thomas of Oklahoma, live in Sacramento. On several occasions they have attended the Gold Discovery Celebrations held in Coloma on the anniversary of the discovery. "The place has changed some since my time," said Monroe, "but the land is still the same."

Grandfather Deserted Ship for the Gold Fields

Eighty-five year old George Green of Placerville has the distinction of having both paternal and maternal grandparents who were Forty Niners.

In a tape-recorded interview with Mr. Green on June 3, 1975 at his home on Cedar Ravine road, Placerville, he spoke of his forefathers' migration to America and of the events he witnessed as a young man in Placerville . . . the Folsom prison break of 1903, the Court House fire of 1910, the removal of the Bell Tower from Main Street, and the advent of electricity in Placerville, in which his father played an important part.

The Migration

"My grandfather Albert Rodemark, Mother's father, was a glass blower in Bavaria. When news of the gold discovery spread around the world he shipped out as a sailor on a German sailing vessel. When they landed in San Francisco the whole crew deserted . . . left the ship and headed for the gold fields and never went back.

"There was another Placerville resident who was on the same ship, a friend of Grandfather's . . . his name was Koletzke. They were almost like brothers. When they landed they went their separate ways. Years later they met again in Placerville.

"They are buried within 10 feet of each other in the Placerville Union Cemetery.

"My mother's mother was born in Massachusetts. She was in California at the time of the Marshall discovery. Her maiden name was Rhine. When her father died, her mother married Joseph Zeigler who had a farm just out of town, across the road from the present Lion's Park on Cedar Ravine road. He also was from Bavaria.

"When he took ill and could no longer work the farm, he sent for his stepdaughter and son-in-law Rodemark, who later became my grandfather. Zeigler gave him the farm and he operated it until he died."

So . . . the glass blower from Bavaria with a dream of making a fortune in gold became a farmer and reared a family in El Dorado county.

A RARE CERTIFICATE belonging to Mr. G substantiates his great-grandfather's status wi the fire department in 1859. Mr. Zeigler die 1902 at the age of 77.

ACIFIC MINE IN 1878

Charles Green, George Green's father, was born in Wales. He was a small child when his parents came to America, circa 1862. "They settled in Pennsylvania," said Green, "and the old gentleman worked in the coal mines. As my father grew up and finished grade school he said he grew tired of what was going on there. He thought the time was right for him to start out on his own. The first job he got was in Tuscarora, Nevada. He worked there for awhile . . . then had an opportunity to come to Placerville and work in the Pacific Mine. He was hoist engineer there for several years.

"While working at the mine he became interested in electricity," said Green. "He built an electric generator . . . a small one . . . but he made a mistake in the construction. He turned it on and it flew to pieces. A man by the name of Price put up the money and Father built another one. It worked and they had electric lights in the mine before Placerville had electricity."

"Soon business men in town formed a company," Green continued. "They bought a generator and Father installed it. He handled the distribution work and became the superintendent of the Placerville Electric Company."

Placerville until that time used gas lights. The gas was generated by burning pitch pine wood in a vast furnace. It was then distributed through cast iron pipe to all parts of the city, according to P. Sioli, circa 1883.

THE MOUNTAIN DEMOCRAT STAFF - circa 1920. Hand-set typography and time-saving devices such as "canned copy" and "boiler plate" were tools of the trade when the newspaper was printed on water-power propulsion presses. Pictured are Miss Mollie Carpenter, owner and publisher (seated at desk), and Clarence E. Barker, who later became owner and publisher of the Mountain Democrat (identified by his grandson, Joe Barker, and other family members). It seems appropriate that the name Clarence Barker appears in this book of pioneers because he was the grandson of Mathias Lauber, who in 1844 enlisted in Company C First Dragoons of General Kearney's forces. He was with Kearney and Commodore Stockton through the Mexican wars and was present when they marched into Los Angeles and raised the American flag over the fort on the hill. After his discharge Mathias Lauber came to El Dorado county. He went first to Big Bar on the Middle Fork of the American River and later located in Kelsey in about 1849. Today the Mountain Democrat masthead reads "Larry Belanger, Publisher & Editor". Mr. Belanger, a native of Wisconsin, was hired as Editor by the Barkers in 1957.

Dr. Fitch, a dentist, had the first electric drill in Placerville for dental work, thanks to Charles Green, who made a small water wheel-generator combination that charged the batteries during the night, building enough power to operate the drill during the day.

"Father was always experimenting with something," said Green, and proceeded to relate in detail the various bucket combinations his father experimented with before he was satisfied that he had perfected the most effective wheel possible. This was the double bucket with the rib in the center. "With this wide bucket he would lose none of the splash," explained Green, "and he would get the full force of the water pressure. He made the pattern and had these buckets made at Morey's Foundry, here in Placerville. Well, there was a man in town then who had been fiddling around with water wheels, and he saw Father's buckets there at the foundry. He either stole them or someone let him get away with them because he went straight to San Francisco and got a patent. His name was Pelton."

It is interesting to note that it was this water wheel design that generated the power to run the *Mountain Democrat* press, prior to the formation of the Placerville Electric Company.

70

El Dorado County Historical Museum Collection

MAIN STREET, PLACERVILLE
This picture was taken on May 10, 1899,
the day of the Foresters Picnic and Parade.
Most of these buildings were destroyed
in the courthouse fire of 1910.

In 1905 George Green's father died at the age of 43. This meant he had to quit school and go to work to help his mother. His first job was with the Morey Foundry & Machine Shop.

He later worked as a mechanic in a garage. After that he worked for W.A. Rantz in a store located in the building now occupied by the Ski Hut. When Rantz sold to Don Goodrich he continued to work in the store for 41 years. He retired in 1959.

Today Mr. and Mrs. Green live quietly in a home built for his father in the mid-1800s. Mrs. Green, nee May Fairbairn, a teacher, taught in the county schools for 16 years. They married in October of 1922 and recently celebrated their 54th anniversary. They have no children.

Among some of their prized possessions are several pieces of furniture made by Mr. Zeigler, who was known for his fine custom-built furniture.

George Green's ties with the past are ever-present for him because his grandfather's farm was a short two miles from his home on Cedar Ravine. And the Pacific Mine, where his father first worked, is just over the hill in back of his home.

THE PELTON WHEEL - According to Mr. Green, the double-bucket innovation
was created by his father, Charles Green, and the original model was later presented
by Mr. George Green to the University of California Hydraulic Laboratory.

71

The Courthouse Fire of May 15, 1910

The fire started when the janitor, Roy Taylor, burned some papers in the incinerator back of the Court House. "I remember it well," said Green. "There was no mechanized equipment in those days. The town had all hand-pulled hose carts, four horse-drawn carts, and the hook and ladder deal. I belonged to the outfit whose hose cart was stationed at the Ivy House. As soon as we were called out we went right down there.

"A strong east wind carried burning papers to the Odd Fellows building, a wooden structure that housed the Limpinsel Grocery Store . . . then a saloon operated by Warren Larkin was next . . . then the Central Hotel located where the city parking lot is now . . . next a blacksmith shop down where the Mother Lode Bank was. Burning paper and shingles were landing everywhere.

"There were a dozen fires going at once. That meant men were scattered out all over town. The farthest one was the Episcopal Church on Coloma street, a burning piece got under the roof. We finally got them all out except the main fire, the Court House, and it burned itself out.

"Because many people complained they hadn't heard the bell on the night of the fire, it was decided it should be moved to a higher location, out of the ravine to a hill somewhere."

The site chosen for the relocation of the town's "alert system" was on Reservoir and Pacific streets. Mr. Green described the results of this transfer as follows: "They rigged up a set of batteries that would press a button and the bell would be tapped six times. Well . . . it worked fine as long as the batteries were fresh. If the batteries ran down or there hadn't been a fire for some time, they wouldn't know if they had batteries or not.

"Of course when the batteries were down the hammer wouldn't work...the bell wouldn't ring, and by the time the operator got to the door and could locate the night watchman to go up the hill and ring the bell...the building would be burned down. So....they brought the bell back and replaced the Tower at the Plaza."

ALARM SPREAD through Placerville on May 15, 1910, when a fire started at the Court House. Fanned by winds, it threatened for a time to repeat the holocaust of 1856 when fire almost laid the town in ashes. This picture, taken on May 16, shows the remains of the Court House, on the right, then the Odd Fellows Hall, Limpinsel Grocery Store, Warren Larkin Saloon, and the Central Hotel. Greatest personal loss was that of District Attorney Thompson whose entire law library was destroyed.

William (Mike) DeNatly Photo

Green Collection

THE TOWN PLAZA - When the tower and alarm signal were moved to Reservoir Street following the 1910 fire, a plaza was designed at the site of the old Bell Tower. This picture was taken by Mr. George Green at noon on July 3, 1912. Right: The Bell Tower rebuilt.

Green Collection

THE FIRST HYDRAULIC PUMP known to exist, according to Mrs. Lane, was built by the Snow brothers Herman, Charles and Joseph.
The Snows were called on when the construction of the railroad line into Placerville reached Weber Creek west of town. Posts could not be
set for the bridge construction until water was removed from the post holes. The problem was solved by the Snow's hydraulic pump.
Pictured at the bridge site are the Snow brothers and members of the crew.

Mabel Snow Lane is the granddaughter of pioneer settlers Samuel S. Snow and Jacob Kyser. Her father was Herman Snow, son of Samuel Snow, and her mother, Helen Kyser, the daughter of Jacob Kyser, a rancher and fruit grower who settled in the vicinity of what is now known as Gutenberger's Corner, southeast of Placerville on the Pleasant Valley Road. Jacob Kyser was a descendant of the Marvin Roberts family, founders of Roberts Island in the Delta area years before the Marshall discovery of gold.

Mrs. Lane referred to an article written by Reva Clar for *The Western States Jewish Historical Quarterly* in 1970 to aid her in telling much of the Snow family's early history.

Samuel Sussman Snow arrived in New York on January 1, 1837 from his homeland, Germany, at the age of 19. There he resumed his studies in medicine (started earlier in France) and earned his diploma. It was in New York that he met and married Paulina Fink, whose Catholic family also came from Germany.

Doctor and Mrs. Snow left New York and settled for a while in Wisconsin, where he established himself as a practicing physician. He also started a fur trading business with the Indians. He received his naturalization papers in St. Croix, Wisconsin, on July 30, 1849.

From Wisconsin they moved to Council Bluffs, Iowa, where he continued his fur trading with the Indians. It was there that he bought a ranch and planned to settle and raise a family.

The winter of 1849 was cold and severe in Iowa, and Paulina Snow, who was now pregnant, suggested that they move to the milder climate of California. Spring of 1850 found Samuel Snow helping to organize a wagon train for California. His qualification as a doctor, and, perhaps, his experience in dealing with the Indians, may have influenced the group to elect him to lead the train. According to Mrs. Lane, he was the only Jewish individual known to head one of the many trains that traveled to California.

On May 15, 1850 the train left Council Bluffs. On that same day Emanuel Snow was born under a wagon. "Don't ask me why, under the wagon," said Mrs. Lane, laughing. "Maybe it was raining."

That the train crossed the plains without difficulty can probably be credited in great measure to Snow's friendly relations with the Indians along the way. One horse was lost on the trip, in Utah, and its place on the team was taken by the cow that was brought to provide milk for the infant Emanuel.

SAMUEL SUSSMAN SNOW
An El Dorado Pioneer

PIONEER WIFE AND MOTHER - Paulina Fink Snow, wife of Samuel S. Snow, was born June 28, 1827 in Germany. She came to America with her parents who travelled with her and her husband by covered wagon to California in 1850.

The wagon train arrived in Pleasant Valley, California in August of 1850. Samuel Snow was now 32 years old, his wife, Paulina, 23. Emanuel, their son, had spent the first two and one-half months of his life traveling to California.

On arrival most of the families stayed in Pleasant Valley. Dr. Snow, his wife and child, and Mrs. Snow's parents and their family continued on to Sacramento, where they took squatters' rights to land located on the present site of the California State Capitol grounds.

Dr. Snow left them there with instructions to wait until he returned. Taking some supplies, he went back to Hangtown to look into the mining situation. When he didn't return after a considerable length of time, the family became concerned, packed their belongings, and returned to Pleasant Valley, thus losing their right to the Sacramento land.

On their return to El Dorado County they found that Dr. Snow had started a store in a tent, selling supplies to miners in Dogtown. Family records show that on September 27, 1851, Paulina gave birth to their second son, Joseph, who was born while they lived in a tent in Diamond Springs.

In the later part of 1851, or early '52, he bought property from a Mr. Smith in Iowaville, a small mining camp that sprang up in 1849-'50, adjacent to another such camp called Dogtown. Both were in the area of what is now known as Newtown. The two-story house on the property was built of the finest Georgia pine lumber which reportedly had been shipped around Cape Horn and hauled to Iowaville by ox team. It was a well-constructed building and Dr. Snow soon was operating a hotel, a store, and a ten-pin alley on the ground floor. He also set aside one room in which he looked after his patients.

It would appear that word of the Snow business establishment in Dogtown had reached other camps, for the following item, written by Archer B. Hulbert, appeared in *The Chronicle of California Trails* in 1931.

> "We were prospecting on the north fork of Weber or Weaver Creek, twenty-five miles east of Hangtown. It was Saturday; the rain had been falling nearly all day, when Sam Hit came into camp with the joyful news that a white woman had come to Snow's Camp, sixteen miles away. Next morning he . . . . struck out on foot to see such a wonderful thing as a white woman. When he arrived at Snow's Camp it was late in the day, and as Mrs. Snow kept a restaurant, he had dinner at $1.50 . . . . he says he will never forget the day he walked thirty-two miles to see a white woman in California."*

Dr. Snow continued his medical practice primarily in the Newtown area, although he was known to travel great distances to answer a call for medical help.

* Western States Jewish Historical Quarterly

EMANUEL SNOW - *Oldest son of Samuel S. Snow, was a charter member of the Placerville Society of Territorial Pioneers. At the age of 75, in 1925, he was the oldest "covered wagon baby" to be honored at the California Admission Day Diamond Jubilee.*

JOSEPH SNOW *was born in 1851 in a tent in Diamond Springs. He was the 2nd son of Samuel and Paulina Snow, and the first of their nine children to be born in El Dorado County. After his father's death in 1892, Joseph Snow, then a successful miner and cattle raiser, paid tribute to his father's memory by registering as his cattle brand the initials "SS".*

Lane Collection Photos

THIS ORIGINAL SNOW HOME was located in Iowaville. Seven of the Snow children were born here. Unidentified members of the family appear in this picture, taken in 1895. It was here Samuel Snow conducted his many business affairs, and carried on his medical practice until his death in 1892. In 1906 his son, Jacob, built a new home here, using much of the fine Georgia pine that was used in the construction of the original home in 1850.

RMAN AND CAROLINE SNOW - Herman ame a miner. Caroline (Carrie) assisted her ber in his medical practice. She later married bbi Herman Davidson of Stockton, California.

THE NEW SNOW HOUSE, built in 1906, was still standing in 1914 when an article in the Mountain Democrat reported its location as being south of the North Fork of Weber Creek on the east side of Snows Road. Another report in the June 29, 1970 issue stated: "Andrew Taylor, who resides in the Snow home, was kind enough to show visitors some of the Snow mementos, including a Double-S branding iron, used on all Snow cattle." The home was destroyed by fire in 1974.

By 1861 the Snow family had increased. There were now six children, five boys and one girl, Caroline. Dr. Snow had also increased his interests in the county. He held one of the first riparian water rights in El Dorado County. In 1940, the State Water Resources showed this to be the oldest water right in the State of California. Five miles of ditches ran from the North Weber Creek to the Snow ranch house at Iowaville. Large reservoirs were built above the house for storage of water to fill the flumes.

Placerville Synagogue

In 1854 Samuel Snow joined with others to form the Placerville Hebrew Benevolent Society. They bought and fenced a small plot of land for a cemetery and fixed up a synagogue in time for the High Holidays.

The original synagogue was located on a .17 acre lot at the corner of Cottage and El Dorado Streets in Placerville. On April 30, 1878, Michael Simon, Edward Cohn, and Samuel Snow, trustees of the Society, sold the lot to James Bailey for $25.00. At the same time they bought a larger lot from Henry and Pauline Louis on the south side of Mill Street. When a freak storm, a hurricane, destroyed the synagogue that year, they built another one on the new lot. *

Asked about the mining, Mrs. Lane said, "I remember Father saying it was quite an undertaking getting the gold transported. They always had the women carry it. They'd put as much as they could carry on their persons and pack the rest in suitcases. They had to go by horse and buggy from home to Placerville, where they changed to a stagecoach. They never sold gold in Placerville. They took it on to the Sullivan mint in San Francisco. When they changed from the buggy, and again when they left the stagecoach in San Francisco, the men would walk alongside, with the women in the middle, just in case of a holdup.

"My father often told stories about mines. One was the Sailor Jack mine and was operated in my father's day by three sailors. After two of them died and the other was killed, accidentally, the owner of the mine refused to permit anyone to operate it.

"In the 1930s, during the Depression, the mines opened up again. The Sailor Jack was taken over by Edgar Kimball of Camino. My oldest brother, Charles, and a friend of his ran the Sailor Jack for Mr. Kimball, who was an engineer on the train then and didn't have the time to run it himself. That was a rich mine in the early days, but they found that the channel was cut by another channel that was picked up by a Mrs. Blakely on the other side of the hill. She became fabulously rich from that mine.

* WSJH Quarterly.

78

HELEN AND HERMAN SNOW raised their family of three in El Dorado county. They lived in Fairplay, Diamond Springs and finally on the Snow ranch near Newtown. Herman Snow was crippled by childhood spinal meningitis. Because he could not do the heavy work done by his brothers, he was assigned to handle the monitor in all the family hydraulic mining operations, and soon became a specialist. In 1890, he and his brother Jacob, using some of their mining capital, bought timberland, built saw mills, and went into the lumber business in the Sly Park Area.

CHARLES SNOW, born September 23, 1868 was the youngest of the Snow children who throughout their lives continued their activities in mining, ranching, stock raising and lumbering in the county. He died in 1932.

Lane Collection Photos

A WEDDING PARTY that experienced a shock. Helen Kyser and Herman Snow were married in Byron, California on April 18, 1906, the day of the San Francisco earthquake. Identified in the front row of the picture on the left, in dark suit, is Herbert Kyser, father of the bride, next to him is Adanan Houston, bridesmaid, Helen Kyser, the bride, Herman Snow, groom and, next to him his brother Charles, the best man. The identification of other members of the party was not possible due to the loss of records during the years.

MEMBERS OF THE JACOB KYSER FAMILY were photographed after the funeral of their mother in 1893. Back row from left: Roxana, Helen (mother of Mabel Snow Lane), Bert, Adanan, and Emily. Front row from left: Duane, Lena, Jacob Kyser, and Lora. Jacob Kyser was a rancher in El Dorado County, near Gutenberger's Corner on Pleasant Valley Road. According to family records, he was of the Roberts family that had settled Roberts Island in the early 1800's. Duane was 90 years old in 1976 and living in Sacramento, California.

"My father's and grandfather's mines were mostly hydraulic, and weren't named. The Snows hydraulicked all over El Dorado County — Newtown, Placerville, Diamond Springs, Coon Hollow. People called on them when there was any important hydraulicking to be done. My father was an expert. He always manned the monitor . . . that's where the water comes out. He could place that water any place he wanted it.

"There was a cave-in, once, and one of the miners was trapped inside the tunnel where they were hydraulicking. I remember Dad laughing about that . . . he said the only way he could get him out was to put the pressure on and wash the dirt from in front of the tunnel, which he did. When he got the dirt washed away, he called to the miner and told him to come out . . . and the miner called back, 'Well, put me on a nice clean board so I won't get dirty.' Of course, the poor man was already covered with mud from head to foot, but he came out laughing."

"Once when we were going through some old things in the attic of the old house," said Mr. Lane, "we found receipts that amounted to $100,000 from the mint. That was during the hydraulicking days. The attic was full of old books, ledgers, receipts, and different things . . . somehow they all disappeared. We do have a few mementos left . . . a scale they used to weigh the gold, a pan . . . and we have the old Pelton wheel used on the farm. And we believe we have the biggest flag in the county. It's about 13 by 21 feet in size. The folks stripped a big pine tree up on the hill and used it for a flag pole. It could be seen for miles."

Directional signs in the county reading Snows Road, Snows Ridge, and Snows Mill all testify to the activities of this pioneer family. Dr. Snow surveyed the road that bears his name. When they were mining and making frequent trips to Lake Tahoe, he surveyed that road through to Camino to avoid going into Placerville.

It was this hill that Mrs. Lane had to climb when she was a small child attending school. She said, "We walked a mile and a half to school . . . where the Camino Community Church is now. We lived on the other side of the hill and on the other side of the creek, but still they made us go to the Camino school instead of the Pleasant Valley school.

"When my mother thought the hill was too much for me, she sent me to my aunt's home. She was Mother's younger sister, Mrs. Ed Sherwood. They lived in the Summit school district, so I went to school there. The school is on the Springer and Bucks Bar roads, near the George Dean place. The Deans are related to the family too."

RELICS RECOVERED from the attic of the old Snow House before it was torn down include this scale and pan. Dents in the pan were made by the weight of gold pieces hitting the pan.

CLARENCE A. LANE, husband of Mabel Snow Lane.

POUNDING DAM - Members of the Snow family are pictured at the dam they built on Weber Creek.

Lane Collection Photos

FLUME running above the Snow Ranch from Weber Creek to Snow mine operation.

The Snows Mill sign is located in the Iron Mountain area. "We haven't been in that area since they renamed it the Immigrant Trail. We don't know whether the Forest Service left the marker there or not, but the family had a good-sized mill there until it burned. There was a sawmill on the ranch at one time, too, but the Snow boys never made too much money in lumber. They always lost it some way or another.

"The only one of the Snow boys that made money in lumber was "Jake", that was Jacob. He was born in 1853. He made and lost several fortunes. They say he was quite a colorful character."

Today, from their hillside home on Fort Jim road, Mr. and Mrs. Lane look out across the vast acres that were once the Snow Ranch (1200 acres at one time). Mr. Lane, a native son, was born in Chino and lived most of his life in the Santa Ana area. "I came up to El Dorado County during the Depression years with my sister and brother-in-law, Mr. and Mrs. Mendenhall," said Mr. Lane. "We didn't know much about mining but we made a go of it for several years. Then when times got bad I picked pears for Clarence Larsen in Camino."

The Lanes are confronted daily with the past. Less than 20 feet from their door they can pan gold whenever they wish. Behind the house can be seen an ancient river channel uncovered by the early day placer miners. The channel has been authenticated to be the prehistoric bed of the American River, when its course ran north and south.

Because of his other interests, Dr. Snow restricted his practice to residents in the Newtown area but was known to care for anyone who called on him, including the miners, the Indians, and especially his close friends. His daughter Caroline, who assisted him in his practice, told a story of his going out on horseback one night to treat an Indian woman whose husband had asked him for help. The man brought a horse for Snow to ride and a rawhide pouch of gold for payment, both of which Snow refused, saying that he would ride his own horse and that he wanted no payment. The Indian, in gratitude for the care given his wife, would often stop at the ranch and offer his help by cutting wood or doing any necessary chores.

Mrs. Lane remembered another story . . . "When my Dad was about four years old, Grandfather Snow came down with scarlet fever, so they sent all the kids over to Grandmother Fink's in Pleasant Valley. While they were there, my dad took an ax and chopped his finger off . . . almost off . . . all that was holding it was just a little piece of skin. Grandmother Fink didn't know what to do, so she sent him back home. Well, Grandpa Snow doctored that finger and he didn't lose the finger or even the joint . . . that had been cut in two. He saved the finger, but of course Dad got scarlet fever."

82

*Bureau of Mines

HYDRAULIC MINING-Herman Snow is shown operating the monitor during some hydraulic mining done on the Kimmer land adjoining the Snow property. This land became part of the Snow holdings. In hydraulic mining the dirt is torn down by water pressure, broken up, and carried on to the sluice where the gold is extracted. Reservoirs, built at a higher elevation than the claim, supply water for the operation. The force with which the stream of water rushes from the pipe attached to the hose is so great it will kill a man instantly and tear down a hill more rapidly than 100 men with shovels. In the foreground, in the photo on the right, the destruction of trees and all else in the path of the destructive force is quite visible. In 18? the State of California passed legislation prohibiting hydraulic mining. Driving through any part of the Mother Lode country one can see what some people describe as "pretty bluffs." In reality they most always are remains of some old hydraulic mining operation.

Lane collection photos

FILL FOR A DAM - Herman Snow, operating the monitor, washes away a hillside on the Snow property west of their home. The dirt was used to build the Weber Creek dam located between Newtown and Snows roads. Mrs. Lane could not identify the other man in the picture but believed it to be her uncle Charles.

MARY SILVA BACCHI was born April 2, 1878. The historic old Vineyard House in Coloma traditionally observes its anniversary on April 2nd, the day of its official opening in 1879. On April 2, 1972, Frank and Virginia Rimple, then owners of the Vineyard House, held open house honoring Mary Bacchi. This picture was taken at the Vineyard House on her 94th birthday.

Bacchi Collection

84

Bacchi Family Heritage

WILLIAM BACCHI, a native of Switzerland came to America prior to 1849. He came to El Dorado County and started raising cattle in 1861, a business that has been carried on by his sons and grandsons for more than a century.

NATIVES OF THE AZORE ISLANDS Manuel Silveria deAvilia and his wife Maria Narcissa Peinheiro met and married in Pilot Hill in 1877. Although both were from the Islands they met for the first time in Pilot Hill.

Mary Bacchi, nee Silva, was born April 2, 1878 in Pilot Hill, El Dorado County. She was nearing her 97th birthday when she granted an interview in her home located on the Bacchi Ranch, where a cluster of Bacchi family homes dot the land that was known as Michigan Flat during the Gold Rush. She asked that her son Byron be present during the interview, on January 15, 1975. "Because," she said, "his memory is better than mine." However, she needed very little prompting, as she and Byron, who then was 65 years of age, reminisced.

Her father was a whaler. "He was born on an island in the Azores. He often told me that when he was a boy he'd sit for hours watching the big sail boats pass. The bigger the sails, the more he dreamed about going to sea." She said he was still a young boy when he got a job on a boat and soon was sailing the seas as a whaler. "He whaled all over the world."

In 1850 the ship sailed into San Francisco. When the crew heard about the gold strike, they deserted. Her father worked on Telegraph Hill for a time, then settled in Pilot Hill.

"Father's name was Manuel Silveria deAvilia," said Mrs. Bacchi, "but the only time you will see it is on his tombstone in the Pilot Hill Cemetery. He changed his name to Manuel Silva. He said his name took too long to write.

"My mother, Maria Narcissa Peinheiro, was a native of the Azores too, only she lived on a different island than my father. They didn't meet until they were living in Pilot Hill. That's where they married in 1877. Her name was shortened too. Everybody called her Mary and her last name kept changing until they finally had it down to Pine, Mary Pine." "Lots of people changed their names when they came here," said Byron. "Some because their names were unusual and hard to remember or spell and some for other reasons . . . who knows?"

When her father's interest in mining waned, he turned to ranching. "Mining wasn't the big thing with father. He mined for a while at the Marshall claim in Pilot Hill Canyon, when he lived in Cooper Ravine. Later he bought some cows from someone down at Clarksville and started raising cattle. When it got too much for him I helped. He didn't ride a horse and I did, so I took over . . . more or less."

When she was 16 years old she owned her own cattle. She thought she had about 70 head at that time. When she moved them to summer pasture in the mountains, she went by herself. "I didn't need any help. I pastured up at Stumpy Meadows and drove them by way of Cool and Georgetown. It was a two day trip, so I stayed overnight with the Brazils out of Georgetown the first night. They were just below Balderstons. Then the next day I'd drive them on to the Meadows."

Some Childhood Memories: "When I started to school I had to walk three miles to the Pilot Hill School. Later they built the Burner Hill School nearer our home, and I only had to walk a mile and a half." She recalled the names of teachers, Maude Lovejoy, Mr. Adams and Mr. William Dunn, who, she said, came from Kansas. Byron said that when he attended school he had to walk about a mile and a half to the Union School, which later was called the Lotus School.

"I remember one time . . . my father took me with him to Placerville to pay the taxes," said Mrs. Bacchi. "We went in a horse-drawn cart. On the way back I got cold. I can't remember ever being so cold. Father stopped at the Long Garden gate and the lady there . . . what's her name . . . Mrs. Hawke, I think . . . she gave me a cup of hot tea and that kept me warm 'til we got home. It was a long way to Placerville then. We started at daylight and didn't get home until dark.

"Then there was the time I was so sick they had to get a doctor. I was about 12 or 13 years old, I guess. The doctor told them to put me in a tub of salt water and for me to exercise, walk or ride a horse. And he gave me some little pink pills that were full of iron. He said I'd lost my vitamins or something." When asked if she thought the salt baths helped, she said, "Well, they couldn't hurt you."

Did she ever meet Marshall? "No, he was before my time. He died in 1885. I was only about six then but I remember them talking about him. There was something going on at Coloma one time. Wagons passed the place all day. They said it was about Marshall but we didn't go. It was a long way from Pilot Hill to Coloma." Because of the dates mentioned, it can be assumed the event was the funeral of James Marshall.

"Very few people today understand what it was like then," said Byron. "There were no trains out here, no busses, automobiles, telephones, TV, and the like. You take, even in my time, when we moved the cattle to the mountains we packed the wagon with what we would need and stayed all summer. You could go for months without seeing anybody but the members of your own family. If someone happened to stop by, that was an event. We had our work to do and we stayed home and did it. Now-a-days when something happens in Europe you'll hear about it quicker than we'd hear about something that happened fifteen miles away in those days."

HENRY BACCHI points toward the Bacchi homestead on top of the hill where he was born.

MARY BACCHI designed and made a divided skirt so she could ride western saddle while driving her cattle to range in 1906.

86

Bacchi Collection

THE BACCHI RANCH is situated at the site of the early-day mining camp in the heart of what was called Michigan Flat. It was here the Stanford brothers operated a miners' store.

Bruce Robinson Photo

THE BAYLEY HOUSE on Highway 49 at Pilot Hill was built by A. J. Bayley in 1860 and was the private residence of the Bayley family. Constructed of bricks, the colonial-style mansion was reported to be second to none in the state at that time. When rumor had it that the proposed transcontinental railroad was to follow the Fremont Route through the Sierra, Mr. Bayley built, intending to operate it as a hotel. When the railroad by-passed Pilot Hill, going through Auburn instead, he retained the three-story, 24 room palatial residence for his family. There have been several owners through the years. The most recent, Alexander & Baldwin of Honolulu, presented the historic landmark to El Dorado County.

Landmarks

"The Old Bayley House at Pilot Hill was there before I was born," said Mrs. Bacchi. "I knew the Bayleys. Mama used to send me there to get things from the store. They had a store in the kitchen part of the house. It was a big house. The family living part was upstairs. The Bayleys are buried in the cemetery on the hillside there. Tom Stevenson owned it for a while. I knew him too and then John Wagner bought it and his family lived there. I knew them all. I guess there isn't much left of the place now with all the vandalism that's gone on there. They've taken about everything but the bricks, and I guess they're too heavy to carry away."

Michigan Flat, now part of the Bacchi Ranch near Lotus, was once the 'shopping center' for approximately 500 people who lived there in 1854 and later. Miners who worked the Red Hill, Coyote Diggins, and Rich Gulch mines came into town to buy from Charles Smith, who was the first merchant reported to have opened a store built of canvas.

The Stanford store opened later and it was here the Stanford brothers, Thomas W. and Leland, laid the foundation of their wealth.

From Michigan Flat, El Dorado County, Leland Stanford went on to become the Civil War Governor of California from 1861 to 1863. In 1885 he was elected to the Senate where he served two terms. When he died, he left 9000 acres of Sacramento property and $21 million to the State. Stanford University stands as a monument to Leland Stanford.

The Bacchis have a monument of sorts, just inside the gate at Mary Bacchi's house. It is a granite stone that stood outside the door of the Stanford Store at Michigan Flat. Many old-timers said men had won or lost their entire earnings, in gold, betting on a man who thought he could lift the rock. The rock is not large in size but weighs over 440 pounds. Byron said they had heard that only two men ever succeeded in lifting it.

Bacchi Collection

In 1908 Mary Silva married Henry Bacchi. They had three children, Byron, Francis, and Bethel. Asked about their courtship, she said they went to the dances held in the Community Hall at Pilot Hill, and when she worked at Forni's he'd stop by to see her.

"Yes, I worked. I cooked at a traveling house where the cattlemen passed . . . it happened like this. It was a real dry year. They shut the water down at Georgetown and the cattle people had to do something . . . so they moved their cattle up early. Forni had a place up there and he said if I'd go up and do the cooking and take care of the place, he'd furnish everything and in the fall we'd divide half and half, and that's what we did.

"I cooked the meals, served them family style, and kept the rooms ready. That meant washing the sheets almost every day. We didn't have washing machines then. I heated the water in a wash boiler in the yard and washed on a wash board. And then I had to look after my cattle. I made sure they were all right. I put out salt for them and in the fall, of course, I had to wean the calves and put them to meadow. Yes, I worked."

The Bacchi Family Heritage

William Bacchi, a native of Switzerland, lived in the town of Rodi in the Swiss Alps. He emigrated to America and was mining in Trinity County when news came of the Marshall gold discovery in Coloma. Before making his home in Garden Valley, El Dorado County, he lived in Diamond Springs and the town of El Dorado, where he met and married Virginia Pini, who also was a native of Switzerland. They had two sons, Henry and William, and three daughters. One died at the age of 12. Virginia and Elizabeth grew to adult age.

Like most Swiss people the Bacchis kept dairy cows. William Bacchi is said to have likened the foothill land of El Dorado County to

THE BURNER HILL SCHOOL-1891- MARY SILVA was 13 years old when she attended the Burner Hill school in the Pilot Hill district. Prior to the building of this school she had to walk three miles to attend the Pilot Hill School. Burner Hill was located near Foster Corral and Ridge Field in the Pilot Hill district and only one and a half miles from her home. Students standing are, from left: Mary Silva, Florence Briggs, Harriet Revoir, Louise Coster, Mary Foster, Manuel Coster, Joe Foster, August Coster, Manuel Silva, Frank Coster, Horace Burnett, Joe Coster, and George Burnett. The girl on the horse is Dollie Foster. Joseph Mario is the man holding the horse. Seated in the buggy at the left are Mrs. Catherine Perry and Mrs. Laura Aubertus. The teacher at that time was Mr. John Adams (not shown).

Bacchi Collection

MARY AND HENRY BACCHI at their ranch after checking a herd at pasture. Picture taken about 1950.

THE MANUEL SILVA FREIGHTER - Manuel Silva, brother of Mary Bacchi, started his freight-hauling business in 1907. He made regular runs between Georgetown, Cool, Pilot Hill, and other Mother Lode towns and Sacramento. This picture was taken in Sacramento about 1909.

that of the Swiss Alps. He foresaw the promise it offered for raising beef cattle, a commodity he believed would be in demand as more and more families continued to arrive in the county daily. Mr. Bacchi homesteaded and purchased land as did his children when they followed in his footsteps.

An article published in the Sacramento Bee in 1956, an interview with Henry Bacchi, made it quite clear that it was not always easy. He told how they had started selling, first to the mining and lumber camps, and then to the stores. As competition grew they found their market held because of the superior quality of their meat. They had started with Durhams and bred to Hereford bulls; they also raised swine. They took their cattle and swine to high country where grass and birch were plentiful, producing a high grade quality of meat.

The article also carried Mr. Bacchi's opinion of the red tape imposed upon the ranchers by the government at that time. He told about the time a federal man came to the ranch and told him he would have to tear out a small dam that they had built on their property. Mr. Bacchi then told the federal man what he thought of the idea, refused to tear out his dam, and ordered him off the ranch.

The Bacchis are a close family. The ranch business is run with the cooperation of all family members. At one time during the interview with Mary Bacchi, she said of her sons, "Francis is the cowboy and Byron is the mechanic. It takes both to make it work . . . ."

Today, her son Byron and his wife Carol, their son Eddie, his wife Virginia, and children, and her son Francis, his wife Betty, and their children, Henry, Nikke, Cherie, and James are a part of the Bacchi heritage. With the exception of Nikke, they all live in their separate homes within the Bacchi Ranch compound at the foot of the hill where the first family homestead was located.

89

He Drove the Tahoe Stage

Marion Burgess, who celebrated his 83rd birthday this Bicentennial Year, enjoyed talking about Coloma, its people, and his life while growing up in a town that had survived the stampede of the California Argonauts in 1849. He also talked about Placerville — with its dirt roads filled with cobblestones, gas street lamps, and board sidewalks — where he worked in 1916 as a mechanic and drove the Pierce-Arrow Stage to Lake Tahoe and Camp Richardson.

Marion was one of three sons born to Rufus and Stephanie Burgess of Coloma. They were Edgar, known as 'Tod', Rufus, and Marion. He does not remember his grandparents' names but remembers hearing his father say that they came to California across the plains with a wagon train. They were slaves and traveled with their owner in 1850.

His father, Rufus Burgess, did some mining at first, but he soon bought land and started to farm. "Our farm was on the hillside across from where gold was discovered," said Burgess.

"Father terraced that whole hillside by hand and then planted fruit trees. We packed the fruit at home and hauled it by horse and wagon to Placerville.

"My father had a blacksmith shop, too. It was there where the Coloma Community Hall is now, by the bridge. He used to do all the tool sharpening, horse shoeing, and anything in general repair work. They used to have lots of trouble with wagon wheels. The spokes would get loose . . . so he'd tighten them up. He'd heat the rims and put them on a spindle to shrink them. And that tightened the spokes up. They had heavy wagons then. John Wagner had a six-mule team. He used to haul freight. He'd haul anything . . . but mostly that heavy mining machinery."

Very little mining was done at that time, with the exception of the Chinese, who were working the river.

"They had sluice boxes with ripples in between. They'd throw the dirt in, then wash the dirt out, and the gold stayed in the ripples," said Burgess. "I guess nobody knows how much gold they took out. They'd pack it in old suitcases and bags and take it to San Francisco. Some of them had to walk all the way."

Old timers who know Marion Burgess will remember his hearty laughter, his jovial nature, and his ability to see the humorous side of life. Today, at 83, he has lost none of that youthful spirit. But he wonders why people can't get along together as they did in Coloma in the early days.

THE STAGE - On the way to Lake Tahoe with a party from Placerville.

RUFUS BURGESS joined the US Army following the declaration of war June 6, 1917. He returned to Coloma March 19, 1919. Other young men of Coloma who enlisted were Gavert Grother, Clarence and Alvin Marchini, Joe Hooper, Howard Ashley and Joe Hansen.

Yohalem Collection

AS LATE AS 1883 residents in Coloma indulged in some mining. Pictured working a drift off the American River near town are, from left, Charles Johnson, a fruit grower, Phil Teuscher, a miner, Rufus Burgess, local blacksmith and farmer, and Commodore P. Young, a miner. Visible in the far background are the suspension bridge and the buildings of Coloma.

Marshall Gold Discovery Park Museum

MONUMENT OF NATIVE STONE was erected the State Park, designating the location of the tter mill where James W. Marshall discovered ld in 1848.

"Coloma was a quiet town. Everybody was good, no problems . . . unless some one came in from outside and started trouble. It was the most wonderful place in the world to live. I wish it could be like that now.

"I remember how the people would come and visit one another. Everybody had a jug of wine. They'd take a glass and sit . . . and talk . . . and talk . . . and talk. They'd tell what they'd done, where they'd been, how many miles they'd traveled. I think they told some pretty big whoppers. But that was their way of having a good time. They didn't fight like they do now. In those days, getting together was just having a good time.

"The kids, too, they had to make their own amusement. They didn't have play parks or picture shows, but they had fun. I remember one time . . . you know, the Chinese liked to play cards and gamble. Well, one night when the Chinese were sitting out there gambling, the kids got real close and tied their queues together. Then they snuck up with a big bunch of ashes and threw it all over them. Well, the poor men . . . they couldn't see . . . they jumped up, pulling each other this way and that, trying to get their queues untied. It was really something."

Marshall? "No, I don't remember my folks talking about him. He was before my time. He was buried, I think, about 1885. I wasn't born

91

until 1893. People used to come down to Coloma, though, asking to see where he found the gold. My brother Tod, that's Edgar. Everybody called him Tod. We used to take people down by the river and show them where the mill used to be."

Mr. Burgess said that when he was older he worked with a crew of men assigned to locating the site of the saw mill, because the state had erected a monument to Marshall and proposed placing a marker at the mill site. However, the South Fork of the American River had changed its course from time to time, and floods had carried away all surface evidence of the structure. It was while digging in the river bed that Burgess struck a metal object with his shovel. It was a saw that had been used at the mill. Further digging uncovered other evidence that established the original mill site, and a marker was installed.

The fact that the saw had not rusted while under water all those years was attributed to the fact that it was buried in heavy layers of sawdust. The seven-foot artifact is now on display in the County Historical Museum at the county fairgrounds in Placerville.

Mr. Burgess spoke of the many times the bridges in Coloma were washed out, making it necessary to ford the river. When a new bridge was built in 1915, he and his brothers worked on its construction.

He recalled working in Placerville as a mechanic when he was about 18. "I worked at the Class A Garage, across the road from the Ohio House. I must've been there for almost five years. Then I worked for others too . . . drove a truck for Fitzlawf, and for Louis Enzler. He operated a transfer company. I think it was about 1916 or '17 I drove the Pierce-Arrow Stage Coach, for Richardson, to Lake Tahoe. My brother Tod drove it from the beginning. He'd take it from Sacramento to Placerville, then to Lake Tahoe and Reno. He did that a long time."

He laughed as he remembered the time he was making a return trip from the Lake in the Pierce-Arrow and someone had drained the oil from the engine and forgotten to replace it. "I was this side of Phillips and there was this whirring, grinding noise. I got off the road just in time because it just wouldn't turn no more . . . all the bearings was burned out."

He used to watch the sheriff as he patrolled the Chinese section of town and "where those ladies lived." He watched him when he turned on the street lights at night. He doesn't remember his name, but said, "He was a little short fella, kinda crippled. We used to call him 'Step-and-a-half'. He'd walk along with this long stick . . . the lights were fastened to a pole . . . then he'd stick this stick up to the lamp and it would light. It must've had something on it, like carbon or something, and the light would come on. They were gas lamps."

When he spoke of his friends he mentioned Irma Lawyer, whom he had recently visited at Lotus, Edward DeLory, Jones Wilder, a teacher named Carver, Simon Hunt, the Hoopers, and the Papinis.

"I don't remember too well," said Mr. Burgess. "I'm 83 years old now . . . and I can look back and see where I could have bettered myself, especially where money was concerned . . . but I'm too old to think of that."

FORDING THE AMERICAN RIVER at Coloma below where the bridge is today. Picture was taken about 1916.

SUSPENSION BRIDGE over American River w for foot traffic only. Three bridges had previou been washed away by flood waters.

Yohalem Collection

Marshall Gold Discovery Park Museum

Yohalem Collection

THIS WHIP SAW, found buried in sawdust in the American River at Coloma, in 1929, revealed the site of Sutter's sawmill. A memorial marker was placed at the site. The men who recovered the saw are, from left, Henry Labiff, who was the County Surveyor, Marion Burgess, Henry Gallagher, Joe McGonagle, Henry Kane, and Frank Spencer. The man on the right in back of Spencer is believed to be either Albert or George Johnson.

Descendant of the Winters Family

Claire Freeman's interest in the history of El Dorado County and its pioneer families is well known to local history buffs. She is a descendant of pioneers. Articles written by her appear frequently in the Heritage Association feature column "Reminiscing" in the Mountain Democrat. Claire Freeman was born Claire Rosier in Placerville in 1898. When interviewed at her home on Coloma Street in Placerville, she said, "My grandfather, Levi Rosier, came to California across the plains in 1850. His wife, Zelpha, and their two little daughters Laura and Jane came later by boat across the Isthmus in 1859. My aunt said a big storm came up on the trip and they were terrified. There was a cow in the hold of the ship and it kept bawling all the time. She said later when she had nightmares she could hear that cow bawling.

"When the Rosiers first arrived they lived in White Rock briefly, and then went to Columbia Hill in Nevada County. That's where my father Charlton (Charles) Francis H. Rosier was born. They came back to White Rock and lived there for many years. They moved to Placerville in 1875.

"My father was a surveying steward on a boat at Lake Tahoe for years. He married Clara Winters, who was the daughter of Joseph Winters, at Virginia City, Nevada. My mother died when I was just three years old."

When she spoke of her grandfather Winters' early days at Lake Tahoe she said, "He was a partner with Captain Augustus Pray and in 1861 they built the first sawmill near Glenbrook. In 1863 he and Lee Colbach built the first hotel, Hotel Glenbrook House. It remained the finest hotel at Lake Tahoe until 1875, when it was moved across the lake by barge in 1897. Then it became known as McKinny's Resort."

In September 1960 Mrs. Freeman paid a visit to her cousin Mrs. Gertrude Kurt in Nevada and they talked about the family. She said, "Great-grandfather John Deivers Winters and his wife Elizabeth, for whom the town of Elizabeth, Illinois, was named, operated one of the longest stagelines in the world. It ran from Galena, Illinois to Washington, D.C. Great-grandmother was a woman of great courage and executive ability. One time when there was a flood the driver was afraid to ford the stream, so Elizabeth took over the reins and drove the team across. They were carrying the mail.

LEVI ROSIER crossed the plains to arrive in California in 1850. He was a native of Wisconsin, a miner and farmer by trade. In 1859 he sent for his wife Zelpha 'Johnson' Rosier and their two young daughters Laura and Jane who arrived by way of the Isthmus of Panama.

CLAIRE ROSIER at age two. Her grandfather Joseph Winters was one of the original six signatures of the Ophir Mine. (inset above)

THE HOTEL ROSIER in 1895 was located where the El Dorado Savings and Loan building is today (1976). Mrs. Claire Freeman's mother Clara and her father Charles Rosier operated the hotel in 1895-96. They are shown with friends in the front of the hotel. Mrs. Rosier (in white dress) is standing next to her husband. The hotel faced on Coloma Street and the board-sidewalk at right led to what is now Center Street parking lot. At that time it was a street of barns, chicken houses, stables and similar buildings. The city had public toilets at that time. They were built over Hangtown Creek at the rear of the buildings.

THE ORIGINAL STRAWBERRY STATION *when owned by Will Watson, Mrs. Freeman's uncle, was an overnight stop for people traveling express or freighter from Nevada through Lake Valley to Placerville.*

Photos from Freeman Collection

"It's hard to understand why J. D. Winters left his prosperous business and came West," said Mrs. Freeman. "He dealt with presidents and was a person of importance. There was one thing . . . he went on a $100,000 bond for a friend and had to make good on it . . . so perhaps he figured by leaving the whole business and going West that he would settle things. Nevada County history tells much of the life and success of the Winters family.

"Their sons, Theodore, John and my grandfather Joseph, had come West ahead of the parents in 1847. There is one story they tell about my grandfather. He was 15 years old when his father caught him gambling with the guests at the Illinois Hotel, owned by his father in Sacramento at the time. His father disapproved violently and threw him out. He tried gambling on the river boats and amassed quite a sum of money. He and John Clark were partners in a restaurant at Foresthill when Joseph got word of the silver strike in Virginia City. His brother John was teaming over the mountains at the time, and they went to Virginia City.

"They tell stories about how he, my grandfather, gambled with the Mormons and won all their money and traded it back for shares in the Ophir Mine, at that time only a hole in the ground. He retained these shares and had them when the mine came in. Then we heard the story of Grandmother's mother . . . that was Elizabeth's mother. She was stolen by the Black Hawk Indians. The Indians killed the children who were with her. She had another child while she was held captive. She nursed the Indians through a smallpox epidemic and they may have relaxed their guard on watching her, because she escaped with the baby, but in fording a stream the baby was washed from her arms and she returned alone.

"To me," said Mrs. Freeman, "one of the most important bits of El Dorado history about our family would be my aunt Viola Rosier's marriage to Will Watson. He was the son of Charles Watson, the stage coach driver who figured in the Bullion Bend Holdup in 1864. The robbers presented him with a receipt for silver bullion and money in the Wells Fargo strongboxes stating it was to be used for the Confederate Army fighting in the Civil War."

The robbers were traced to the Somerset House where, in a shootout, one deputy sheriff was killed and another wounded. The men were later arrested but the bullion and strongboxes were never found. For years men searched the hills between Sportman's Hall and Somerset House trying to find where the loot was hidden. It has never been found or reported found.

"My aunt gave me a whiskey bottle that was fastened onto the stage driven by her husband's father, Charles Watson, when the stage was held up. She pointed out that a thong was laced through the eyelets on the flask and it hung on the stage for first aid. I suppose that was in case any of the travelers couldn't stand the wild and woolly rides down the mountains."

96

CHARLES A. WATSON - Stage coach driver who was given a receipt from the robbers of the stage at Bullion Bend in 1864.

DELIA WHALEN WATSON was born in Liverpool, England in 1841. She came to America in 1857 and married the legendary stage coach driver, Charles A. Watson, in 185

ZELPHA BARLOW BOSQUIT, Daughter-in-law of El Dorado County sheriff A. S. Bosquit and cousin of Claire Freeman. The Bosquit family raised Mrs. Freeman following the death of her mother when she was three years old.

DELIA WATSON–whom Mrs. Freeman affectionately calls Grandma Watson. This picture was taken prior to her death in 1917.

OUVENIR OF THE BULLION BEND LDUP - This flask hung somewhere on the e coach driven by Charles Watson on the oc- n of the holdup at Bullion Bend. It was n to Mrs. Freeman by her uncle Will Watson, of Charles the stage driver. The holdup : place June 30, 1864. Two coaches were ging silver bullion from Virginia City, da, when they were stopped above Sports- 's Hall by six armed men. Ned Blair was ing the first coach and Watson the second. robbers were captured but there is no rd of the bullion ever being found.

THE BARLOW HOME in Upper Town about 1875. Pictured are, from left: Levi Rosier, Mrs. Claire Freeman's grandfather, next the five Barlow girls: Grace, Zelpha, Bertha, Rena and Etta and their mother Laura and father George Barlow. The home was among many removed for the construction of the freeway through Placerville in 1952.

About Placerville: "When I was a child, Placerville was a very beautiful place. I'm sorry to see so many of our lovely buildings have disappeared. Especially I regret that the freeway took so many of the homes in Upper Placerville. In those days it was always Uppertown or Lowertown. Old-timers said it was like two separate towns. In the old city directory put out by the Fitches Printers they were listed that way. There was quite a bit of rivalry between them. They ran a bus then between the two towns. The fare was 25 cents to go to Uppertown or Lowertown or reversed.

"Stella Tracy wrote an article about the homes in Uppertown. J. W. Sigwarts had a beautiful home there, as did C. W. Brewster. The Parkhurst Crosby home was on the main road. It had a 260-foot frontage. The house sat back from the road. My grandfather Rosier bought it in 1875 and it was destroyed in 1952 to make way for the freeway. Mr. S. A. Brown owned it at that time, and he was a partner with Truman Wilcox who had a grocery store.

"Mrs. Brown was quite a gardener and she had a conservatory on the east part of the property. It was a beautiful home with croquet grounds and the young people of Placerville used to gather and play croquet there, but the freeway took it all. I was a little disappointed that some of the old-timers didn't have backbone enough to get up and fight it even though they knew it would lose money. I did, but I didn't get anywhere."

Photos from Freeman Collection

The Ivy House: "Well, I can only tell you what we've heard about it. It was called Upper Central House at the time my father and uncle Will Watson bought it. It is so often referred to as the Conklin Academy. Well, the first Conklin Academy was on Bedford Street, where the telephone company has a service building now. It was on the west side of the street. When I was a child I used to visit the Bosquit home that was there and Molly Thorndyke had the old Bedford Inn. That was the first Conklin Academy there on Bedford Street. Jessie Maynard was the librarian here at one time. My cousin Etta of the Kramp family in Diamond Springs and Maggie Kelley, who was the Superintendent of Schools, were instrumental in establishing the Marshall Museum in Kelsey. When Maggie was no longer able to take care of it they tried to sell, but it seems no one had money to buy the things and they moved them or returned those that were on loan. The state had given some money toward the museum which they named "The James Marshall Museum". We had supposed that most of the things would go to Sutter's Fort in Sacramento, but they were dispersed and were not available when it came time for the museum that was built in Coloma."

Early Days: "It's interesting in a way to see the reenactment of the wagon train, but that is just to publicize a road . . . they never say anything about the beautiful sights along the road. I can remember in the early days when the crowd would get together and we'd go up to Kyburz and all the fishermen and hunters got together and camped down there in the meadow.

"Then it was so interesting to see 'Old Sugarloaf' . . . they never feature that or say anything about it . . . and it's such a famous old rock. Crowds would go up . . . they would take a picnic lunch and hike up to 'Sugarloaf'. When the men would reach the top they'd put a flag up there and it was really something to see.

"And today you see pictures of Strawberry Lodge. The way it looks now would lead you to believe that that's where the lodge was, but it really wasn't. That wasn't where it was at all. The building was right up close to the mountain, the original Strawberry . . . and you could look up at the rock and feel that you were right under the cliff.

"I remember the snake hunts too. Alice Pugh and a bunch of us went out one time. The men had guns and knew right where the snake dens were and they'd shoot down there and I remember they brought back a whole sack of snakes, yes, rattlers.

"I do wish they would feature 'Sugarloaf', 'Lovers Leap' and 'Riverton' and some of these beautiful sights along the road instead of glorifying a road."

THE CONKLIN ACADEMY FACULTY - This rare photograph of the faculty is believed to have been taken in 1880. Identification was listed giving last names only in some cases. Those identified are, from left, standing: Prof. John P. Munson, ...Ball (music teacher), Charles E. Markham, ...Redman, ...Bartholome Munson. Seated, from left: Mrs. Wilson (English), Prof. E. B. Conklin, Mrs. Conklin, and Mrs. Egleston. The first Academy was located on Bedford Street and later moved to the Ivy House building.

Freeman Collection

HAVING THEIR PICTURE TAKEN with "Grandma" Watson at Strawberry in 1901 wer from left: Mrs. Will Watson, Hazel Watson, sta ing at Grandma Watson's chair, Jane Rosier an young Gladys Watson. Strawberry Lodge at that time was owned by William Martin, husband of Olive Watson, who was the daught of Charles A. Watson, stage driver.

El Dorado County Historical Museum Photo

Freeman Collection

THE IVY HOUSE on Main Street in Placerville was operated by Mrs. Freeman's uncle, Will Watson, and her father, Charles Rosier, from 1893 through 1895. The surrey met the trains and stages that arrived and transported the guests to the hotel. Meals were served for 25 cents.

THE ROSIER FAMILY HOME in Uppertown, known as the Brown Home was built in 1875. It was among the homes condemned to make way for the freeway through Placerville. Mrs. Claire Freeman, nee Rosier, identified those in the picture, from left: Eddy Bonker, Mrs. Rosier on the porch holding Hazel Watson, Grandma Rosier, Will Wigglesworth (sitting on stones), Grandfather Kevin Rosier, in foreground, Grace Barlow and Zelpha Barlow.

Freeman Collection

Marguerite Hoxie Pho

Salmon Falls Pioneers

It was not the lust for gold that brought Mary Sullivan to America from County Cork, Ireland. It was the desire to flee from the devastation that the potato famine had caused in Ireland. Miss Sullivan had an uncle living in New York and, according to Mrs. J. Frances Wagner, her granddaughter, she joined him there in 1850.

After working for her uncle a short time, she had an opportunity to work in Boston, Massachusetts. The news of the migration to California fired the imagination of the young Irish girl, and one day she boarded a sailing vessel in Boston and sailed to San Francisco by way of the Isthmus of Panama.

She found employment in San Francisco but did not stay long. She was offered an opportunity to go to Sacramento to work and accepted. Again her stay was short. When she was offered work with Mr. and Mrs. Joseph Taylor who operated the Wakasha House in El Dorado County, she accepted.

The Wakasha House was one of the main stops for travelers going to the Mother Lode.

"While she was employed at the Wakasha House she met my grandfather, Austin Taylor Leachman," said Mrs. Wagner. "He was a nephew of the Taylors. They married in 1859 and purchased a ranch and buildings located where Brown's Ravine is today. They established the Leachman House and were successful in operating it as long as the stage and freighters traveled the Overland Road. Grandfather served two terms as Supervisor of the 4th district.

"They had one daughter, Jennie, who was born May 10, 1861. In 1900 she married my father, Walter F. Cirby, only child of Jennie Frances Cirby, also of a pioneer family," said Mrs. Wagner, who today makes her home in Folsom, California.

THE GAINS HOUSE was formerly the Orr Hotel of Salmon Falls built by Thomas Orr who in 1855 sold the property to Mrs. Mary Gains, widow of J. W. Gains. The building was Mrs. Gains' home at the time this picture was taken. A store operated by Mr. J. T. Silberborn was located nearby, and the Salmon Falls school was across the road. In 1930 the property was owned by William A. Miller, a grandson of Mr. and Mrs. Gains.

JENNIE LEACHMAN

AUSTIN TAYLOR LEACHMAN arrived in California in 1850 by wagon train. He operated the Leachman House, a stop-over place on his 220 acre farm in the Salmon Falls area. Active in politics, he was twice elected supervisor of the 4th district.

THE ROLLING HILLS in the Salmon Falls area in El Dorado County were turned to farm land in 1884 when William B. Plumb and his wife Sophie, whose maiden name was Silberhorn, acquired 280 acres on the south fork of the American River. Pictured in the field on their farm are Mr. and Mrs. Plumb and their daughter Addie, who in later years became Mrs. George B. Hoxie. The Plumb home, barn and out-buildings can be seen in the background. The Chinese handyman, in background to left, lived in a cabin on the farm. When the water was high he rowed Addie across the river to attend the Salmon Falls school.

THE CROOKS FAMILY HOME IN SALMON FALLS - This picture was taken about 1885 when Mr. George Crooks, (standing left of center) was ditch tender on the Natomas ditch. Mrs. Crooks is seated on the extreme right of the picture with one of their married daughters, Ada Joerger. Mrs. Ida Wulff, left, is with her friend Addie Plumb and Mrs. Ella Anderson, seated center, whose husband also was a ditch tender on the Natomas ditch. The ditch is visible on the left of the picture.

THE SALMON FALLS SCHOOL in 1857 had 62 children in attendance. This picture, taken about 1884, indicates the drop in population in that area following the exodus of the miners. Addie Plumb, who later became Addie Hoxie, is standing in the front row, second girl on the right from the chair, center.

Marguerite Hoxie Photos

Rudy Schlein – 49'er!

Rudolph Schlein was born May 1, 1884. He was nearing his 92nd birthday when interviewed at his cabin home on Auburn Ravine in Auburn, Placer County. At the scheduled time for the interview he was napping in a hammock under a big oak tree in front of his cabin. Mr. Schlein's appearance and his stories make him the examplar of a man who searched for the El Dorado.

"I was born in Georgetown in back of the Odd Fellows Hall in a two-story white house. When I was two years old the family moved to Garden Valley, where I spent most of my life. My dad had a mining claim down there. Oh, I've been all over California . . . I know every rock by name . . . and Nevada. I tried mining there and some in Idaho.

"I panned my first gold when I was six years old. I only went to school for two years. I couldn't see anything in it . . . I was about nine then. I learned more outside than I did sitting in a school room. My mother didn't like it but my Dad said, "What are you going to do?" I told him I wanted to mine . . . so that's how I started.

"In my time there was Indians and Chinese all up and down the creeks around Garden Valley . . . the Chinese, they were pretty smart. The white men would work the creeks and go on, and the Chinese would come in after them. They dug up the bed rock and got a lot . . . they made all the money. The white men went through too fast."

In 1910 Mr. Schlein married Ruth Kidder (also known as Ruth Burlingham after the grandparents who raised her). After her death in 1917, he married Lillie Nathlich in 1921.

"Then we had a spell of hard times. There was no work. We had poor years, couldn't mine, we had no water. At that time it mostly was ground sluicing where there was water and pocketing . . . and sometimes you had to pack dirt four miles to sample it. Well, I took out several pockets but that never appealed to me much. It was too much work. You'd run up a trace and it'd take maybe a week to turn it up. When you find where it comes from it's gone. I did it back in the '20's. Oh, but it was tough . . . I even made whiskey.

"Yes, I made whiskey. I just sold enough to keep bread in the house. It was good stuff I made . . . I did a little selling in Placerville and Shingle Springs. All them places were bootlegging all over, you know . . . some were caught and some wasn't .

RUDY SCHLEIN panned his first gold at the age of six and mined in El Dorado and Nevada counties from the time he was nine years old. This photograph of him is the official trademark of the El Dorado Savings and Loan Association.

RUDY'S TIN CAN VIOLIN - After he proved to himself that he could make a good violin, he experimented with unusual materials, making a violin out of a gas can and a harmonica out of a flashlight.

102

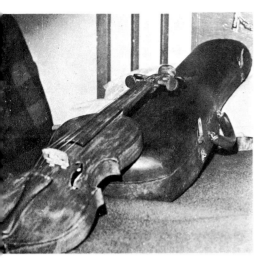

SCHLEIN VIOLIN - The violin and case were made by Rudy Schlein, a self-taught violinist. He made twenty-nine such instruments. All proved to be rich in tone, although Mr. Schlein had never studied the craft. Each was made by hand from selected woods. He used no varnish, preferring to treat the wood by rubbing it with the palms of his hands.

"I went into all kinds of things. I bought cattle and butchered and sold the meat to the mines." Occasionally he would sell a calf or steer to the slaughter house or butcher shop in Georgetown or Placerville. A calf would bring about $10.00 while a prime 600-pound steer would bring as much as $30.00. They paid $2.00 to rent a team to go to Placerville where they bought staples . . . flour, sugar, and clothing. A pair of work jeans would cost 45¢, a good sturdy workshirt, 25¢, and a heavy pair of socks, 5¢. A glass of beer could be enjoyed for a nickel while a double shot of whiskey was only 10¢, with a free lunch.

"I made my first violin after I married my second wife," said Schlein. "She played the piano, so I decided I'd make a violin. I looked around and got a big manzanita and made my first violin."

His natural ability to make things has kept him busy through his long life. He is an accomplished, self-taught violinist and had made 29 violins, all hand carved. Being one of the last of the old-time gold miners, this colorful figure with his flowing white beard and bright miner's garb is in constant demand to participate in various Gold Rush type activities. In 1952, at the age of 72, he appeared in New York City on the popular television show, "What's My Line."

His father, George Frederek Ernest Augustus Schlein, was called "Alphabet" Schlein because of his many names. He was a native of Germany and came to America in 1841. His two brothers had preceded him and urged him to leave Germany.

His mother, Mary Nathlich, also of Germany, arrived in America in 1868, after the sailing vessel she was on went aground off the Shetland Islands. A birthday celebration for the Captain of the vessel had resulted in all hands imbibing too much. The passengers made their way up the steep cliffs of one island with the help of ropes. They were transferred to a larger vessel and returned to Germany. All of their personal belongings — household goods, hand embroidered linens, china, and a 100-pound sack of prunes the family was bringing to the new land — went down with the ship. They received $250 from the government for the loss of their property. Mary Nathlich's family finally arrived in New York on August 13, 1868. She married George Schlein in Hartford, Connecticut in 1873, and they came to California in 1879.

Mr. Leonard Davis, Rudy Schlein's nephew, wrote of his great uncle, "He has lived on and about Georgetown Divide all of his life, pursuing farming, mining, and building. In addition to building his own home in Garden Valley, he helped build innumerable houses, cabins, barns, etc. for residents of the area."

Rudy Schlein is one of the last surviving members of the hardy breed of rugged individuals who helped make the West what it is. When he departs, it will truly be the end of an era.

When asked to what he attributed his longevity, he chuckled and said, "Whiskey and wild women!"

Photos Rudy Schlein Collection

103

LOGS BEING UNLOADED into the pond at the Danaher Pine Company

Cola Smithflat House

El Dorado County Historical Museum

Joe Cola was born in El Dorado County and raised in the logging camps of the Danaher Pine and El Dorado Lumber Companies. He is the son of Angela Fossati and Joseph E. Cola and the third generation of the Fossati family to be born in El Dorado County. His grandmother, Sarah Fossati, was the daughter of Napoleon and Candida Lombardo, who homesteaded the land and built the Old Stone House that today is the Boeger Winery, on Carson Road east of Placerville. Another such landmark, the Smithflat House, has been in the Fossati family since 1878. In an interview with Joe Cola and his wife, Beverly, in their Smithflat home in December of 1975, they talked about their family and recalled stories about "the-way-it-was in my grandparents' days."

"According to family records, my great-grandfather, Napoleon Lombardo, came from Genoa, Italy, to California in 1856," said Mr. Cola. "He tried mining and didn't like it, so he and my great-grandmother, Candida, who was a native of Switzerland, homesteaded a place about two miles from Smithflat. They built their home of natural stones found in the area. I remember my mother telling me that her mother, Sarah Fossati, helped by carrying stones for the building. They must have been little ones, because she was about six years old at the time.

"They farmed the land and started a small winery. My cousin, Elmo Fossati, and his wife still live on part of the ranch. His children are the fifth generation of the family to live there. Elmo's father, John, carried on the distilling of fine wines and brandies started by our great-grandfather, Lombardo, who furnished the sacramental wines for the Catholic Church of Placerville.

"Yes, the Colas were early settlers, too. My grandfather on my father's side was Pietro Cola. He was from Italy and received his naturalization papers when he was in Amador County, before he came to this county. But I can't say what year he arrived here. He married my grandmother in 1872. Her maiden name was Asunta DeBernardi. They homesteaded on Newtown Road at the intersection of Fort Jim Road. The old barn is still standing. The original home burned and they rebuilt. They raised their family right there on the ranch.

CHARLES FOSSATI, who in later years inherited Smithflat House

NICOLA FOSSATI AND HIS SISTER, MRS. BESSEMA,
Joe Cola's grandfather and great-aunt

SARAH FOSSATI AND CANDIDA LOMBARDO,
grandmother and great-grandmother of Joe Cola

JOE COLA at age six had the lumber camps and forests for his playgrounds. He is pictured standing beside a giant sugar pine cut and loaded for hauling from Camp 5 at Pino Grande.

ANGELA FOSSATI, *mother of Joe Cola, at age sixteen*

JOHN NAPOLEON LOMBARDO AND HIS WIFE CANDIDA *homesteaded land two miles from Smithflat about 1856. He was a native of Italy and she of Switzerland.*

CANDIDA AND NAPOLEON LOMBARDO, *right, are pictured with three friends at their home. The house, now an historic landmark, was built of stone in 1872 and sold to Greg Boeger 100 years later.*

Photos from Cola Collection

"Grandfather had the contract to supply firewood for the county courthouse in Placerville. That was the old courthouse that burned in 1910. His son, my uncle Henry Cola, had a stage line from Grizzly Flats to Placerville. My aunt Eva married and lived in Grizzly Flats. There was a tragedy there . . . her first husband, Ed Stafford, was killed in a fight in a barroom in Grizzly. They said he was stabbed. My uncle John Cola was a contractor and built the stone wall around the Placerville grammar school. Many of the early-day concrete bridges had his name stamped on them.

"My dad and his partner named Stivers had the Palace Saloon at Georgetown in 1910 and 1911. I have the old saloon ledgers and it's quite interesting to see how many familiar names are listed on the pages. It sure gives you an idea of a man's drinking habits, and his credit rating too. There were quite a few that didn't pay their bills.

"Mother and Dad were married in 1917 in Placerville by Rev. M.J. Cahir. I was born in 1918 and my brother in 1924. We lived in Smithflat in the winter, then in the summer we lived in the logging camps. Dad was working for C. D. Danaher or the Danaher Pine Lumber Companies then. Later it was the El Dorado Lumber Company and then Michigan-California Company.

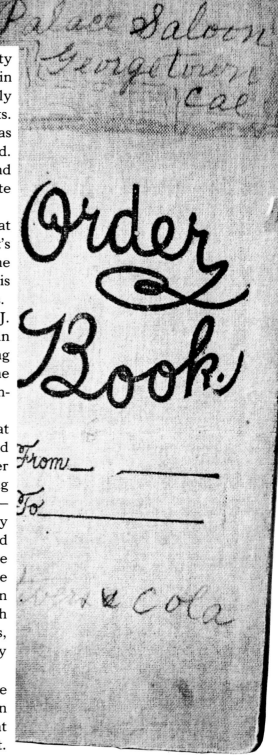

"It was soon after I was born that they went to a camp located at Stumpy Meadows. We lived in every camp except Camps Six and Nine. And the only reason we didn't live in those was that the other camps were operating at the same time. Dad was the company logging superintendent and I grew up learning the ways of the woods — woodburning logging locomotives, our houses on skids for easy movement from camp to camp, camp cook houses with milk, meat and eggs delivered by the Bacchis, canned foods coming in by the Camino, Placerville and Lake Tahoe railroad and sent out by the return logging trains to South Cable Point, carried across the river on the cable crossing to be picked up by the logging train on the north side and delivered to Pino Grande and to the camps, gandy dancers, spar poles, donkey engines, highlines, calks — all were a part of my life in those days.

"In the winter months when we lived in Smithflat I went to the Smithflat school, the same school my mother attended. In 1878 when my grandparents Sarah and Nicola Fossati bought the Smith's Flat House it was a 25 by 50 foot, two-story building with a full basement. It was one of a chain of wayside stations that were established along the road to Genoa, Nevada and Placerville."

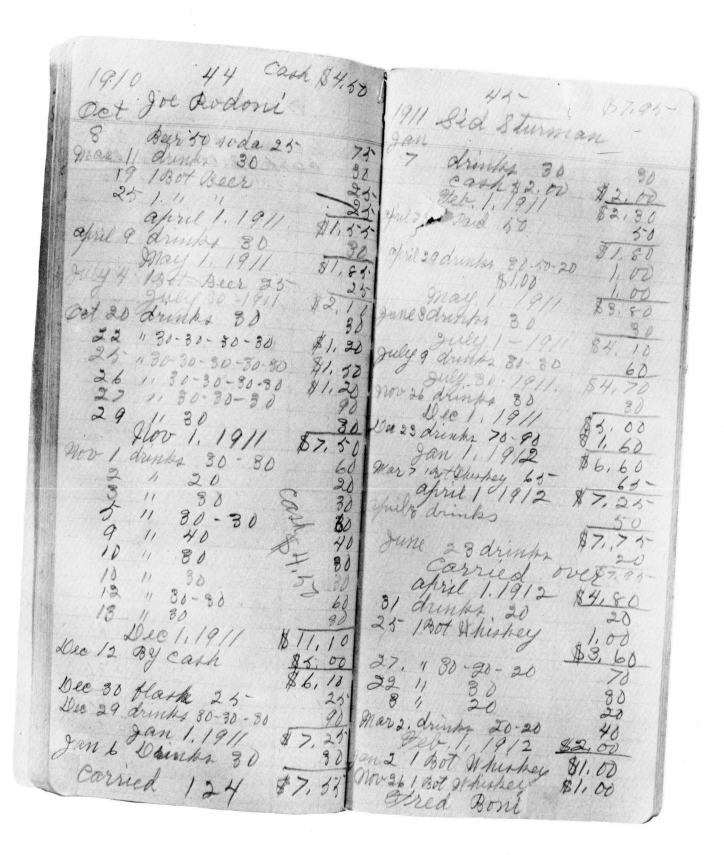

THE PALACE SALOON at Georgetown fared very well, if one can judge from the charges placed in a ledger kept by owners Cola and Stivers. Perusing the pages of the old ledger one may also speculate on the drinking habits of the community.

THE SMITHFLAT HOUSE in 1876.
The present owners, Joe and Beverly
Cola, Bill and Lavonne Cola, and Jim
and Mickey McNatt, are restoring the
historic landmark.

Then, referring to a report compiled about the property, Cola read segments of the material:" 'Three Mile House, the old inn, store and post office located in Smithflat, is the last of the original "Mile Houses," stopping places for the miners, teamsters, freight carriers, and coaches during the California Gold Rush and the development of the Comstock Lode in Nevada. The main part of the building, the general store, the post office, the living room, bedroom, dining room, dance hall and rooms upstairs, the full attic and the basement, was built in the early 1850's. In 1892 the northwest wing was added, which included the kitchen, pantry, ironing room, hall and two bedrooms downstairs and five bedrooms upstairs. This addition was nailed with square nails.

" 'In 1895 the northeast wing was added to include a saloon and cardroom on the main floor and bedrooms upstairs. Round nails were used in the construction of this addition. An annex was added to the basement at that time.

" 'The post office was installed in 1876 in the corner of the general store. It was moved to a larger space in the family living area in 1946. In 1964 it was moved again to still larger quarters in the area that had been the saloon.'

"Here's one record that's real old," said Cola, "something about the post office. The post office celebrated its 100th birthday this year (1976). It wasn't continually in the Smithflat House. You see, my grandfather was a Republican and the people down the street were Democrats. When the administration changed, it was moved down the street to Mr. Potts' house . . . when the Republicans got back in, it moved back to the store."

The barn at Smithflat could accommodate about forty horses. The house had twelve bedrooms, which were rented, three others were used by the family. Everyone, the family, their guests, and the "paying guests," ate in the dining room, which had two large tables. There was a trap door and stairs from the dining room to the basement for ready access to the milk, butter, cheese, meat, wine, apples, potatoes, etc., needed upstairs. Foods which needed to be kept cool were lowered from the dining room to the basement on a dumb-waiter. The basement had a bar, which was used before the 1895 wing was added, which included a bar. The old stone steps leading into the basement, at the end where the bar was, are very worn from the traffic to the saloon and to the storage places. Two small tunnels served as a storage place for the blasting caps and mercury needed in the store.

SARAH AND NICK FOSSATI
(seated center), grandparents of
Joe Cola of Placerville, were photographed with family and friends on
the porch of Smithflat House in
1895. Angela Fossati, seated next
to Mr. Fossati, became Joe Cola's
mother. Others identified were,
in back row from left, Dosie Potts,
Art Lyon, Bill Potts, unidentified
man, Bert Carpender, Sam Mialia,
young John A. Fossati, Mrs. Frank
Raffetto, who was an opera singer,
unidentified boy at window. Seated
in the front row, from left, were
Bob Jones (wearing dunce cap),
Sarah Fossati, Nick Fossati, Angie
Fossati, and Frank Raffetto (behind
post).

STEAM-DRIVEN TRACTORS were used for hauling lumber prior to the advent of the railroad in Placerville.
This picture was taken at the corner of Broadway and Washington Streets where Crocker Brothers had their store.

Cola Pho

The famous old Three Mile House changed hands many times. In 1862, F.J. Peipmeyer sold to Fredericka Dollmeyer. In 1864, Henderson sold to Martha Saul, and in 1872 Albert M. Saul and Catherine Saul sold to G.B. Raffetto and Nicola Avansono. In 1873 Luigi Campini, rather than Nicola, was co-owner with Raffetto. In 1878 Luigi Campini sold his share to Nicola Fossati - the building was then known as Raffetto and Co. Hotel and Store. About 1885 Nicola Fossati became sole owner. The sign "Fossati's Three Mile House" is preserved at Smithflat House today.

"I often heard members of the family remark about my gentleman grandfather (Nic Fossati) sitting on the front porch entertaining or visiting while Grandmother (Sarah Fossati) waited on the store and the mail customers, baked all of the bread, cooked and served meals for the family and all of the boarders, did her sewing and all of the laundry, kept all of the books, and managed to go to church on Sunday. They called those 'The Good Old Days.'

"Grandmother Fossati was an astute business woman in the days long before women were supposed to be. There was always plenty to do at Smith's Flat House. The corrals for cattle, stables for the horses, the blacksmith shop and room for the freighting wagons, as well as the hotel rooms, the saloon and card rooms, all demanded her supervision. One improvement she instigated was a roof extended across the road so that ladies could alight from the carriages without getting wet in inclement weather.

"After Grandmother passed away in 1947 at the age of 84, Uncle Charlie inherited the property and carried on with the post office and grocery, as well as having a dynamite business and interest in mining. After Charlie's death my Uncle Nick was left the property. My brother Bill, his wife Lavonne, Jim and Mickey McNatt, and my wife Beverly and I purchased the property from him in the spring of 1975 and are slowly restoring it. We hope to make it one of the most popular tourist attractions in the area."

William (Mike) DeNatly P

THE P. G. & E. POWER HOUSE on the American River, now the site of the Chili Bar dam

Cola Photo

DRIFTING LOGS washed into shallow waters were recovered by the river drovers, who pulled them out to deeper water. These pictures were taken in 1889.

El Dorado County Historical Museum Photos

RIVER DROVERS - When the logs left the chute they hit the water with great force, creating many log jams. The twenty-eight men aboard the river boat belonging to the American River Land and Lumber Company were drovers, who broke the jams and kept the logs moving.

THE LOG CHUTE at Chute Camp, northeast of Camino on the American River, known today as North Cable Point. Outlines of where the chute stood are still visible. Logs slid down the chute into the dam, where the drovers moved them on for loading.

The Smithflat Mines

"The Blue Lead Mining Channel runs north and south through town and is the channel on which many of the mines were located — the Bendfeldt Mine, the Kum Fa, Carpender, Toll House, Rogers, Granite, Hook & Ladder, and Deep Channel. The Bendfeldt Mine was on the south side of the freeway on my brother's property. One of the early mining records shows that Patten & Taylor filed for the right to run a tunnel from Weber Creek on the south, along the Blue Channel under Smith's Flat, to White Rock Canyon on the north. This is the tunnel which runs beneath the Smithflat House basement. There is a concrete slab on the basement floor over the shaft which went down into the tunnel.

"When I was young, Bert Bryan, son of an early Smith's Flat pioneer, did a lot of mining here, and I can remember him having an old steam boiler with a tall smoke stack on it. He would build a big roaring fire and close off the draft, which would then pull all of the stale air and powder smoke out of the tunnel through a pipe running down into the mine. He mined in Smith's Flat until his death. One of his family has recently given the museum a name plate from the J.M. Bryan's Rolling Quartz Mill.

"I don't know when we would have had electricity here if the Carpender Mine hadn't needed it. That was about 1924, I think. Before that the South Fork Canal provided water for most of the power used in mining operations. The Creighton Blacksmith Shop that ran with water was next door. When I was a little boy, we carried water for our house from a leak in their pipeline.

"The miners often spent their winters as boarders, and the spring and fall cattle drives always brought the cattlemen to Smith's Flat House. One of the last boarders was Henry Barton, a brother of Bill Barton who lived and summered his cattle at Lake Tahoe. His cattle ranged where the airport is now located. Barton Memorial Hospital at Lake Tahoe is named after their family."

For years there has been some confusion about the name of the town. Mr. Cola said, "Gold was discovered in Smith's Flat in 1852. The town is located on Hangtown Creek, which heads in Smith's Flat, or Smithflat as it is known today. When miners moved in and a town sprung up, they called it Smith's Flat because the only man living there at the time was a farmer named Smith . . . who was farming on the flat. A post office was established for Smith's Flat in 1876. Then the Postal Department in 1895 asked that it be changed to one word, 'Smithflat', because of confusion with another post office in the state, Smith Field. Thus the change."

THE BENDFELDT MINE - In 188. P. Sioli wrote: "The Bendfeldt Blu Gravel claim, one of the finest grav mines in El Dorado County, is in itself a monument of industry, plu and perseverance for the owner, Mr. Fred Bendfeldt."

Cola Colle

Cola Photo

THE CARPENDER MINE was located on Airport Road east of Placerville. One of several mines that worked at full capacity during the Depression years, it was the property of W. P. Carpender, El Dorado County judge, and great-grandfather of Jack Carpender.

*WANDA & MARY CARPENDER
daughters of Bert Carpender*

Bert Carpender Photo

SILAS LARSEN FARM in 1887

Rose Larsen Corbell Ph

THE LARSEN RANCH IN CAMINO in 1909

Rose Larsen Corbell Ph

Larsen Valley

*NEILS THEODORE EMIL LARSEN
The patriarch of Larsen Valley, grandfather of Rose Larsen Corbell*

*MARNE L. DAHL LARSEN, wife of
N.T.E. Larsen, with her daughters Mary,
on left, and Louise*

(Inset) ROSE LARSEN, age 6

Mrs. Rose Larsen Corbell, when interviewed in her home on Larsen Valley Road
in Camino in February of 1976, said, "This
is the house that my father built in 1885
before he married my mother. I was born in
this house. All this land around here was
known as Larsen Valley. I don't know why
they ever called it Apple Hill . . . there are
no hills." Mrs. Corbell said that her grand-
father, Neils Theodore Emil Larsen, and Marne Louise Dahl were
married April 10, 1851, in the church of Glengine, Norway, by provost Larrs Christian Arup. They left Fredrikstad, Norway, in 1853,
resided in Liverpool, England, for one year, and sailed on the
"Crinelcutes" for America. On arrival, they crossed the continent by
ox team to Utah, where they stayed and where several children were
born to them.

When they prepared to leave Utah for California, they left under
the protection of American soldiers. Because her grandfather did not
subscribe to the Mormon practice of having several wives, "he was
persecuted and he had to have protection in order to get out of the
place."

The family arrived in El Dorado County in July, 1860, at what was
known as "Johnson Meadows," a few miles east of Placerville.

"As I remember, there was a large house on the place. It had at
least three stories and fireplaces in every room, and of course it was a
Mecca for our pilgrimages as children. The house was in a bad state of
disrepair. The story went that it was haunted, and I believed sincerely
that it was."

The Larsens later settled on a homestead in the area known as the
(Jack) Barkley place. Mr. Larsen acquired land up to several hundred
acres. Mrs. Corbell recalled, "There are deeds where he only paid
$2.50 an acre for some of it, and that now sells for $3,000." She told of
"ne'er-do-well homesteaders," one of whom, "being a lazy sort,"
would take fence posts, poke one in the stove, "and then when they
burned out, he'd poke in another." The barns on the present Barkley
place were built by her grandfather.

Her father, Silas Larsen, bought up the land now occupied by the
Engstrom Christmas tree farm, Santa's Acres, and adjoining land.

"When I was a small child, that was all in wheat. It came to my waist. I remember walking through it when we were children, making a trail, and then we were in great trouble." She continued, "I can remember when all this was forest where the orchard is." Her father had cleared it all, helped by her mother, who would "put the baby in the clothes basket and take it out with them."

Her grandfather, whom she characterized as "very stern and a very hard worker," who worked his sons very hard, was also "devout in his religious beliefs, and he wanted and expected everybody to do the same."

N.T.E. Larsen was the first man to plant pear trees east of Placerville, "a venture for which he was ridiculed," Mrs. Corbell recalls, "because they felt that the climate was too rigid and cold." Today, Larsen Valley is widely recognized for the superior quality of its pears and apples. "One apple tree, planted by our grandfather, is over 100 years old and still bearing fruit." She said that the fifth generation of the family, many of them orchardists, now resides in and near Larsen Valley.

"I guess you could say it started when each of Grandpa's sons was given 160 acres of land when he married. They built their homes, planted orchards and reared their families. You see, my uncle had a large family, nine children — seven boys and two girls — and I believe he allotted them certain portions of land as my father did my two brothers. He gave them each orchard land. Now it's known as Larsen Valley.

"My cousins converted the old barn their father built into a packing shed and cold storage. It's called Larsen Apple Barn . . . it's located on Larsen Valley Road. The family has always had its roots here.

"When the Chapter of the Placerville Fruit Growers Association was initiated in 1914, his sons, Emil E. and Silas C., my father, were two of the fourteen original members."

Early Days Recalled – The old Blair School at "Six-Mile Stone" was an important part of her life, as was the County High School on Clay Street in Placerville. "I think it's called Government Center or Civic Center now," she said, and pointed out a large urn in her yard that once stood in front of the high school. "It was given to my sister by James Irving, a well known local orchardist, who was on the high school board."

She recalled the old Five Mile House, a road house for travelers and dairymen who moved their herds "right on the highway."

"One of my most pleasant memories of my childhood is the winter evenings around the fireplace. My mother and father both had very pleasant singing voices, and they'd sing to us. Some of the songs I can still remember are 'My Sweet Kitty Wells' and 'The Ship That Never Returned' — that was a very sad song. We were always a very closely knit family.

SILAS C. LARSEN AND SADIE DAVEY LARSEN *on their wedding day*

WILLIAM DAVEY *was constable in Placerville for many years.*

THE BLAIR SCHOOL, 1903 - *Three generations of the Larsen family attended the school that stood where the Adventist Church is today on Highway 50. Mary Larsen was the teacher at the time. She is seated in the center. Others identified were, from left, Rose Galuppi,.......Jones, Ollie Davey, Lucy Hartwick, Hazel Davey, Edna Davey, Ollie Jones, Rose Larsen, Mabel Larsen, Bertha Davey, and Grace Davey.*

THE OLD FIVE MILE HOUSE *was one of many mile houses built during the Comstock Rush in 1859. It was a road stop for travelers and dairymen who moved their herds to higher pasture in the summer. Mrs. Corbell said that the school was near the roadhouse and when the cattle came up the highway, the teacher let the children go to the fence to watch. Pictured on the porch are, from left, Millie Blakeley, A.J. Blakeley, Rose Davey, and Robert Blakeley.*

MARNE LOUISE DAHL LARSEN

HENRY H. DAVEY, great grand-
father of Rose L. Corbell

HENRY H. AND SADIE G. DAVEY
with their children, John H., Rosina
and infant Rose

ROSINA DAVEY, Rose Larsen
Corbell's maternal grandmother

SILAS AND EMIL LARSEN

SADIE AND JOHN DAVEY, referred
to by the family as "a pair of peaches"

ROSE DAVEY AND
ELLEN LARSEN

"When the El Dorado Lumber Company was established at Camino, that made quite a difference in our lives, because they had a small store there. Before that, if you wanted a hairpin or a loaf of bread you had to go to Placerville to get it. And that was quite a trip, because the road always had about a foot of dust in the summer and a foot of mud in the winter.

"And we used to get very deep snow here. It's not so bad now. I remember one time my uncle and a friend went hunting and got lost in a snow storm. My father and some friends tried to find them. They were out in that storm all night . . . Mother was so frightened."

Other reflections: "Another time we were frightened was the prison break at Folsom. We heard about it from this man Festus Rutheford. He was a good friend of the Davey family . . . in fact, his sister married my uncle later. Well, anyway, my brother had to deliver milk to Camino every day, and when these convicts were loose, we didn't know where they were, of course . . . so Father would gather us all together, take his gun, and we'd all walk clear up to the end of the meadow, which was just below the town. We'd wait there until we'd hear him hit the railroad tracks with a milk can, then we knew he was safe and we'd wander down to meet him and we'd all go home."

She laughed as she recalled 'the donkey' — "Tom Hartford bought a donkey for his little girl, Nellie, to ride to school. Her brother would ride with her as far as our house, then he'd get off and let me ride with her to school. Sometimes the donkey would stop, just refuse to go, and when they stop . . . they stop. Lots of children went to the Blair school, the Rupleys, the Lupes and Hassler, Barkeley, Adams, and the Van Vlecks. It covered a large area because at that time it was the only school up here."

HEADED FOR SAN FRANCISCO and the 1905 Mid-Winter Fair are Emil E. Larsen Sr., driving, Mary Larsen, and an unidentified man. In the back seat, from left, are Ella Larsen Davey, Sadie Davey Larsen, and Silas C. Larsen. The family traveled from Placerville to San Francisco by stage.

122

50th WEDDING ANNIVERSARY OF SILAS AND SADIE LARSEN (of Larsen Valley) in 1936

CLARENCE S. LARSEN

When she spoke about her teaching career she said, "After my four years in high school, where I took the regular academic course preparing me for college, I went to Los Angeles and entered what was then known as the Los Angeles State Normal School. It is now part of the University of Southern California. When I graduated I returned home. This was still summer school out here. Something happened to the teacher and they hired me . . . so I was teaching two weeks after I graduated.

"I taught here until the school closed in November and then I went to Stanislaus County until my school opened here in April. I taught at both the Blair and Camino schools, from 1934 till 1958." She then showed one of her cherished mementos and said, "When I retired, the Parent-Teachers Association at Camino gave a reception for me and presented me with this book, 'Rose Corbell, This Is Your Life'." It contains comments made by pupils and parents on a tape recording. Reading it, one recognizes not only that Mrs. Corbell is a descendant of El Dorado County pioneers, but also that she made a personal contribution to the community by devoting her life to teaching.

Point Pleasant Beach

Fancher Collection

Mrs. Virginia Papini Fancher of Coloma said, "Our family has lived on this land for more than 125 years. My great-grandfather, Luther Davis, came to Coloma in 1848 from Boston, Massachusetts, at the age of 32. When word of the gold discovery brought '49ers moving into Coloma, he established the first bakery and confectionery store where the Episcopal Church is today.

"My mother's father, William Hooper, came here in 1850. Grandfather Hooper was an orchardist. He had his own vineyard and drying house. He also had the early-day water ditch that brought water around Coloma. He grew fruit and vegetables and took them as far away as Virginia City, where he sold to the miners and stores."

Today, the land is known as Point Pleasant Beach, a Coloma resort. Her grandfather's orchard and vineyards included the present resort area and the land where the Sierra Nevada House stands today.

She said there were lots of Chinese there at that time. "Grandfather had two Chinese villages on the property and a Chinese mine. We still have one on the ranch part around the Sierra Nevada House. When they put Highway 49 through, it divided the property. One Chinese village was on this side going toward Georgetown and a small one used to be where we have the rest room here at the resort, down by the river. They mined there along the river.

"Actually, they turned the river. They dammed the river and the rock dam is still at the same place. Its original bed is right here where our house is today. Today the river is about 500 feet from here."

Marshall – Her mother, Dorcas Hooper Papini, often laughed at one incident that happened when she was about nine years old. She said that when she attended the funeral of James W. Marshall, she had to cry. But she confessed it was because her mother had insisted she wear her new shoes, and they hurt her feet.

"Mr. Marshall was a frequent visitor at our home," said Mrs. Fancher. "I remember Mother said when he called her mother would have tea and a little cake or biscuits. He was a nice man. I know my parents thought he was ill-treated by the government. They charged him with drinking and refused his pension when he needed it most. I know my grandmother and mother said they never saw him drunk. He was always a gentleman."

Mrs. Fancher still lives on the land that was her grandfather's orchard. The family home also serves as the office for the beach resort. Throughout the years, thousands of tourists and campers have no doubt enjoyed their stay at Point Pleasant Beach, never knowing the history of the ground they were on.

(inset) MRS. DORCAS PAPINI was 84 years old when this picture was taken in 1961. She was the daughter of William Hooper, rancher in Coloma as early as 1850. She was born in Coloma on March 11, 1877, and lived there all her life. Her four daughters, Emma, Cecilia, Margaret and Virginia, were all school teachers.

THE VINEYARD HOUSE was the center of social activities in Coloma. It was built by Robert Chalmers in 1879 as a hotel and family home after he married Louise Allhoff, widow of Martin Allhoff who had a large vineyard and made wine on his property near Coloma. Mrs. Fancher's great-grandmother, Jessamina Adelaide Ferrier, was a sister of Mrs. Robert Chalmers, nee Catherine Ferrier, whose husband built the Vineyard House. Mrs. Chalmers is pictured standing on the porch with her daughter, Louisa Allhoff, and her sons, Martin and Joseph Allhoff (on steps.) In archway at the Saloon entrance is Frank Seeley. This picture is believed to have been taken about 1881.

Yohalem Collection

124

Yohalem Collection

A MEETING AT THE BRIDGE — The occasion for the picture taken at the new bridge over the South Fork of the American River at Coloma, is not known. Ladies present for the event were from left, Josephine Norris, and Mrs. Hall (seated on rail), (standing) Annie Thole, Julia Johnson, Cora Thomas, Louise Gallagher, Gallagher child, Hattie Colwell, Angie DeLory. (On right front row, from left) Ollie Thomas, Jane Stearns, Lizzie Crawford, Mamie Thomas. (Back row standing, from left) Sadie Anderholder, (seated on rail) Cecilia Papini, Dorcas Papini, Mrs. Stolfus and Annie Thomas.

WILLIAM HOOPER, Mrs. Fancher's grandfather, at one time worked in the Eureka Slate mine at Slatington, before the town was named Kelsey.

Marshall Gold Discovery Park Museum Collection

125

Photos from Frances Cross Lee Collection

THOMAS, SR., AND CATHERINE ORR of Paisley, near Glasgow, Scotland, of the clan McGregor, emigrated to America about 1835. As members of the Brigham Young train of 700 wagons they made the historic trip from Nauvoo, Illinois, to Salt Lake City, Utah. They later followed the Mormon Trail on to California, arriving in 1850, and settled at New York Ravine in Salmon Falls.

The Orrs of Shingle Springs

SALMON FALLS RANCH OF JAMES ORR, taken prior to 1890. When Thomas Orr, Sr., and his family settled at New York Ravine in Salmon Falls in 1850, they planted the first barley in El Dorado County. The seeds were brought with them from Scotland. Orr land holdings are said to have totaled 1340 acres at one time. As Mr. Orr's children grew and married, each was given a parcel of land. Pictured in the foreground is Miss Katherine Orr, prior to her marriage to Frank Cross. Her brother Thomas is seated in the wagon.

FRANCES CROSS LEE (Inset above)

When fragments of a 35-family wagon train from Salt Lake Valley, Utah, pulled into Pleasant Valley, El Dorado County in 1850, Thomas Orr, Sr., looked the countryside over and took his family to Salmon Falls, where he established their home. His wife, Catherine Jackson Orr, and children, John, James, Thomas, Jr., Katherine, and Isabel, had just endured the hardships of a four-month journey across the plains. Thomas Orr, Jr., was 18 years old when they reached California. In later years he wrote his autobiography, a document that is a prized possession of Mrs. Frances Cross Lee, great-granddaughter of James Orr, the son of Thomas Orr, Sr.

From this autobiography Mrs. Lee gleaned most of her information about her pioneer family. "My mother, Lotta Weihe, married my father, LeRoy Benjamin Cross, in Lodi, in 1921. He was born in 1890, the son of Katherine Orr and Frank Cross. I don't know what year it was, but my great-grandfather, James Orr, and his brother John established a stage line from Sacramento to Marysville and one in Placer and El Dorado Counties. They were in competition with the California Stage Company.

"I was told that Grandpa Orr was a whiskey-drinking driver," said Mrs. Lee. "He liked his nips and they said he sat with a shotgun and a keg between his legs, and a knife in his belt. His brother, Thomas, Jr., enjoyed telling stories about his brother. He especially liked the one about the time in Georgetown when a man called one of the dancehall girls a very obvious name. Grandpa insisted he apologize to her, saying no matter what she was or where she worked, she was still a lady and he should apologize. When the man refused, Grandpa pulled his knife and stabbed the man. And another time . . . we never did hear what unraveled Grandpa, but he took after a man and chased him out of town, spraying him with bullets all the way, and ordering him never to come back. I guess he was one 'hellacious' stage driver."

Mrs. Lee continued, "It was on one of the stage runs into Auburn that my grandmother was born. James' wife, Avis Safronia Davis Orr, wanted to go to Auburn one day to do some shopping. Well . . . she had misjudged the date, so Katherine was born in the Auburn station. They remained in Auburn for a few days and then returned to the ranch at Salmon Falls."

127

The Orr Ranch at Salmon Falls was established by Thomas Orr, Sr., when the family arrived in California in 1850. In his autobiography, Thomas Orr, Jr., wrote:

"We got into Hope Valley, followed up and camped over night. We bucked snow all day in getting up the grade and camped at the summit. The next morning we started down, negotiating snowbanks twenty feet deep. We could hear the water running beneath. We rough-locked the hind wheels of the wagons, took the lead cattle off and chained them to the hind wheels in order to hold back. That day we passed out of the snow belt and then followed the '49 trail to Leek Springs and came on through Sly Park to Pleasant Valley and arrived there on the Fourth of July, 1850.

"When we got to Shingle Springs we saw a man at a place above the present Planters House splitting shakes to build a cabin. We went on to Deer Creek. Father met a man he had known in Illinois and Salt Lake. He was keeping a trading post there and Father called him by name, Porter Rockwell. He was alarmed and told Father to call him Brown in the future because he was one of Brigham Young's destroying angels and his life wouldn't be worth much if people discovered his real identity. Father asked Brown about the best place to settle and he told him there was no need to go any further . . . that place was as good as any.

"Father and my oldest brother, John, went to Salmon Falls and met two old mountaineers. They had pitched a tent on New York Ravine and were keeping a trading post. Their biggest sales were in provisions and whiskey. Father took a liking to the place and made an offer of $500 for their two quarter sections secured by them on a squatters' right, and the deal was made.

"After Father bought the place at New York Ravine we moved from Deer Creek. We started the road from the old emigrant trail to Green Springs on the Coloma road.

"We started mining at Mormon Island and Father rented the trading post at New York Ravine to McFarland. When we arrived in this country, men were mining up the American River from Mormon Island. Placerville had but a few tents and log cabins and was first known as Ravine City and then later Hangtown.

"Father saw the possibilities in the hotel business and rented a hotel at Salmon Falls and added a log cabin to accommodate the guests. He served the general traveling public with meals, costing $1 each. Mother secured some dried apples, which had been shipped across the Isthmus of Panama and made apple pies, which readily brought from $1 to $1.50 each. Barley sold for 25 cents a pound and hay cost $1 for one night's feed. Whiskey sold for 25 cents a drink. We had brought a dozen chickens with us from Salt Lake, carrying them in a

KATHERINE ORR CROSS WITH LE ROY CROSS, father of Frances Cross Lee. The original of this picture was in a brooch owned by Mrs. Lee's great-grandmother. The brooch was made of gold from New York Ravine at Salmon Falls and was worn by her for years.

Photos from Frances Cross Lee Collection

ORR HOME AND HOTEL IN SHINGLE SPRINGS - In 1893 Thomas Orr, Jr., was proprietor of the Meyers Hotel in Shingle Springs. He purchased an old winery and converted it into a rooming house. In later years it was torn down and a small cottage built. Standing on the porch on the only three-story building in the county at the time are, from left, an unidentified hired hand, William G. Taylor, husband of Lillie Jane Orr, Thomas Orr, Jr., and his brother, James Orr.

129

coop, and they proved gold-getters. Egg-nog sold for 50 cents and milk punch the same. Cigars sold for several dollars each and they were poor weeds at that. Nothing sold for less than two bits.

"Father kept the hotel business running for two years and during that time brother John started mining, the popular diversion. Later he was put up for deputy sheriff with Henry Larkin and served in that capacity under Sheriff Dave Buell.

"Our family raised the first barley in El Dorado County, planting out the seed in 1851 which we had brought with us.

"The mining excitement was intense, and thousands of men were going up the Georgetown way.

"The money used was Mexican silver quarters and half dollars and $50 and $10 gold slugs, but the principal medium of exchange was gold dust.

"After Father had gotten well established in the hotel and bakery business at Salmon Falls, he bought the property from Henry Larkin for a consideration of $2,500. We had the only bakery, store, hotel and feed stable in town and made money rapidly. There were days when we would take in $1,000 to $1,500.

"It was an unwritten law of the country that if any man came around the Horn, across the plains or Isthmus, he was to be grubstaked by the ones who had prospered and by this avenue Father spent $85,000 in the twelve years he was in business, loaning money to miners, feeding the new arrivals and grubstaking them, and he never so much as received one penny in return.

"Father rented the Salmon Falls business to the McKenzie boys, residents of French Creek now, and started farming at New York Ravine and I went back with him. James got married and took up a ranch nearby, devoting his time to farming.

"The homestead was located near the New York Ravine and was one of the richest claims in El Dorado County at that time. He said the Ravine was part of the homestead but they thought the gold should belong to everybody . . . not to any one person or family. Believing this, they always let anyone who wanted to pan for gold and take what they could find.

"The Orr children were, of course, Mormons . . . and that is how Father raised all his children, right on down," said Mrs. Lee.

When and how the Orr family joined the Mormons is told in the Thomas Orr, Jr. autobiography that covers eighteen years of their life prior to coming to California. The first paragraphs in his account tell of the family departure from Glasgow, Scotland in 1832 and the purchase of a farm in York State in America. After farming for four years they moved to Illinois where Orr had purchased government land.

THOMAS ORR, JR., was three years old wh[en] his parents left Scotland for America, and eig[ht] years old when they owned and operated a far[m] in Illinois. When he was fourteen his family, w[ho] had converted to the Mormon faith, left Nauv[oo] Illinois, with the Mormon pioneers. Four year[s] later, in 1850, they arrived in Pleasant Valley, California, and settled at Salmon Falls.

LE ROY B. CROSS, father of Frances Cross Le[e] was two years and nine months old when this picture was taken in 1892. A piece of tartan, brought from Scotland, was draped on the chil[d] to create the effect of a Scottish dress.

"Father built a log cabin and commenced to split rails to fence in his field. He could get no rails to lay a roof on the cabin, so he placed clap boards (now called shakes) with the logs placed on top to hold them down. The cabin had a dirt floor and the doors were made of wooden puncheon with hinges of wood.

"I was eight years old then and our family, with father and mother, consisted of three boys and two girls. At that age I split rails and otherwise did a man's work. After we built the cabin, we snaked logs in with yokes of oxen. Father bought a left-handed wooden plow for working the soil and I had to drive three yokes of oxen and walk on the plowed ground to avoid getting my feet full of thistles.

"My mother spun wool yarn from the sheep hides to make our clothes. Her spinning wheel had been brought to York State with us from the old country and was among our effects taken to the new land. Incidentally, my mother was the first woman in Illinois to use a spinning wheel.

"Considering the sparse settlement in our vicinity, there were no schools, churches or community houses of any kind. We never saw any strangers in those days and, only rarely, our nearest neighbors, who lived at a distance of several miles, came to visit us. We were located seven miles northeast of Commerce across the Mississippi River from Fort Madison, Iowa. We raised corn, wheat, oats and buckwheat in abundance.

"When the Mormons were driven out of Missouri, they came to our neighborhood in large numbers. Some of them squatted on land, while others purchased tracts from the government. Father helped them build twelve cabins in one season. In locations the Mormons organized school districts, the teachers conducting schools in cabins. We children got our first education from them while attending school in the winter time.

"The Mormons were intense on religion and preached it everywhere and at every opportunity. After considerable persuasion they induced my father and mother to embrace their faith and they became converts. My people were Presbyterians before they left the old country and after becoming Mormons they were so pious they wouldn't even let us children whistle on Sunday, let alone perform manual labor. We got along first rate with our new neighbors and in hardly no time we had quite a settlement.

"At the place called Commerce on the Mississippi landing, the Mormons build a city after their exile from Missouri, and they subsequently changed the name to Nauvoo. Joseph Smith, as president of the Mormon church, was called the prophet and resided in Nauvoo with his twelve apostles. I remember on one occasion playing basketball with him.

Joseph Smith Executed

"The Gentiles in the vicinity resented the encroachment by the Mormons and on some pretense arrested Smith and associates and took them to Carthage, where they were imprisoned in the county jail. While confined there, a mob of Gentiles broke into the jail and shot Smith and his brother Hiram. Smith had jumped out of a window to escape, but the infuriated mob apprehended him and stationed him against a well curb, where he was executed.

"We lived eighteen miles from Carthage at the time and the news of the execution was quickly carried by couriers. Father was among the number who went to Carthage to view the remains of Smith. I was not taken along, but I have a clear recollection of the incident, and the intense excitement caused by it. The perpetrators of the crime were never punished.

"The Mormons elected Brigham Young as Smith's successor as president of the church, and after he took office there was continuous trouble over religion. The Mormons finally decided to leave Illinois and go westward in their religious worship. Some of the Mormons sold their places for a mere pittance while others abandoned their homes and belongings.

"In 1845, after a decision had been made to move westward, the Mormons commenced rigging up their wagons for the anticipated long overland trip.

"In the spring of 1846 we left Illinois and crossed the Mississippi River and took up our westward journey. Our crossing place was at a little place called Des Moines. From there we proceeded on to Pisgie, where the Mormons located. The whole country seemed alive with wagons and tents. We continued on to Sarpees Point or Mosquito Creek, Iowa.

"In view of the council of the Mormon heads, the place on the east bank of the Missouri was later named Council Bluffs.

"At this period in the trip, Uncle Sam was calling for volunteers in the Mexican War. A liberty pole was raised in front of a big tent, flying the national colors. Five hundred Mormons enlisted as recruits, and went to Fort Leavenworth to join the Regulars."

After the volunteers departed, Mormons set up an encampment called Winter Quarters, since changed to Omaha, Nebraska. "My folks were the first to build a cabin on the present site of Omaha."

When his father bought some cattle from a neighbor in exchange for the sale of their cabin, they were forced to find grazing land. "There was no feed for them at Winter Quarters. With twelve families we started up the Missouri River and traveled 125 miles before we found a favorable place to winter the stock . . . We started to work building cabins and prepared for a winter's retreat. We arranged the cabins in a square and connected them so they served the purpose of a fort.

"As a fortification we dug moats or ditches and set posts as protection against the Indians . . . We got along quite comfortably until about the middle of winter when our grub began to run short. Someone must go to Winter Quarters for provisions and my father and I were given the assignment . . .

"The cold was intense during the trip, and we suffered from exposure. Father and I would build the fires when we camped, and keep them going at night-time, to keep us from freezing. We slept in the open. In order to get fodder for our horses, we had to hew the outside bark off the trees so we could get to the tender lining . . . we felled cottonwoods and let the oxen browse off the tops."

It took them a week to travel the 125 miles back to Winter Quarters, where they laid in a supply of provisions and started back. When they were one day out "a blizzard struck us with great fury and we were compelled to return." It was two days before the storm abated.

"Father was advised to cross the Missouri on the ice, and meander upward along the wood trail and he followed their advice . . . we left the river bottom and proceeded up a hill so steep we could not follow with our heavy wagon loads. We decided to go back to the river and cross to our own side. We made our way through an almost impassable barrier of underbrush, frozen swamp, cane brake and fallen timber and finally arrived at the frozen river. The ice was so glassy and smooth the stock couldn't keep a firm foothold and would sprawl all over the surface. We had two axes and with them we tediously chopped and hacked the ice until it was rough enough for the stock to stand. By following this method we crossed over to a sandbar and followed it as far as we could. We had to hack the ice again until we reached another sandbar and followed its length and then on our own side of the river we had to use our axes on the ice surface. There were no more sandbars for us to use and we entered timber and brush so thick we were forced to halt."

His father left him with the wagons while he searched for the road back. It took him half a day to find the trail. They were still forty miles from their camp. "We left the oxen behind but took the horses with us. I rode one and led the other, packed with all the provisions it could carry." It took two days to return to the fort. When they arrived, they learned that while they were away Omaha Indians had located the fort and come across the river in great numbers. "They drove off what cattle they wanted and stole the last horse in camp but did not molest the folks."

Thomas Orr wrote in considerable detail of incidents that occurred while they waited for spring and their return to Winter quarters. When spring came, they started back down the river. "A bunch of Indians came to us and when they saw their efforts to drive our cattle off were futile, they started shooting them with arrows. They killed the oxen drawing our wagon.

"That was the last trouble we had with Indians until we returned to Winter Quarters in the spring of '47. We found everyone there in a turmoil of excitement, making preparations to resume the overland trip to California. Father loaded a three-ox team with supplies.

700 Wagons Start For California

"The caravan started out with *seven hundred wagons*. I was then 16 years of age. We got along very well as far as Loup Fork of Platte River. At that season of the year the river was too high to ford so we unloaded some of the wagons and tied the wagon boxes together to make an improvised ferry boat, and used it to transport the train piece-meal across the river.

"The next halt was made on the North Platte, a river about a mile and one-quarter wide, but shallow enough to ford. The quicksand was treacherous and we were cautioned against letting the horse and stock stop even for a minute. In one place the sand washed away and took a wagon and oxen with it, though the occupants were rescued.

"In order to get across the river it was necessary to hitch six yoke oxen to each wagon and two drivers were stationed on each side to whip them and keep them going. The train eventually got across after considerable delay and then we went into an open country and followed the course of South Fork Platte for 500 miles on level plain, without trees or mountains to vary the monotony of the landscape.

"Several times Sioux Indians came to us on the plains but caused no trouble because of our force. We saw herds of buffalos in countless numbers but killed only the ones we needed for actual necessities, such as meat and hides.

Brigham Young In Command

"While on the plains it was decided to organize the caravan into companies of 100 wagons, and certain ones were placed in charge of each. Brigham Young was commander-in-chief. John Taylor was captain of our company.

"During the daytime eight men were kept with the herd of cattle and ofttimes experienced difficulty in keeping the buffalos from mingling with the stock. A stampede of our stock was a frequent occurrence.

"We proceeded across the plains double file, fifty wagons to the side. There was no timber and we were compelled to use buffalo chips as fuel for our camp fires. We continued the use of these chips until we arrived at an island in the South Fork, covered with timber. This place was later named Grand Island, a Nebraska town. We killed buffalo there, dried the flesh and jerked it with wood fire. We camped at Grand Island a week. The young men made side excursions to Scotts Bluff above Chimney Rock.

"We crossed the Rockies at Sweetwater, came on past Pacific Springs, (east of Fort Bridger) down Big Sandy Creek, through Echo Canyon to Green River, Wyoming.

"Without special incident, we got to Fort Laramie on the old Oregon Trail, and only two or three men were stationed there. They were the first whites we had seen outside of our own train since leaving Winter Quarters. The train divided at Fort Laramie. We next went to Fort Bridger, then to Sublet's Cut Off, and headed into Salt Lake country, and it took all summer for the hundreds of wagons to get in.

"We arrived at Salt Lake July 27, 1847. Brigham Young was first on the ground and acclaimed the place as the Zion for which they had been seeking. He ordered a halt and said no further progress of the caravan would be made that year if at all. The men folks started building adobe houses, arranged as fortifications. There were three divisions of forts, each one-half a mile in length.

"Fall wheat was planted, seed which had been brought across the country. A strict order had been issued against anyone killing cattle for beef because we depended on them to pull the wagons.

"The authorities resorted to an emergency measure in order to conserve the supplies and examined each man's larder and apportioned the rations evenly to all the families. We were compelled to subsist on oatmeal and occasionally we killed rabbits, prairie chickens and crows to vary the menu.

"We went through a mild winter and when spring opened up we found an abundance of thistles with roots resembling parsnips. We boiled them with tops and roots intact and found them delicious. This vegetable is called segoes, or Indian turnip and in size it resembles an English walnut. We found wild berries in quantities sufficient to satisfy.

"In the spring of '48 the wheat crops came up but not with much success and in places it was so sparse it was not thick enough to cut so we pulled it up. Our thrashing facilities were crude. We pounded the wheat out with sticks and cleaned it in the wind. Some corn had also been planted and we ground it and the wheat in the Orleans old-fashioned coffee mill."

He wrote that in the spring of 1849, fifty families went over the ridge into Utah Valley and located on the Provo Creek. They made a treaty with the Utah Indians — the Indians would refrain from stealing their cattle and the white man was to kill no wild game. All went well until a Dr. Stoddard and a man named Lorentsky killed a deer. This led to a quarrel with an Indian who confronted them. When the Indian attacked Lorentsky, Dr. Stoddard shot him. They hid his body, which was soon found by the Indians.

"That was a signal for warfare against the whites. One man was killed in the fort and in response to an appeal for assistance the Government sent soldiers and recruits to our relief and prevented a wholesale massacre. The Indians were hunted out and in one battle on ice at the south end of the lake, twenty-five of them were killed at one time. Our casualties were light in comparison. During the winter's campaign practically all of the Indians were exterminated. During one engagement with the Indians my brother, John, got shot in the foot and James was wounded in the shoulder, but both recovered.

"In the spring of '50 my brother, John, was anxious to proceed to California, the original objective. The gold discovery there had been reported in Utah but there was little excitement among the Mormons as Brigham Young advised his followers to keep quiet and remain isolated from the Gentiles.

"After much coaxing John finally prevailed on my father to make the trip, and with my mother, two brothers and two sisters, we started to California.

"We left Provo and came to Salt Lake before the snow was off the ground and remained there until the grass began to grow. Thirty-five families joined our caravan to California and elected my father, Thomas Orr, as captain of the train.

"Bill Prouse, who was working for General Sutter when gold was discovered at Coloma by J.W. Marshall, had gone back to Utah with pack animals to meet his folks. He said he was familiar with all the stopping places on the emigrant trail and after joining our train was made pilot.

"Our first stop was on the present site of Ogden, but no settlement existed there then, only small roving bands of Indians held possession of the country. In order to recuperate our animals we camped at Ogden several days and then proceeded on to the Bear River. To cross over we used the wagon boxes as a ferry boat. Our next stop was at a steep ravine, Malad. We were compelled to unhitch the oxen and then lowered each wagon down one side with ropes and pulled them up on the opposite grade with five or six oxen to each wagon.

"Thousand Spring Valley was our next stop and there our cattle and horses stampeded, pulling the wagons with them. After much trouble we stopped them and got the wagons back into the road. We traveled on until we came to a sink on the Humboldt River and then had a forty-mile desert to cross. Bill Prouse told my father the best course to pursue was to carry grass as feed for the livestock and travel all night long.

"We followed his advice and discovered several sloughs about half-way across where we watered the stock and rested. We finally got across the desert and came to the Carson River. This river makes a bend around a desert twelve miles across and we reached the edge about noon. The locality is called Gold Canyon now, and is west of Virginia City.

"Prouse said the country there strongly resembled the California gold fields and a few of us went down with shovel and pan and dug a little pot hole the size of a post-hole and panned out two or three pans of dirt. Every pan showed color and we brought the gold for father's inspection. He was not much impressed with the find, so after our stock had a good feed on grass, we ate our lunch and started across the twelve-mile desert to avoid following the tortuous course of the river, out of our way a good many more miles.

"We came up with the Carson River again at dusk after a weary half-day's journey and unyoked our oxen to feed. This location was later called Empire City. We stayed there all night and in the morning when we gathered the stock up to start out we discovered one horse missing and looked for it everywhere but to no avail until somebody saw it down in a whirlpool, floating around. It had fallen over a twenty-foot cliff and broke its neck.

"Instead of going to where Carson City is now located, we cut across to Carson Canyon toward the Sierra Nevada range of mountains.

"Half way across the plains below Carson we met three Indians going that way and they told us the oxen could cross the mountains but the snow was too deep for the wagons. We drove on to a little creek, with fine bottom land and stopped at a place near Lake Tahoe, now called Genoa. We were there three weeks waiting for the snow to disappear from the mountains. Some of us went up a canyon and felled trees. We used the poles in making a corduroy road across a creek and in other places bridges would be constructed by men in our company.

"My brother John, accompanied by men named Bill Prouse and Nick Kelly returned to prospect the place where Prouse had made a find of gold. My brother was lucky in the first hole, panning out a nugget which later showed a value of $8.25. This was the first piece of gold ever found on that side of the mountains and my brother's sons living in Sonoma County, still possess this nugget, which has been handed down to them."

The story of the Orrs' arrival and settling in Salmon Falls, El Dorado County, is told in the first chapter of this entry.

Fairplay Recalled

Merritt Dean was born May 1, 1884. He was three years old when his father Willis and his mother Josephine LaBor Dean moved from Pinole, Contra Costa County, to El Dorado County in 1887. There they homesteaded 160 acres of land on the Omo Ranch road southeast of Fairplay and west of Indian Diggings. When interviewed at his cabin home on the Mt. Aukum road on February 15, 1975, Mr. Dean was looking forward to his 92nd birthday. He talked about mining, the opening up of sawmills in the area, his fear of Indians, and the capture of a kidnapper.

The Indians

"When I was old enough to start to school," said Mr. Dean, "I had to walk four miles through heavy brush and timber to go to the Fairplay School. They didn't have roads then like you have now . . . and there were lots of Indians. I was scared to death of those people . . . No, they didn't bother anybody, but I didn't know that then. I was only seven years old.

"We lived down in a canyon and in the morning when it was time to leave for school I'd go outside and listen. If I heard voices I wouldn't go . . . my mother or father had to walk with me up the hill and down to Cedar Grove where the Barneys lived. Will Barney had a mine there and I'd go to school with his kids. When school was out my folks would have to come over and get me. I wasn't going on that road alone. No sir, I was just plain scared of Indians.

"I sometimes wonder what happened to them . . . moved away . . . or died off I guess. There were lots of them here." He said that there was a encampment at Omo and another at Nashville, and they often visited back and forth. "Sometimes there would be 25 or 30 going up and down the road, singing and laughing . . . just having a good time. When they held their powwows, Indians came from Plymouth, Volcano, Nashville, some from Modesto and Nevada. They really whooped it up. They were a happy people . . . never bothered anybody. Oh, once in awhile they'd get into a fuss among themselves, but I never heard of them in trouble with a white man.

"I remember a man named John Levington . . . He ran a hydraulic mine at Cedar Grove. They had 100-foot banks they piped against with a 200-foot water fall pressure. The water came from Perry Creek, from a ditch that ran right through our home place. I was still a

County Historical Museum

THE TOWN OF FAIRPLAY was located on Slug Gulch road about two miles from the present Fairplay Store. Many members of the town's pioneer families are buried in the Fairplay Cemetery located on the hillside at the rear of the hotel building.

APTAIN COPPAH HEMBO was one Indian o child or white man needed to fear. He uided emigrant trains over the roads and saw at they came to no harm from unfriendly dians. This picture belonged to Judge T.F. ewis of Placerville and was given to him by is mother, Mrs. Laura Lewis Coombs, a iend of Coppah. Judge Lewis and his other attended Coppah's funeral, about 886. He was buried on a hill near the old roft home in the Garden Valley area of l Dorado County.

kid, but I remember standing on a hill over there when they were piping on a bank 60 or 70 feet high. They piped around the bottom maybe 10 or 20 feet and that whole hill came down. That was something to see. There were two of those hydraulic mines up at Indian Diggings. Other mines around here were the Lucky Jack, the Glorianna, and of course the big Crystal Mine at Fairplay."

He said there was gold on their property, but his father didn't mine much. "It was just hard work . . . with no equipment or nothing, and when they started cutting the trees, little sawmills started up. There was Staten, Farnum, and then Wetzel came in. My father worked in the woods logging. He got $40 a month and board.

"Some of the biggest trees of the county used to stand on that hill on our place. I remember we took a rope one day and measured one. It was nine feet in diameter, and must have been two hundred or close to three hundred feet high . . . a sugar pine, as round as a dollar. That was beautiful country then . . . but it's been logged off. All the big ones are gone."

When he was 21 years old, he said, his father gave the homestead to him and they moved to a home on the Fairplay road. "That house is still standing. The Frank Hicks family lives there now. After awhile I sold the place to Mildred and Jacque Conliffe. They did a lot of work on it and made it real nice. They built their house out of trees they cut off the place and ran through a little sawmill they had there. When her husband died she later married a Ted Gallion, from Sacramento. I guess they're doing fine there."

135

He said that when arrests were made around Fairplay, when trouble started, they held court in the Odd Fellows Hall. He drew attention to the changes he believed had taken place in people. "We were free then," said Dean. "You see how it is now . . . you can't do this . . . can't do that. Why, you could lay your tools down in our day and leave them there a month, and nobody would touch them. You couldn't do that now . . . No, it's all different."

He laughed as he told about the time Mr. Wetzel caught the kidnapper of a little boy. Because he did not recall names or dates, reference was made to a newspaper account of the incident that was prominent in all newspapers in 1942.

Marc de Tristan, Jr., the three-year-old son of Count and Countess Marc de Tristan, was kidnapped from the street in Hillsborough, San Mateo County while his nurse had him out for a walk. A $100,000 ransom note was left, and the kidnappers drove away in a two-door Ford sedan.

The following day a deer hunter reported his car stolen at gun-point on the Ice House road above Riverton. This brought the hunt to El Dorado County. According to the report, the FBI did not release the news until Wednesday, six days after the kidnapping. Once released, it was published in newspapers and on radio.

Having heard the news, Cecil Wetzel became suspicious when he and Ellis Woods found a man standing by a car on a logging road above his sawmill in the Omo Ranch area. When he saw the golden-haired boy in the car, he started questioning the man. "When he pulled a gun, there wasn't any doubt that he was the kidnapper," said Wetzel. "He was close enough for me to reach out and grab him. So I just grabbed his head in both hands like a football and flipped him to the ground. As he dropped, I fell right on top of him and reached out and took the gun. It was only a second and Ellis was there. He had another gun in a shoulder holster. We tied him hand and foot and went to the nearest telephone, which was in the River Pines Grocery Store. We kept him until the officials from San Francisco arrived to pick him up."

Cecil Wetzel, the 200-pound lumberman, was a former Washington State College football star noted for his flying tackles.

The kidnapper was Wilhelm Jakob Muhlembroich, a German alien who spoke four languages and was a barber by trade. There was a big reward out for his capture, but Wetzel and Woods refused it.

Mr. Dean said he never married. He had one brother, Lonnie Dean, who was well known in the Fairplay area. "Lonnie had two sons, Ben and Bill," said Merritt, "Ben's son Kenny lives with his wife and children, Karen and Kenny, right next door to my place here, so I get to see them often." He said he often takes rides around the countryside with friends and never ceases to note the changes that have taken place.

FAIRPLAY — Court was held in the Odd Fellows Hall. Trouble-makers were thrown in jail until they "cooled-off," and on election day 500 votes were tallied in the precinct. The busy mining town was a short distance from the Crystal Mine on the Cosumnes River. Owners of the mine at that time transported Chinese from San Francisco in wagon loads. It is reported they blindfolded them just outside of Plymouth to avoid their knowing where the mine was located.

FAIRPLAY AFTER THE STORM - Sidewalks were washed away, supplies in the store and hotel damaged, the Opera House ruined, and a number of homes flooded when a nine-day storm hit the town in the early 1800's. The hillside in the background, stripped of all its virgin timber and ground cover, may account for the damage done.

County Historical Museum

LOTUS AND COLOMA SCHOOL PICNIC, 1911, at the historic Vineyard House.

1. Gavert Grother
2. Irma Turnbeaugh Lawyer
3. George Grother
4. Woman (back of George Wagner)
5. George Wagner
6. Woman (back of George)
7. Man (alongside George)
8. Sophie Veerkamp (teacher)
9. Leroy Thomas
10. Hazel Howland (Goethe)
11. Ralph Dunkum
12. Annie Thomas (Jaeger)
13. Sam Sommers (in back)
14. Lorena Wagner (Smith)
15. (back) Elsie Uhlenkamp (Colwell)
16. (front) Martha Turnbeaugh (Grover)
17. (back) Carl Michael
18. (front) Wesley Grother

19. Lottie Galleher
20. (child) Albert Herzig
21. Bill Immer
22. Bill Amstalden
23. Mamie Galloway
24. Man (unidentified)
25. Elmer Colwell
26. Mary Gallagher (teacher)
27. Melvin Nethercott
28. Tod Burgess
29. Everett DeLory
30. John Bayne
31. Rufus Burgess
32. & 33. Men behind shrubbery
34. Mamie Thomas
35. Ella Norris
36. Herbert Wagner (hat)
37. George Luneman (hat)

38. Ed Thole (holding Alice Gallagher)
39. Alice Gallagher
40. Man (unidentified)
41. Ralph Colwell
42. Angie DeLory
43. Hattie Colwell (Mrs. R. Colwell)
44. Walter Wagner (back)
45. Lady (unidentified)
46. Martha Gray
47. Jane Stearns
48. Fredericka Wagner
49. Frank Wagner
50. Alice Veerkamp
51. Louise Gallagher (holding Marie)
52. Marie
53. Frank Veerkamp
    (dim view of tiny child Hilda Herzig)
54. Man (unidentified)

55. George Colwell
56. Maud Veerkamp (Panning)
57. Man (unidentified)
58. (boy) Russell Spatz
59. Josephine Norris
60. Bob Johnson
61. Charley Howland
62. May Howland
63. Boy (unidentified)
64. Raymond Gallagher
65. Fred Thomas
66. Saunders Moseley
67. Frank Amstalden
68. Albert Norris
69. Traver Goethe
70. Marion Burgess
71. Frank Gallagher
72. Melvin Gallagher
73. Buster Galloway (in front)

Traver Goethe was the youngest brother of Charles Goethe of Sacramento who was a great philanthropist and has a school, street, and park in Sacramento named after him. Their father was a Sacramento real estate broker.

138

WILLIAM W. WAGNER, a native of Illinois, made two trips to California.

JESSE WAGNER at age 16

JOHN WAGNER, miner, farmer, and dairyman, bought the Bayley House in Pilot Hill in 1917. It was the family home until 1946, when he sold it.

Photos from Wagner Family Collection

Mrs. Lorena Wagner Smith and her brother, George Wagner, remember that their grandparents settled in the Gold Hill and Lotus communities in El Dorado County, but only after they had made a second trip to California did they decide to remain, to build their homes and raise their children in the new state. Their maternal grandfather, Charles Tobener, arrived for the first time in 1850. After a number of unpleasant experiences, he went back to Missouri. He returned in 1862 with his bride. Of his first crossing they said: "When Grandpa Tobener was 17, he went into partnership with two men in St. Louis, Missouri. Each invested an equal amount to purchase the needed equipment and provisions to get them to California by wagon train. When they reached eastern Nevada, the two men had a bitter quarrel. They agreed to dissolve the partnership. They cut the wagon in two and made two carts. Each man took a cart and a number of oxen. Grandpa got one ox and a dog for his share."

She said Charles Tobener went to Hangtown, where he sold his ox for $50, and then went on to Coloma. His luck wasn't much better there, because he worked with some men digging a tunnel through a hill between Coloma and Lotus, known today as Tunnel Hill. The plan was to turn the South Fork of the American River through the tunnel, leaving the river bed at the horseshoe-bend exposed for surface mining. After a number of cave-ins (some still visible today), the tunnel was abandoned. The men started fighting and there was a lack of funds, so it was never finished.

Tobener went back to Missouri after the tunnel incident and did not return until 1862. This time he brought his bride with him. They came by way of the Isthmus of Panama. "He bought a donkey for her to ride and he walked across," said Mrs. Smith.

They went to San Francisco by boat and then traveled across country by stage to Coloma. He bought land and settled on a farm in Gold Hill, where he planted fruit trees and grapes and did some mining. Charles and Mary Tobener had twelve children. The first seven were born on the farm in Gold Hill, El Dorado County, and five were born in Gold Hill, Nevada, where Tobener went to try his luck when news of a gold strike there was made known. "Our mother, Fredericka Tobener, was born at the Gold Hill farm here in California," said Mrs. Smith.

"Our grandfather, William Wagner, was 24 years old when he left Illinois to come to California in 1850. We have no idea what means of transportation he used to reach here that first time, nor do we know why he went back to Illinois, but family records show that he did return, and while there he married Drucilla Thomas in 1855.

"In 1862 they came to Lotus, California, arriving by wagon train. They had five children. The older two died while very young and are buried in Kinderhook township, Illinois, where our grandparents lived before coming to California. A daughter named Alice and a son named Jesse Franklin were also born there. They made the trip to California. Jesse, who was always called 'Frank,' became our father. The family enjoyed telling how he learned to walk while crossing the plains. He was one year old at the time." Their daughter Alice later married Francis Veerkamp, son of another well known pioneer family. John, their youngest son, was born in Lotus in 1864.

All three children attended the Uniontown school. "It was the only grammar school the Frank Wagner children attended," said Mrs. Smith. "The building still stands on the hill, surrounded by oak trees. The school had a marvelous bell in its tower. It could be heard for four miles if the wind was right. Its tone was sweet and clear. We children, living three miles away, often heard the 8:30 bell at home and, by running, got to school before 9 o'clock."

The Wagners settled on a small 40-acre farm in Lotus. Their property expanded until the family holdings totaled 1900 acres. "Grandfather Wagner and his partner, 'Doc' Fairchild, built the original Lotus Store sometime between 1888 and 1890," said Mrs. Smith. "John and Francis Veerkamp took it over in 1900 and then later it was sold to Chris Uhlenkamp."

Rare Gold Mine

Frank and John Wagner discovered gold in a quartz mine on the original 40-acre Wagner ranch. "The gold they found there is unique," said Mrs. Smith. "Mining engineers agree that the two quartz mines near Lotus are the only place in the world where gold has been found in roscolite, instead of in quartz."

Roscolite, she explained, is a dull black mineral. It is the oxide of vanadium and it eats up all the minerals it contains but the gold. So the gold contains no silver, copper, or other minerals, and is practically pure. Gold from the Wagner mine brought a higher price, $21 per ounce, while other gold brought $16 an ounce.

"When they quit mining in 1917, our father and his brother John went into the beef cattle and dairy business. By taking their cattle to the summer range in Union Valley, they were able to make butter in the summer time. John bought the Bayley House in Pilot Hill and the spacious 24-room house, built by A. John Bayley about 1862, became their home until 1946.

ON THE WAGNER FARM IN LOTUS
George and Lorena had their picture taken with their grandfather, William Wagner, and their father, Frank Wagner. The family land holdings eventually totaled 1900 acres.

LOTUS SCHOOL

Wagner Smith Collection

THE LOTUS SCHOOL Class of Spring 1911. In the back row, from left, are Walter Wagner, Lorena Wagner, Wesley Grother, George Wagner, Frances Gallagher and the teacher, Miss Mary Gallagher. In the front row, from left, are Albert Herzig, Vera Harris, Martha Turnbeaugh, and George Harris.

HE ORIGINAL LOTUS TORE was built by illiam Wagner and his rtner "Doc" Fairchild 1893. It was taken er around 1900 by hn Wagner and Francis erkamp, and later sold Chris Uhlenkamp. The ildren in the foreground e Alice and Charles gner and (on right) sie Uhlenkamp. Alice gner later married ancis Veerkamp. Stand- near the store are Mrs. lliam Wagner (on left) d Mrs. John Wagner.

Wagner Smith Collection

"Our father stayed on the home ranch at Lotus and continued in the cattle and dairy business. He formed a partnership with his sons, Herbert and Walter, and in 1947 the ranch was sold to a Mr. Stodick from Nevada. Herbert and Walter, now both in their eighties, are still ranching near Elk Grove, California. George and I, the two younger children of the family, have been retired for some time, George from ranching and I from teaching."

"When the old-timers were alive, you could hear a lot of stories," said Mr. Wagner. "I remember one . . . I don't recall the man's name, but he had a house about a mile down the river from Lotus and he had a mine. They say he went to the blacksmith one day and had him make a land auger the size of an oyster can. A land auger that size made the blacksmith curious and he said the only thing he could figure was that the man was putting his gold in oyster cans and burying it.

"Well, one day they found the man dead . . . his body was in the water at the bottom of the waterwheel at the mine. Soon everybody started looking for the gold . . . buried in oyster cans. You'd have to check the records to find out how many times that man's ranch sold. His place was just a mile below Lotus on the river road, but not on the Bacchi side. Champ Castle was the last one I can remember who tried to find it. When they didn't find anything on his ranch, they looked on the next ranch, Herzig's place. Then Valentine bought the parcel . . . it was sure funny to see everybody wanting to buy that ranch. All they did was dig, looking for oyster cans. Nobody ever found any that I know of."

An incident that both remember, but with somewhat different versions, was the prison break of July 27, 1903 when convicts escaped and were reported seen in El Dorado County. They robbed a store at Pilot Hill to obtain ammunition for weapons they had taken from the prison armory. The National Guard was called out and it was the men of the Guard that they both recalled.

George Wagner said, "The way I remember it, I was about three years old. They say a kid don't remember too much when he's three, but I remember them soldiers . . . the blue uniforms and white stripes on them. There was thirty of them with Captain Swisler. They come up to the place in a bunch. Not straggling along, they were a solid mass. And they come to the house and stacked their guns . . . you know how they stack their guns. They left one man on guard and the rest went into the house and ate . . . ate everything we had. They didn't sit down to eat. They stood around the table and ate everything. I remember Mother sent us down to gather more eggs. We took the nest eggs, rotten eggs, and anything we could find. They ate all the potatoes, bacon, biscuits, and bread . . . there wasn't anything left when they finished."

Mary Miller Wagner Collection

(Above) THE SLATER STONE HOUSE, built by George Slater in 1862, is still standing on Reservoir Hill on Mosquito Road near Placerville. The old home and farm remained in the family for over 100 years. George and Susanna Slater, great-grandparents of Mary Miller Wagner, came to America from England in the early 1840's. They came to California by wagon train by way of St. Joseph, Missouri. Their son, Edward, married Rosanna Shanley of Utica, New York, and Mary Elizabeth, the only child of Edward and Rosanna Slater, married Mark Miller of Placerville. Mrs. Wagner is one of eight children born of this union. Today the old Stone House has changed in appearance. A wooden structure has been added and the original native stone has been covered with shingle siding.

(Above) A FAMILY PICTURE OF THE
WAGNERS taken in 1899 shows John
Wagner, his wife Sophia, and their two
children, Charles and Alice, on the left.
Jesse "Frank" Wagner and his wife
Fredericka Tobener Wagner are on the
right with three of their four children.
The infant is Lorena (now Mrs. Smith),
the child standing is Herbert Wagner, and
the boy in foreground is Walter Wagner.

GEORGE AND MARY WAGNER

Both recalled that a Mrs. Jurgens who lived on Weber Creek had "a bunch of daughters." The convicts went to the house and Mrs. Jurgens, not wanting any trouble, permitted them to come in. "She thought if she treated them nice there would be less trouble," Mrs. Smith said. "They were just as gentlemanly as could be. They were convicts, but they were as nice as anybody you'd want to know. They played the piano and they stayed there several days before they left."

"There was a reward out for them," said Mr. Wagner, "and the store owner at the time, Chris Uhlenkamp, and someone else thought they'd get some money. There were said to be thirteen in the bunch. They sure could have gotten shot. They found where the convicts had bathed one day down by the river. Their clothes were spread out on the rock to dry, so they had to be near, somewhere around in the woods. They were probably watching Uhlenkamp all the time. If they had spotted them, they would have shot but they didn't. They were lucky."

Mr. Wagner remembered the dusty streets of Placerville and a Mr. Bill Day who drove the horse-drawn sprinkler wagon to keep the dust down. "It was quite a thrill for us when they put gravel on the street, especially in the winter when the mud was so deep. The sidewalks were built up high — they were board walks — and then they'd put two twelve-inch planks across the street so you could walk to the other side. When the slate mine was working, that was something. They'd bring those loads of slate through town and dust would ream out . . . it was awful."

Mrs. Smith said she went through all grades at the Lotus school and then attended a school in Stockton, where she took the teachers' examination. "I started teaching school and taught continuously, with the exception of two years I took off to go to college and one year after I married. All together I taught twenty-one years in the El Dorado County and Folsom schools."

Today George Wagner and his wife, Mary Miller Wagner, often drive from their home in Placerville through the familiar countryside, reflecting on their childhood days when they traveled many of the same roads by horse and buggy. Mrs. Wagner is a descendant of the pioneer Slater family of Mosquito Road.

Lorena Wagner Smith lives in the home her late husband William Joseph Smith built at the site of his machine shop at the El Dorado Y, south of the town of El Dorado. She has many relatives and friends, and enjoys sharing her knowledge of the county and its early-day families.

A Banking Pioneer

Mr. Lloyd Raffetto of Placerville remembers the ingenuity and determination exercised by his grandparents when they settled on a homestead in El Dorado County in the early 1800's. He is the grandson of Dominico Raffetto and the son of John and Adela Creighton Raffetto. During a three-hour interview on June 16, 1975, he laughed heartily at some incidents, but he was quite serious when he referred to the Depression years and described how the Raffettos refused to be deterred by conditions. "When my grandparents lived on the Raffetto homestead in the Newtown area," said Mr. Raffetto, "I used to stay there at times and I was always amazed at the self-sufficiency that they enjoyed. They raised their own wheat . . . it was hard wheat, or sometimes called winter wheat. They'd cut it by hand, pile it in a circle and have the horse walk around on top of it . . . then they dusted it off and hauled it to Pleasant Valley, where they made it into flour.

"My grandmother made her own macaroni. She used to make this big pile of dough, then roll it out thin, slice it, and hang it on the clothesline outside to dry so they could store it. They raised their own meat, too. They were particularly careful when they killed an animal to save the brains, because that went into the stuffing in the raviolis. My grandfather made a thousand gallons of wine a year from his own grapes. On Sundays he used to have about fifty people call on him.

"Their only income was from selling wood. Their biggest customer was one of my aunts, Aunt Ida, who had the Arcade Bakery on Main Street. My uncle would haul the wood for a great stone oven in the bakery and he'd build a tremendous fire. When it burned down, he'd rake the ashes aside and shove the dough in and bake the bread."

The Arcade Bakery was on the ground floor in the I.O.O.F. building on Main Street, where Arian's Department Store has been located since 1952. The stone oven stood in the rear of the building on the east wall, next to the City Hall parking lot.

"My father was a remarkable man. Every summer, when he was young, he used to walk over to Genoa to work in the wheat fields. He got $30 a month, and room and board. He would bring $60 home . . . Boy, that was a welcome thing in those days. It took him two days to walk over there; Genoa, you know, is over the mountains from South Tahoe. He said one time he made it back in one day — that was about

DOMINICO RAFFETTO

ADELA ISADEEN CREIGHTON RAFFETT and an attentive son, Lloyd Raffetto, in the yard of the Ivy House, late 1897 or early 189

LACERVILLE HOTEL, now the Raffles Hotel

OLD CARY HOUSE, 1857, Wells Fargo and Co. stage depot in Placerville. $90,000,000 from the Comstock mines stood on the porch awaiting shipment to San Francisco. The Cary House was torn down in 1915 to make way for the Placerville Hotel.

90 miles. When someone asked him how he did it, he said, 'I ran part of the way.' Then when Dad started to work in the mines, he got a dollar and a half a day. When he had saved a thousand dollars, and a friend named Potts had saved a thousand, they bought the Conklin Academy and turned it into the Ivy House."

Born In The Ivy House

"About 1890 Dad bought out his partner. I was the first child to be born in the Ivy House. All my brothers and sisters were born there, all without a doctor, just a midwife. Four of us are still alive. There's my brother Elwyn, or Mike, who is next to me. He gained quite a reputation in radio and television appearing in "One Man's Family" and "I Love a Mystery." My brother John lives in Auburn, where he is the president of the Placer National Bank. He has two sons, one works for Xerox and the other is a stockbroker in Sacramento, Peter Raffetto; you may have seen him on television. My sister Isadeen lives in Placerville. She married A.H. 'Sandy' Murray. He's a native son — his ancestors were settlers in southern California. They have two daughters, Patricia and Moira. My wife, Ethel, and I have one son, Danno, and a grandson Kurt. Mrs. Raffetto was a Quigley before we married. Her family also played a part in the early-day history of the county.

"When Dad had the Ivy House, they served meals in the dining room for 25¢ and then he raised it to 35¢. 'Jack, you can't do that. People won't pay 35¢ for a meal.' Well, they did, and the Ivy House did a big business with the miners. They'd have breakfast in the early morning and go out to the mines. My dad would put up a lunch in what they called a 'three tier' . . . did you ever see one? It was a round lunch pail with three sections that fit together. In the bottom part, he'd put the sandwich, in the middle the dessert — a piece of pie or cake, and on top . . . well most anything — soup, coffee, or whatever. You know, those guys used to come home with that middle section filled with gold.

"In later years my brother, John Raffetto, took over and operated the Ivy House and built the Ivy Motel on adjacent property. It was torn down in the 1950's." His father bought the Cary House in 1911 and tore it down in 1915. "He built the Placerville Hotel on the site of the old Cary House. My Aunt Ida, who had the bakery, had remarried by that time, and she and her husband, Mr. Beck, operated the hotel. When their lease ran out, my dad wrote me and asked if I would come back and run it. We closed it for one month while we redecorated and refurnished it, and then we opened it as the Raffles Hotel."

(Above) THE IVY HOUSE was purchased about 1890 by John A. Raffetto. He is seated by the door, holding his oldest child, Lloyd. The Raffetto children, Lloyd, "Mike," John, and Isadeen, were born in the Ivy House. It remained in the family until it was demolished to make room for a parking lot.

THE RAFFETTOS - about 1934 - Standing, from left: Elwyn, John, John Sr., "Sandy" Murray, and Lloyd. Seated, from left: Isadeen, wife of "Sandy" Murray, Pauline, wife of Elwyn, Ellen, John Jr.'s wife, and Ethel, Lloyd's wife. John, Sr. lived to be 92 years old.

(Below) THE WINNER - Lloyd Raffetto breaking the track record at El Dorado High School, 1917

ELWYN AND LLOYD RAFFETTO, 1901
Elwyn, known as "Mike," became an actor
and his name was a household name to the
radio audiences of "One Man's Family" and
"I Love a Mystery."

ADELA CREIGHTON RAFFETTO and son
Lloyd Raffetto, home from the service

Photos Raffetto Collection

School Days – Lloyd Raffetto attended Mrs. Dormody's Private School for his first-grade education. "I started late," said Raffetto, "because I had trouble in my youth and they finally traced it to the raw milk we used to drink. Milk wasn't pasteurized in those days, you know. I had TB in a kidney that was removed when I was 10 years old. My brothers Mike and John both had tuberculosis when they were young . . . all from milk.

"After my term with Mrs. Dormody, I went to grammar school and to El Dorado High School. Mother insisted we all go to college. I'll never forget my dad when I got ready to go. He said, 'How much is this college business going to cost?' When I told him I had no idea, he said, 'Well, here's a check book on my account. You know how I'm fixed.' And that was it — he sent four of us through college."

When Mr. Raffetto attended the University of California at Davis there were 600 students enrolled. "598 boys," said Raffetto, "and two girls. I recently received a letter telling me that this year 1975 there were 16,000 enrolled and 2,000 turned away. I graduated in 1921. There was a depression on then. I don't think it was as bad as the one we are in now, but a job was a difficult thing to get. I talked to the head of the dairy industry and he suggested that I teach. So I taught for three years and it was good experience."

While at Davis, he and Grover Turnbull wrote a textbook, *Ice Cream*. It was published by John Wyle Publishers and was a big seller. "Then an outfit from Singapore wrote the University. They wanted someone to come there to advise and install the system used for repackaging the milk, cream and ice cream. I had worked this formula out at Davis, so I went there. I was five months putting the thing together — it was fantastic. Going by boat it took 31 days to get there, with stops in Japan, Shanghai, Hong Kong, and the Philippines.

"Of course, I think the bank was the greatest thing I ever did . . . that was the Mother Lode Bank. I didn't think we would ever raise $225,000, but we did. We met in my office for two years here, once a week, and we made a mistake, although I don't think too bad, by setting the price of the stock at $175 a share. Well, we decided that if they didn't have the money, they couldn't afford to be associated. So, the guy that bought one share of stock at $175 now, through stock dividends and stock splits, has 150 shares. And the first of this month, (July 1, 1975) he will get $40 a share for it."

Today Lloyd Raffetto, ignoring obstacles or overcoming them, continues to direct the business affairs of Raffetto Enterprises. His memories of grandparents who "lived off the land" and a father who walked 90 miles to work to earn wages to support his family, have provided an incentive to match their initiative.

147

She Waited 12 Years

JAMES CREIGHTON who was surprised to find his wife and children made a hazardous trip to California and found him in Nevada in 1862.

Martha Jane Creighton waited twelve years for her husband James to return home to Rockland, Maine, from the gold fields of California. When he did not come back or arrange for her to join him, she booked passage for herself and her three children and sailed for California. This and other events in the lives of Shirley Douglass Gianelli's great-grandparents established the fact that the Creightons were among the first settlers in El Dorado county. "Martha Jane had received many letters from James," said Mrs. Gianelli, "each containing money for her and the children, much of which she apparently saved through the years and used for passage to California." With nothing more than a postmark on an envelope indicating that a letter had been mailed from some place in California called Smith Flat, El Dorado County, Martha left Rockland, Maine.

Crossing the Isthmus in 1862 was as hazardous as it had been in 1849 or '50. Surviving that ordeal, Martha then found a boat to take her and her children to San Francisco. From San Francisco they traveled by river boat to Sacramento, then by stage to Smith Flat, El Dorado County. Upon reaching their destination, Martha learned that her husband was not there. He had gone to the Comstock Lode in Nevada.

ELIZA AND WILLIAM TAYLOR crossed the plains in 1861. Six year old Mary Isadeen Taylor, Mrs. Gianelli's maternal grandmother, was hidden in a sugar barrel when Indians attacked the wagon train

"Nothing I could find in old letters," continued Mrs. Gianelli, "revealed what happened or how they finally got together. I think Mr. Creighton, as she was still calling him when he died, knowing the dangers he encountered when he crossed the Isthmus, was reluctant to have his family come to California. But Martha came . . . and James gave her a large silver belt buckle made from Comstock ore, with her engraved initials. We still have the buckle today . . . it is a treasured possession."

From news clippings Mrs. Gianelli learned that James Creighton, her great-grandfather, built the first flour mill in Placerville. It was run by water-power from the city waterworks at the top of the hill.

Her grandfather, James Samuel Creighton, was a blacksmith and wagon maker. "A lot of the old wagons you see around here today were made in his shop at Smith Flat. The old surrey and another wagon made by Grandpa are on display at the County Historical Museum in Placerville. He was active in civic affairs too. I think it was in 1910 that he was elected supervisor and served 12 years, from 1910 through 1922."

MARY "MOLLY" ISADEEN CREIGHTON mother of Shirley Gianelli, and Mrs. Gianelli's aunt Leila "Pet" Taylor, who, after being widowed, in 1876 married Seth Beach, founder of the Beach Box Factory in Placerville.

(Inset) MARTHA JANE CREIGHTON who traveled from Maine to California in 1862 only to find her husband was in Nevada.

148

Photos Shirley Gianelli Collection

Photos Shirley Gianelli Collection

THE CREIGHTON HOME AND BLACKSMITH SHOP AT SMITH FLAT where John, June and James Creighton were born. The children in the picture are (from left) Jessie Murdock, John Fossati, James Creighton, Perry Potts, June Creighton, and Hazel Potts. While children's hats were quite the fashion, they were removed for photographic reasons. Gentlemen on right are Harvey Hogan, James Creighton (the blacksmith), and John Creighton astride "Old Bird".

JAMES S. CREIGHTON, son of Martha and James Creighton, was noted for his building of exceptional wagons and his work as a blacksmith. He was a county supervisor for 12 years. Pictured with him is his wife Molly.

SMITH FLAT SCHOOL class of 1925. The students standing in back row are, from left: an unidentified boy, Evelyn Stancil, Lawrence McDonald, Marie Jacquier, Inez Ferrari, Bernice Rupley, Ed Jones, and Reggie Jackson. The teacher, May Fairbairn, back of students.
Seated are, from left: Herbert Jacquier, the next two boys could not be identified, Florence Rupley, Lillian Silva, Elsie Bongetta, James Bongetta, Joe Cola and Raymond Jackson.

SALOON AND DANCE HALL owned by Will Potts in Smith Flat. Ladies' fashions place the era in mid 1800's. It was noted on the back of the picture that the establishment was later to become the Frank Raffetto place at Smith Flat.

A Brief Look at Tahoe History

Before the white man came to Lake Tahoe, and long before it acquired the name Tahoe, the lake — teeming with native silver and cutthroat trout, and surrounded by forests of virgin giant sugar pine where deer, bear, and other wild life roamed undisturbed — was the summer encampment site of the Washoe and Paiute Indians. The first recorded sighting of the lake by a white man was that of Captain John C. Fremont on February 14, 1844. It is said that he stood atop a high peak north of Carson Pass with his topographer, Charles Preuss, at the time of his historic sighting. He christened the shimmering, crystal-clear waters below "Lake Bonpland" in honor of a French botanist.

There are reports that other white explorers seeking new routes across the Sierra Nevada had sighted the lake at earlier dates, some as early as 1831. One such sighting by James Madison Harbin is described by his great-grandchildren, James, Elbert, and Euell Gray, now residing in Placerville.

Another early-day explorer, John C. "Cock Eye" Johnson, blazed the first trail from Hangtown to the south end of Tahoe, over what is now Echo Summit, in 1848. Johnson's explorations resulted in the first road, called "Johnson's Cut-Off," into and out of the valley. The valley and the adjacent areas soon became known as "Lake Valley."

In 1851, Martin Smith established a trading post and became the lake's first white settler. Others associated with him through the years were Jim Muir, George N. Douglass, and Ephraim "Yank" Clement. In 1857, the first stagecoach was driven over Johnson's Cut-Off. During this decade, Lake Bonpland was renamed Lake Bigler, in honor of California's third governor, John Bigler. It was not until 1945 that the name Tahoe was officially accepted. It was deemed most appropriate, as Tahoe, in Washoe Indian dialect, means "Big Water".

The discovery of silver in Nevada's Comstock Lode in 1859 started a stream of people, animals, stagecoaches, and freighters over Johnson's Cut-Off on the way to the Comstock. This "head-to-tailgate" stream into the basin over Johnson's Cut-Off continued in an uninterrupted flow until 1868, when the Central Pacific Railroad over Donner Pass was completed, thereby easing what has been described as "the greatest mass movement of men, wagons, animals, and materials known to history."

Photo courtesy of Cross from "California Inns"

OVER THE SUMMIT IN 1860 - This was a familiar scene of men, horses, mules and cargo on the way to the Comstock.

"THE EMERALD", launched in July of 1864 by owner Ben Holladay, made excursion trips to Tahoe City and Glenbrook. The 55-foot steam-operated boat made 12 miles an hour. Later used to tow logs the Glenbrook saw mill, she was operated as a work boat until 1935 when she was retired and scrapped.

Photo William (Mike) De Natly Collection

A HORSESHOE TURN on Meyers Grade (Highway 50). Norman Celio recalls seeing the first of the twenty cars that tried to make it from Placerville to Lake Tahoe in 1906. They were two weeks on the road, and some did not make it.

THE WINTER OF '52 - One can only imagine what Sierra winters were like in the 1800's, but the winter of 1952 is still remembered. The Lake Tahoe Historical Society noted that houses could not be seen from the streets, and people were skiing from second-story roofs.

GRAZING on the Upper Truckee near Lake Tahoe - 1920

Photos Yohalem Collection

In the 1860's Lake Valley developed a haying and dairying economy, and fertile ranches operated by Tahoe's earliest pioneer families dotted the area. The mouth of the upper Truckee River (now Tahoe Keys) became the site of a nationally famous trout fishing industry that, each year, took hundreds of tons of native trout from the lake's waters.

Steam navigation was first used on the lake during the 1860's, and over the decades proud steamers served as important links in the lake's lifeline, providing passenger, mail, and freight service to various shoreline points. The last of Tahoe's "Queens of the Lake" disappeared from the area in 1941.

Mark Twain visited Tahoe during the 1860's and in his book, "Roughin' It," described his personal feeling for the lake's beauty, serenity, and magnificence: "I thought it must surely be the fairest picture the whole earth affords."

With the Comstock Mines going full swing, the demand for lumber for the mine shafts, tunnels, and chasms that honeycombed the lode was phenomenal. Since the Tahoe area contained the only nearby source of timbers, the lumbering industry came to Tahoe. Entire forests were devoured as trees were felled, loaded into hand built logging wagons, transferred to the narrow gauge Lake Valley Railroad, and hauled to the pier at Bijou; from here the logs were discharged into the lake and towed to the mills at Glenbrook. It was estimated that timber exported from the Tahoe Basin and used in the mines at Virginia City alone totaled enough to construct 40,000 six-room houses.

By the turn of the century the timber reserves were down to only a few quarter sections, and large scale logging in the region was over. A limited operation did continue, however, into the early part of this century, with most of its production going into the expanding resort and summer home development.

Names synonymous with this era are those of famed resorts such as Lucky Baldwin's Tallac Hotel, the "Summer Resort of the World" (1898-1927); Glenbrook Inn (1906); Fallen Leaf Lodge (1907); Camp Richardson (1923); Young's Bijou Lodge (1915-1951); Globin's Al Tahoe (1924-1957); and spacious private residences such as "Vatican Lodge" and "Vikingsholm."

Lake Tahoe catered primarily to the summer residents and, except for a few caretakers on the large estates, few people remained in the area during the winter months. The area was undeveloped: there weren't any doctors, nor was there a drug store; mail was delivered only three times a week (via steamer, provided it wasn't stormy); there was an elementary school (a one room schoolhouse), but a high school was nonexistent, and students of high school age had to continue their education off the "hill". The end of World War II, however, found greater numbers living year-around at the Lake.

John Winning Photo

Marjorie Johnson Springmeyer, granddaughter of Chris and Celia Johnson, and daughter of Knox and Stella Johnson, said of Lake Tahoe, "As a child I spent every summer here. My fondest memories are of the Washoe Indians who worked on our ranch. Mother had an Indian cook and the whole Indian family worked for us. From them our family learned to appreciate the land. Every summer I lived here I thought how fortunate we were that our grandparents made it possible for us to grow up in these mountain meadows." Chris Johnson, a native of Norway, came to California in the 1860's and raised cattle in Nevada. When the dry summers and lack of water forced him to search for water and pasture land, he went to El Dorado County and the fertile meadow lands around Lake Tahoe, then called Lake Bigler.

"The lumbering industry at Tahoe was being phased out by the time our family came here," said Mrs. Springmeyer. "It was in 1908 that Grandfather Johnson bought his first land here . . . so, you see, we really are not among the very first settlers in the area.

"He bought the Sibeck parcel that included what today would roughly be the area from Highway 50 through Al Tahoe to Meek's Lumber Yard and Trout Creek Meadow. From there it continued up Heavenly Creek and along the Pioneer Trail to Rancho Bijou, joining Highway 50 again at Young's Bijou (Timber Cove).

"The Sibecks raised a lot of hay on the ranch at Bijou, used mostly to feed the oxen when they were in the lumber business. In fact, it was lumber from here that built Virginia City. It was an interesting old ranch. The old railroad bed ran through the property and the first school at Lake Tahoe was built on Sibeck land. It was called the Lake Valley School." Chris and Celia Johnson had five children, Chris, Jr., Knox, Miranda, Ida, and Annie. Chris, Jr., maintained the land and Knox ran the cattle. Mrs. Springmeyer said that the first irrigation boxes and dams along the rivers were built by Chris, Jr. Throughout the years the family continued to extend their land holdings. At one time they ran 500 head of beef cattle at the Sierra House site.

By the time the family had bought the McComber property, both Chris, Jr., and Knox Johnson were married and had families of their own. Knox had married Stella Van Dyke, who had come to Nevada from Ohio as a young girl. She was teaching school in Carson Valley when they married in 1921. The three children born of this union were Marjorie, William, and Knox.

MR. CHRIS JOHNSON

MRS. CELIA JOHNSON

(Inset) MARJORIE SPRINGMEYER

Photos William V.D. Johnson Collection

CECIL "BOUNCE" WADE was born at Grove, near Tallac. He worked for the Johnson family for about 30 years. A full-blooded Washoe Indian, be can remember when there were no roads at Tahoe and all traveling was by foot or horseback.

THE SIBECK CABIN was built in 1874 when Charles Sibeck acquired a part of the Taylor property, homesteaded in 1861. Chris Johnson Sr. bought the Sibeck holdings and an effort was made to preserve the old cabin. Eventually it was destroyed by vandalism. It stood adjacent to the Happy Homestead Cemetery.

Mrs. Springmeyer spoke of the hard times during the Depression. Her father died in 1931, leaving her mother to look after the interests of the Johnson family and raise her three small children. "Without the help of the wonderful Indian families, who stuck by her, she would never have made it. They were there to get in the hay and they returned in early spring to put up fences. They were the only ones who knew how to round up the cattle from the high country. To this day I have a great reverence for what they taught us about nature and the spiritual feeling of Tahoe. I remember when they camped at Richardson's, and on the meadow at our home. They camped at Bijou and remained there all summer, weaving baskets to sell to the tourists." She said efforts had been made to establish a summer camp for the Indians at Lake Tahoe, but to no avail. After Indians were arrested for taking fish from the lake, a right that was granted them years ago, they grew bitter and each year fewer returned.

"I've always loved Tahoe," said Mrs. Springmeyer, "especially the Bijou meadows where I grew up. When I was a little girl I walked there with my father behind a horse-drawn plow when he made the ditches. Every year, at spring time, I always felt there was something magic about the mountains . . . the way they looked there, across the meadow. That was my favorite spot."

Marjorie married Melvin 'Buzz' Springmeyer of Gardnerville, shortly after he returned from serving as a pilot in World War II.

The heirs of Chris and Celia, Knox and Stella Johnson, found a way to acknowledge their appreciation of the Washoe Indians and the pioneers of Lake Tahoe when they established a memorial to their parents and grandparents. They made a gift of ten acres of their land to the county and city of South Lake Tahoe.

On September 23, 1973, ceremonies were held dedicating a new county and city government complex on that land. It will serve the people of Lake Tahoe and the county for generations to come. The Johnson Memorial Monument, created by Richard Bigler, represents the Indian culture in its design. Present at the dedication were Marjorie Johnson Springmeyer, her husband, Melvin, and their sons, Jon and Frederick, and a grandson, Aaron, who represents the fifth generation of Johnsons. William Van Dyke Johnson, a Supervisor of El Dorado County, was present with his wife, Felica, and their sons, Rod, Kent, and Curtis.

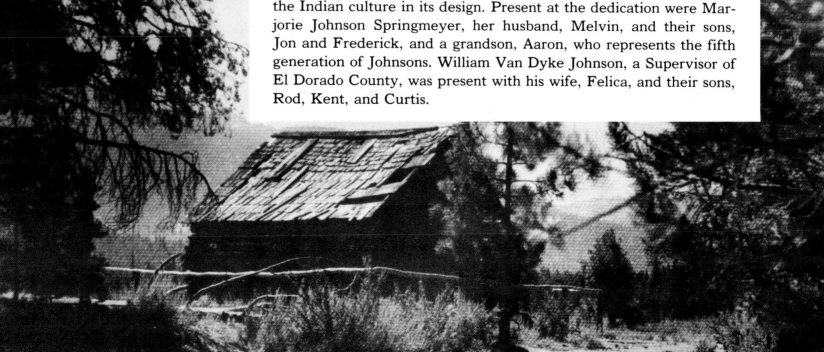

Lake Valley Settlers

When Carlo Guisseppi Celio moved his family to Lake Valley in 1863 there was only a handful of white settlers at the lake. Celio, a native of Switzerland, arrived in El Dorado County in 1853. He first tried his hand at mining on Clear Creek near Pleasant Valley before going into the dairy business with a partner, Marco Varozza, in Placerville. Mrs. Hazel Celio Taylor and her brother, Norman Celio, looked through boxes of old documents, land patents, family ledgers, and old photographs as they recalled stories of their pioneer ancestors. "Grandpa often said Tahoe reminded him more of Switzerland than any other place he'd seen," said Mrs. Taylor.

"About the only inhabitants at that time were the Washoe Indians. As many as five hundred would camp there in the summer. They migrated from Carson Valley and lived in their wigwams along the shores of the lake. As more people moved into the area, the Indian summer migrations grew fewer. By 1920 very few Indians returned. The older ones died off and the younger ones stayed in Carson to work on the highway maintenance crews."

In 1859, Carlo Celio married Maria Giambini Sartori, a widow. In 1869 he bought property on the Cosumnes River between Placerville and Plymouth, known as "King's Store." It was an 800-acre parcel for which he paid the owners, John W. Slaughter and J.E. Peede, $300 in gold coin. When the winter weather at the lake ranch proved too severe for year-round living, the family packed up and moved to the King's Store ranch.

This set a life-style pattern for the Celio family that continued through the years. All members of the family took part in the annual cattle drives. "Come fall, we'd spend days preparing for the trek over Echo Summit with our butter, cattle, and belongings. We always tried to be out of Lake Valley by the 21st of October, before the heavy snows . . . then we went through it all again to get back to the lake home by June. As I say," continued Mrs. Taylor, "to rush up there in the spring and come back in the fall was quite an ordeal in itself. We had to move everything. It was a big job just preparing to move . . . baking for several days so we would have food along the way. When we'd get there, the first thing we'd do was to unpack our 'ticks,' which were like mattresses only they were split down the center, and we'd run to the barn and fill them with timothy hay and make our beds so we'd have a place to sleep the first night. And we always found everything just as we had left it . . . no one ever bothered anything."

CELIO BLACKSMITH SHOP — Many specialty items were made at the Celio Blacksmith Shop at Meyers by blacksmith Joseph Pidgeon (right) and his helper, Rudolph.

THE OLD CELIO LAKE VALLEY HOME was built in the 1800's by former owner Mr. Wenstanley. It was torn down in 1914. Carlo G. Celio is seated on left. On the porch are, from left, Charles Celio, Henry Hager, and other Celio family members, Benjamin C., George, Frank, Henrietta, and Amelia, mother of Hazel and Norman Celio.

(Inset) CARLO G. CELIO at the age of 80. The picture was taken in 1914 at the Lake Valley home.

156

Photos Celio Family Collection

MEYERS STATION as it looked when purchased Celio & Sons in 1903. The Celio family operated hotel, dining room, blacksmith shop, cooperage, general merchandise store for thirty-five years. station was destroyed by fire in 1938.

CATTLE DRIVE headed for Lake Valley

"It was a five or six day drive from the King's Store ranch," said Norman. "We went through Diamond Springs, up over Sacramento Hill, down through the Main Street of Placerville, and out to Smith Flat, where we stayed overnight. Pacific House and Kyburz were our next stops. We'd sometimes try to make it home from Kyburz on the fifth day but didn't always succeed. When we didn't, we'd stop at Phillips, Alice Lyon's place, now called Pow Wow."

When the cattlemen decided, in 1916, that there were too many people and cars in Placerville, they bypassed the town on their drives, taking their herds by way of Stark Lake up to Pleasant Valley. "I remember stops at the Wentz Ranch and the Avansino Ranch at the junction of the road that led to Stark's Grade. By the 1940's very few cattle were driven. They were all trucked."

In the beginning the family business was raising beef and dairy cattle, operating the family dairy, and selling butter, milk, eggs, and cream commercially. At the height of their business the family holdings consisted of 1700 acres in Meyers, 800 acres in Lake Valley, and 400 acres in Big Meadows. It was in 1903 that the Celios bought Meyers Station, originally the historic old "Yank's Station" purchased by George H. D. Meyers in 1873. Prior to that time it was owned by the colorful Ephraim "Yank" Clement and his wife Lydia.

"Our family operated the hotel, dining room, and store at Meyers. They had a blacksmith shop and a cooperage where all the firkins for butter were made. They had their own sawmill and started the Celio Lumber Company. The sawmill was operated by steam power. Most of the lumber used to build summer homes at the lake came from the Celio mill at that time."

In one family ledger they found names of other pioneer families . . . families that purchased supplies from them . . . among them C. Pratt and Henry Schnieder, who bought two bull calves. Mr. Little and Mr. Shattel each bought a cord of wood. Dr. Tiffeney was a country doctor. "He was the only doctor around," said Mrs. Taylor. "He drove two good-looking horses to a surrey. He was from Plymouth, in Amador County."

Photo Yohalem Collection

C. G. CELIO & SONS

CHARLES GUISSEPPI CELIO, JR.
Son of Carlo G. Celio and Maria.

CARLO GUISSEPPI CELIO, *born in Switzerland, came to America in 1852. He stayed one year in New York before coming to California. Of importance to Mr. Celio was the fact that he had witnessed the inauguration of President Franklin Pierce in Washington, D.C. and that there were three inches of snow on the ground at the time.*

FRANK E. CELIO, *son of Carlo G. Celio and father of Florence, Norman, and Hazel Celio. He was born in Placerville in 1862.*

GEORGE CELIO - *Son of Carlo G. and Maria Celio. Born in 1868.*

HENRIETTA CELIO
Daughter of Carlo G. and Maria Celio. Born in 1874.

BENJAMIN CAESAR CELIO
Son of Carlo G. and Maria Celio. Born in 1871.

158

Photos Celio Family Collection

IN FRONT OF THE OLD CELIO HOME about 1908 are, from left, Hazel Celio, her mother Amelia, her father Frank, and brother Norman. Others are Carrie and Camilla Heald and Henrietta Celio.

FAMILY HEIRLOOM - When the children of Carlo and Maria Celio were christened, each wore this handmade dress for the occasion. It was first worn in 1855 and remains in the family today. Pictured is Florence Celio, a granddaughter, on the day of her christening.

Photo from Hazel Celio Taylor Collection

MR. AND MRS. CHARLES VAROZZA
Mrs. Varozza was the stepdaughter of Carlo Celio.

NORMAN, FLORENCE AND HAZEL CELIO, children of Frank and Amelia Celio.

Photos Celio Family Collection

Other bills were made out to J. C. Bailey and W. D. Barton, for whom Barton Memorial Hospital was named. "As I recall, the Bartons were dairying in the Hope Valley at that time (1903), and he evidently came down to buy butter kegs from the Celio cooperage shop," said Norman. "He charged $12.75 for kegs. Other charges on the bill were for 'DRS.' That would be drinks at the bar in the hotel.

"I found this interesting" said Norman. "When the dairy was operating at Sloughhouse ranch, it shows that on March 28 we produced 84 pounds of butter, 82 pounds on March 29, and 84 pounds on March 30. That indicates to me that there were around 80 head of cows on the production line. On April 10th, 111 pounds, showing more cows were on the line. And keep in mind that all milking was by hand. We had no machines in those days." Mrs. Taylor added, "In our grandfather's day butter sold for 8 to 10 cents a pound; in later years I can remember our parents having standing orders for butter from Sacramento to Carson City.

"All the children helped with the livestock, Grandfather's attempted mining ventures, and anything else that he engaged in. Then, in 1895, when they were all 18 to 25 years old, Grandfather formed a partnership with them. The firm name was C. G. Celio & Sons and included our father, Frank, his brothers Charles, George, and Benjamin, and his sister Henrietta." This corporation was set up for a period of 50 years. However, members of the corporation sold all of their properties in 1950, five years before the expiration date.

Norman Celio is sure he was witness to the first cars that ever came over Echo Summit on Meyers Grade. "I remember one morning, as a boy, I was out in the field and I heard some unusual noises . . . sounds I had never heard before. They were coming from up the mountain. Well, I started running to the bottom of the grade at Echo Creek, about a mile from home. I could see these things coming down the grade, pouring out huge amounts of blue smoke. I don't mind saying I was really frightened. As they got closer and closer I'd hide behind the trees and peek out at them. That was about 1906, and I'm pretty sure they were the first cars to make it over the summit from Placerville."

Both Hazel and Norman are retired, but they still spend their winters in Placerville and return to the lake home in the summer. "We had quail, bear, deer, and coyotes by the hundreds," said Norman. "The lake changed when they started coming through in automobiles . . . that's when it all changed."

Hazel Celio Taylor, widowed since the early 1940's, has one daughter named Shirley. Norman Celio has three grandchildren and five great-grandchildren. Thomas, the oldest, lives in Lotus, Norman Richard, Jr. in Placerville, and Christy (Mrs. George Arsenith) in Garden Valley. "Yes," said Norman, "the Celio name will remain in El Dorado County for many more years."

160

FULTON MEAT MARKET was located at the Bell Tower where the bakery is today.

THE MILK HOUSE - "It was built in the very early period when our grandfather settled here and began dairying, sometime in the early 1800's. Here all milk was processed and the butter produced. The early method of separating cream from the milk was by pouring the milk into specially made pans. These pans were put in racks and after 12 to 24 hours the cream would rise to the top. When we had enough cream, it was put into a butter churn to make the butter."

Photos Celio Family Collection

Photos Celio Family Collection

CELIO 10-MULE LOGGING TEAM - Henry Barton, mule skinner. The wagon wheels were solid wood.

CELIO NEW HOME in 1916. In back row, left to right, Carlo G. Celio, Henry Hager, Norman Celio, Hazel and Henrietta Celio, and an unidentified man. Seated on porch, left to right, E.E. "Deacon" Jones, Frank Celio, and, standing at pump, Kirby Catto.

NEWS ITEM - dated Oct. 28, 1965 - "Fifty years ago....Celio brothers brought their first shipment from their mountain dairy leaving 1/2 ton at Limpinsel's Store and sending the rest to the valley."

CELIO WAGONS on their way back to Lake Valley after delivering butter, milk, eggs, and other dairy products to Placerville merchants. The Celio family used horse-drawn wagons as late as 1925.

Alice Lyon of Phillips

There are more trees in the meadow now. The old road and the old way-station are gone. The face of the Sierra resort country has changed greatly over the years, people and places passing from the scene, but Mrs. Alice Elaine Lyon is still very much a part of the Phillips Station resort area.

She spends her summers at Pow Wow and returns to Placerville, where she was born, in the winter. Mrs. Lyon's "Memory Lane" winds back to the days of the beginnings of some of the old Sierra spas, and her family records extend and enhance those memories. When interviewed at her cabin home at Pow Wow in February of 1975 and again at a later date, she talked about her grandparents and her mother, Sierra Nevada Phillips Clark.

"Grandfather Joseph Wells Davis Phillips and Grandmother Mehitable Jane Ball Phillips left Vermont in December of 1851. They booked passage on the "Northern Light", sailed the Nicaragua Route and crossed the Isthmus of Panama on New Year's Day, 1852. Other records, along the way, show that they arrived in California two weeks later," said Mrs. Lyon.

Her grandfather mined in Nevada for a while but then turned his attention to cattle. He spent a summer running cattle on a 180 acre place at the upper end of Grass Lake on the Luther Pass in 1859, then looked for a less severe winter location. "Mother was only six years old when Grandfather brought his cattle over the Johnson Pass and into the meadows in 1859.

"In September of 1862 he purchased the property from E. A. Clark for $2,000. Considering today's market, it is interesting to note there were 160 acres in the parcel. Also interesting is the fact that the land was purchased 13 years before the government survey was made in 1875, a fact that preserved the water rights on the property in the family name for all time.

"In 1863, Grandfather built a two and a half story hotel and five barns on the place. The demand for supplies at the Comstock in Virginia City, Nevada, found a heavy flow of traffic passing the place every day- teamsters with freight, stagecoaches, wagons, people, animals. Mother said they even kept the road open in the winter. This boom made 'Phillips' a going concern."

SHOPPING AT THE TURN OF THE CENTU.
At the sound of a motor car coming through t.
woods, ladies hurried to the roadside to do the
shopping.

Alice Lyon Photos

PHILLIPS CRAG located on Highway 50 betw.
Strawberry and Little Norway, once formed
picturesque backdrop for the Phillips Hotel a.
barns built to accommodate the freighters, sta.
coaches, and travelers on their way to Virginia.
and the Comstock.

Photo El Dorado County Historical Museum

RUBICON MINERAL SPRINGS HOTEL - established in 1886 by Mrs."Vade" Clark. She operated the sixteen-room hotel for 15 years, marketing the mineral water which she said was "better than whiskey." "Wherever Mother set up business her guests would follow," said her daughter, Alice Lyon. "She earned the reputation of being the best cook in the Sierra."

PHILLIPS STATION - Cattlemen moving their stock to higher pastures passed through Phillips almost daily during the spring months.

Alice Lyon Photo Photo

An interesting sidelight of great interest to history buffs, in Mrs. Lyon's reminiscences, is her account of her grandfather's friendship with the historic mail carrier, Snowshoe Thompson, who, she said, "Stayed over nights on his return trips from Genoa and taught my grandfather to ski, using the long pole as a stabilizer and brake. He was one of our closest friends. There was a big pine that was struck by lightning and he used it to make skis. We called it the Snowshoe Thompson tree in his honor. I heard there was a big celebration honoring him in January . . . a Bicentennial reenactment of his historic mail run from Placerville to Genoa."

The "Great Bonanza Road" started losing its importance in the 1880's. When traffic to the mines dwindled, Phillips became a summer resort. There were fires at the resort, the first in 1873 when John J. Sweeney operated the resort under a lease agreement. Fire struck again in 1910. Then the heavy snows of 1951-52 brought about the collapse of the main buildings.

Mrs. Lyon's mother, Sierra Nevada Phillips, had married twice, first A. W. Clark and later James Bryson. Mrs. Lyon was a child of the second marriage. Her mother was known as "Vade" and was an enterprising woman, who established the Rubicon Mineral Springs Hotel and Resort. She marketed the mineral water there, said to be "better than whiskey." At other periods she also managed resorts at Tahoe City and Meeks Bay. She had a natural hospitality and was a good cook, thus assuring a loyal clientele, who followed her in her ventures.

Running a resort in those days was something of a problem. There was no electricity and the refrigeration was an ice house down on the river which, Mrs. Lyon said, "we hoped would hold through the summer." Fruits, vegetables, and meats had to be brought in. Fresh eggs and butter were sent around the Lake by rail and steamer from Minden, to be picked up at Camp Richardson, then called "the Grove." A herd of cattle was maintained, to provide milk. The road situation was often bad, and the maintenance crew consisted of "five men with picks and shovels." When Lampson's Market opened in 1927, it was thought they were "crazy to start up a fresh meat and vegetable stand way down there." (At present "Y".) But they flourished — and they delivered!

Mrs. Lyon was the wife of Henry Lyon, well remembered by many as the District Attorney of El Dorado County for, she thinks it was, six terms. We recall him as a bright and dynamic man. His family had Cole's Station. His mother was Jessie Cole. The Henry Lyons had three daughters, Betty Clark, Jane Brunello and Evelyn Lumley. Each daughter had a boy and a girl, and now Mrs. Lyon has four great-grandchildren.

SIERRA NEVADA PHILLIPS was six years old when her parents left Nevada County to settle in El Dorado County in 1862. She was an astute business woman and when application was made for a post office in Phillips, the postal authorities suggested her nickname "Vade" would do just fine. Thus the U.S. Post Office at Phillips came into being.

MEHITABLE JANE BALL married J.W.D. Phillips in 1851. She sailed with him on the "Northern Light" via the Nicaragua route to California.

JOSEPH WELLS DAVIS PHILLIPS, a native of Vermont, came to California in 1852. He was a cattleman and founder of the historical old way-station on the road between Hangtown and Virginia City during the Comstock silver strike.

WASHOE INDIAN — IDA

Alice Lyon Photos

A FAMILY PICNIC IN THE WOODS was held around 1901.
The members are not identified.

WASHOE INDIAN SUSIE — Her skilled weaving and outgoing personality were described in several books.

"Mother always tried to have a post office wherever she went," Mrs. Lyon recalled. It had to be open on May 1st and Mrs. Lyon said, "I can remember more than once walking through deep snow from Twin Bridges to do it, whether the mail arrived or not." Her mother wanted a post office at Phillips and went to Placerville to talk to the postmaster there, whom she knew. The name "Phillips" was already taken, so she was told to just call it "Vade," her nickname. This she did and the Vade post office remained a well known name in the region.

Guests at the old resort included many notable figures, among them former Secretary of State Frank Jordan and former Secretary Robert McNamara, at the age of 12. Phillips was known from coast to coast. It was a family place, where many returned year after year.

There were Indians in the area, of the Washoe tribe, "a lot of them," Mrs. Lyon recalled. "They just couldn't stand being closed up all the time." One named Ida went home with a Stockton family, developed diabetes and died, living only a short time after her move. It was Ida who had solicitously "cumb'd" Mrs. Lyon's very fine hair and who made a papoose dress, complete with doll, for her one Christmas. "My mother would've trusted Ida before anyone else," Mrs. Lyon says.

Then there was Susie, who washed for Mrs. Lyon's grandmother, and who, she recalled, "loved to tell tales." Susie delighted the guests with her stories. One of her favorite expressions was "I so scare," always leaving the "d" off. She was "so scare" when the white men came in covered wagons. The Indians would go back of the rocks and hide.

And so it was in the old days at Phillips Resort, days of hardship but of fun and fond remembrances.

Memories of Caldor

Lillian Stanley Drew and her husband, William, live in the house where Mrs. Drew was born, in the shadow of the historic Odd Fellows Hall, Lodge No. 9 on North Street and Odd Fellows Hill in Diamond Springs. Mrs. Drew said her grandmother, Mrs. Thomas "Helen" Donoho, came to California from Iowa, via South America in 1852. She was a widow with five children, four boys named Don, Tom, Charles, and James, and a daughter named Ema Adalaide. In 1855 Mrs. Donoho married William Rust, who owned a saloon on Logtown road. "Logtown," said Mrs. Drew, "was one of many active mining camps at the time and apparently Mr. Rust prospered."

She told of her grandfather Rust's sudden, accidental death and prefaced it by saying that her grandfather had always put his gold in cans and buried them, presumably on his property. "One day, sitting in a chair on the porch of his home, he leaned back and fell off the porch. He died before he could tell anyone where he had buried his gold. Numerous attempts to find it failed. They even went to a fortune teller but never found it. There was talk at one time that someone had found it. They were inclined to believe that to be true, but nothing could be proved. They say all the property around the Rust place was sold off in a hurry, and a lot of digging went on for a long time."

This brought to mind another 'gold story' and Mr. Drew continued, "I don't know how true it is, but Jack Hawkins had a piece of property there in Placerville . . . they said it was owned by old John Raffetto at one time . . . but George O'Leary, brother of Sarah Celio, she married Charles Celio . . . O'Leary asked a neighbor to help him blow a tree out, that was on his place. It was an old apple tree. Anyway, this guy came up and put the dynamite in there and blew the durn tree up and gold coins went flying all over everywhere. I don't know how much there was, there's different stories on that . . . but O'Leary sent that guy home right away. At least that's the story told by old timers."

Mrs. Drew said that her father attended school in Diamond Springs when the school house was located where the I.O.O.F. Cemetery is today. She said that for many years, when the school was crowded, they taught school in the I.O.O.F. Hall. It was always one room, all grades, and one teacher. Teachers' names she recalled were Edith Landis and Mr. Moore. "Father was born in 1863. In 1885 he was in partnership with the Smith brothers, operating a general store in El Dorado." Checking an impressive-looking old store record book, she found he had another partner, Mrs. Kinsley, between 1887 and 1889.

AMONG HER MEMENTOS Lillian Drew has a four-inch-thick ledger filled with invoices from the store her father owned and operated in the town of El Dorado from 1885 through 1889. A number of the firms he did business with are still in business, such as Baker & Hamilton Hardware, Betz Bros. & Co., both San Francisco firms. The Lievre, Fricke & Co. invoice shows coffee at 23¢ per lb and one half gross playing cards at $4.00. On June 26, 1888, Stanley's store was billed for sugar at $21.00 a barrel.

THE LARKIN MINE - Before Joseph Stanley worked for Caldor Lumber company he engaged in mining. His daughter, Mrs. Drew, could identify only two men in this group picture. They are a Mr. Dunton, standing by his horse, and her father, Joseph Stanley, seated in front row, fourth from the left.

DIAMOND SPRINGS SCHOOL - Miss Daisy Davenport taught her first class at the Diamond school. The pupils present who could be identified are: 1. Roy Scheiber, 2. Edith Landis, 3. Ivy Jones, 4. Mildred Jones, 5. Tony Pilatti, 6. Fred Stanley, 7. Harry Jones, 8. Angus Bathurst, 9. Elsie Webster, 10. Pearl Scheiber, 11. Amy Harris, 12. Joseph Stanley, 13. Clarence Scheiber, 14. Cedrik Webster. The school house still stands at the corner of Main street and Odd Fellows road in downtown Diamond Springs, and is now a barber shop.

(Inset) ODD FELLOWS HALL

San Francisco, MAR 9 1889

M Stanley & Knisley
E Do

Bought of Wellman, Peck C

Tea Importers
Jobbers of Cigars, Tobaccos, Staple & Fancy Gro

126 to 140 Market Street.
CORNER OF DAVIS.

1	Bbl D Gran Sugar	317	6⅝	
5	lbs Lemon Peel	17		85
1	C Codfish	100	6	6
5 ⅞ lb	S Garden Citys @60°	3 00		
	Less 5%		15	2 85
			9 70

TERMS 10S DAYS. INTEREST AFTER MATURITY.
OR OFF FOR PROMPT CASH.
ORDER NO
AGENT MR Scott

San Francisco, Mar. 16 18

M Stanley & Knisley
Eldora

BOUGHT OF

LIÈVRE, FRICKE & CO.
SUCCESSORS TO CHAS. BERNARD.
IMPORTERS OF

Coffees, Teas & Spices.

707, 709, 711 SANSOME

MOUNTAINEER STEAM COFFEE AND SPICE MILLS

ESTABLISHED 1854

P.O.BOX 2255.
TELEPHONE NO. 873.
NO CLAIMS ALLOWED 3 DAYS
AFTER RECEIPT OF GOODS.

100	lbs roast Nat Coffee	100	23	23	
2	⅌ 12/5 C. T. S.	24	95	22	80
2	Doz small Cologne		1 25	2	50
1	" 1 oz Laudanum			1	50
10	lbs Epsom Salt		07		70
1	⅌ assd tins Dess. Cocoanut	24	28	6	72
6	⅌ No 2 white Macaroni		60	3	60
4	⅌ No 2 yel		60	2	40
	Reams Straw Paper		85	4	25
			18		

John Winning Photo

Photos from Lillian Drew Collection

A TYPICAL SCENE at a Caldor logging camp. A donkey engine and loading equipment was set up in a heavily timbered area. After the choice timber was felled, loaded and transported to the mill, the operation was moved to another area.

Photos from Lillian Drew Collection

A SHAY LOCOMOTIVE - ENGINE NO. 6 heads for the Caldor mill

ANOTHER CALDOR CAMP - Joseph Stanley, Mrs. Drew's father (third man from right). Also identified: Carl Meyer (third from left), and Ray Eldred (left of post).

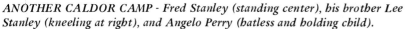

ANOTHER CALDOR CAMP - Fred Stanley (standing center), his brother Lee Stanley (kneeling at right), and Angelo Perry (hatless and holding child).

THE COMPANY STORE at the Grizzly Flat Caldor mill site. Seated The three young men seated to left are Tom Hassler, Gordon Duff ar his arm on his knee, was in charge of the mill's dry kiln. Behind Star

...d of logs from Meyers Flat on the road to PiPi Valley, Lyle Green and Fred Stanley in the cab and Joseph Stanley standing on the first flat of logs.

...eps (from right) are Jim Guest, Jim Abart, an unidentified man. ...ther Carlos (wearing cap). Joseph Stanley, in white shirt resting ...ton Hassler, mill superintendent. Charles Duff was the mill foreman.

THE CALDOR GERMAN BAND - The identification of the musicians was not given. The year was about 1902. Photo El Dorado County Historical Museum

TONY PILATTI waits at a Caldor loading deck.

Photos from Lillian Drew Collection

A TYPICAL El Dorado County mining town. All effort to identify the ravine and camp failed in our research effort. If a reader can identify the location, please communicate with the County Chamber of Commerce.

Photo James Gray Family Collection

John Winning Photos

Covered Wagon Honeymoon

JULIA ANNE PORTER GRAY
Wife of Young Gray, who crossed
the plains in 1854.
Photo James Gray Family Collection

GRAY'S FLAT - The first home built on the Gray homestead off Green Valley road, about 1890. Photo Elbert Gray Family Collection

THE MICKY FREE BIBLE that was given to Polly Gray at the Lone Tree House in 1884, and a flintlock pistol owned by Young Gray of Kentucky are among the artifacts belonging to James Gray, Young Gray's grandson.

MORE THAN 121 YEARS OLD - Heirlooms possessed by James Gray are the boots worn by his grandfather Young Gray and the rocking chair "Aunt Polly" remodeled so she could sit comfortably during their trip across the plains in 1854.

On April 16, 1854, a train of twelve wagons with thirty-six people left Montgomery County, Illinois, for California. Elected to lead the train was a young man named Young Gray of Kentucky. With him was his bride, Julia Anne Porter Gray, of Tennessee, aged eighteen. They had been married on March 2, 1854, and this was to be her wedding trip. When the train left Illinois, Young Gray's younger sister, Polly, later affectionately called "Aunt Polly," was in the driver's seat of one of the wagons. To make her as comfortable as possible, they cut the rockers off a chair, fitting it snugly against the dashboard of a wagon, and it was there she sat while driving across the plains. They crossed the Mississippi River at St. Joseph, Missouri, traveled by way of the Platte River and Fort Laramie to the Bear River and into Utah, where "mosquitoes were very bad . . . had to build smudges to protect the stock." They went through Nevada and into California over the Fremont Trail by way of the Carson River, through Hope Valley, Silver Lake, and Tragedy Springs. They arrived in Mud Springs (now the town of El Dorado) on September 9, 1854.

Three grandsons of Young and Julia Gray, Euell Gray, Jr., James Wesley Gray, and Elbert Gray, all of Placerville, combined their collections of old documents, newspaper articles, Bibles, artifacts, and pictures to aid them in telling stories that preceded and followed the establishing of "Gray's Flat," an historic landmark in El Dorado County.

Soon after Young Gray arrived in California, he bought the Lone Tree House, a tavern and inn built by a man named Ginley in 1852. Located on the then heavily traveled wagon road from Sacramento to Placerville, it appeared to be a sound investment. However, a short time after Gray took possession, the road was re-aligned, bypassing the Lone Tree House. Gray continued to operate the Lone Tree until 1859.

Micky Free, a notorious desperado, who is said to have boasted he would commit more bloody deeds than Joaquin Murietta, was a boarder at the Lone Tree House when Gray purchased the place. However, his identity as the leader of a group responsible for robbing and killing miners in the area was not known at that time. A story, told often by Julia Gray and later by her daughter-in-law, Nora Gray, was as follows:

"Standing on the porch of the Lone Tree House one day, Micky Free gave "Aunt Polly" his Bible. He said his mother had given it to him when he left Ireland and that if he had read it, he might be a better man." This happened just before he went on a rampage, robbing and killing a Chinese man in Coloma. When one of the gang turned State's evidence, he exposed Free, who was captured, tried, and hanged in Coloma on October 26, 1855. When he was on the scaffold, he reportedly made the remark that he had killed the Chinese with Young Gray's gun and shot his dog and wished it had been the owner instead (both Gray's gun and dog were missing from the Lone Tree House on the day of the killing). Mr. Gray is said to have resented the attention Free had been paying his young sister, Polly. Murderer William Crane was hanged on the same day with Free.

The Lone Tree was not Gray's only interest. He acquired land and devoted his energies to farming. As miner after miner moved onto his land and filed mining claims, he realized he was losing much of his land. At that time there was no law prohibiting the filing of a mining claim over an agricultural claim, so Gray applied for and received his land patent in 1890. Much of the homestead land still remains in the family and is known as Gray's Flat. It is located between Ponderosa Road and Cameron Park Drive, just off Green Valley Road in the Rescue area.

On November 27, 1912, Euell Gray, the youngest of the Grays' eleven children, married Nora Harbin, daughter of Madison Pope Harbin and granddaughter of James M. Harbin, a territorial pioneer who crossed the Sierra in 1844.

Madison P. Harbin owned and operated the Diamond West Hotel in Diamond Springs from 1904 through 1907. He also owned the Old National Hotel in El Dorado and later owned another hotel at Bill Potter's in Shingle Springs. After their marriage, Euell and Nora Gray made their home in Placerville and raised a family of five children. They had one girl, Imogene, and four sons, Elbert, Harry (an adopted son), Euell, Jr., and James Wesley.

The sons of Euell and Nora Gray told stories about their father's youth. "In 1892, when he was only twelve years old, he had his own business. He was a butcher. When he got home from school on Friday, he would slaughter the animal he was going to butcher. Then he'd get up at three o'clock Saturday morning, butcher his animal, and package his orders. He had a regular route. He kept a notebook with the names of all his customers. We still have it," said Elbert. "One weekend he'd deliver in Coloma and Lotus and the next in the Latrobe area. Some of his customers lived in the Japanese colony at Gold Hill. He didn't list their names. We guess he didn't know them. He just put down "The Japs" and entered the amount they bought and the price.

EUELL AND NORA HARBIN GRAY
Their wedding picture, 1912.

Photo Elbert Gray Family Collection

IDA JESSIE STONE - wife of Madison Pope Harbin was born in Colorado while her family was on its way to California.

Photo James Gray Family Collection

GOLDEN WEST HOTEL.

Photo from Euell Gray, Jr. Family Collection

THE GOLDEN WEST HOTEL was built in 1856 on the site of the Crescent City Hotel that burned that same year. The stone walls of the building, with the date it was erected was carved over the main door and remained as one of Diamond Springs finest hostelries until it was destroyed by fire in 1937. Madison P. Harbin owned and operated the hotel from 1904 through 1907. He also had the old National Hotel in the town of El Dorado and the hotel at the Potter House in Shingle Springs.

GOLDEN WEST HOTEL-Mr. and Mrs. Madison P. Harbin (center), have their picture taken with friends (from left) Alex Dodds, Bill James and an unidentified young man. Gentlemen standing between two unidentified ladies is Bill Springer. The people in this picture are the same as in the larger photograph.

Photos James Gray Family Collection

EVIDENCE - El Dorado County Game Warden Euell Gray displays the evidence for charges made against the Hotel Placerville in 1915 when fish were killed by lime that was flushed into the creek by the hotel. Pictured with the Warden are, from left: Louis Reeg, Fiori Raffetto, Ralph McNaughton, Judge Clark Howard, Mr. Compton, Art Koletzke, and Euell Gray.

The King of the Mountains.

The above headlines and autobiography in the San Francisco Examiner of Sunday, June 27, 1897, provide the Gray family with still another story about one of their ancestors, James Madison Harbin, who was Mrs. Nora Gray's grandfather.

He wrote, "Profoundly disgusted with dealing with men, I determined to turn to nature . . . Off into the wilderness, eighty miles up among the mountains, I traveled three days of hard riding from the nearest settlement. When I could look the earth in the face and not see man's image there, I halted on the bank of a pleasant creek and made my home. I had a rifle, a shotgun, plenty of ammunition, some blankets and a bit of steel. . . . I had no candles, no kerosene, nor wanted any; pitchpine torches served me well. Along the streams and in the glades I found vegetables to my liking. . . . When I was lonely I turned to the stars and flowers and the water for comfort.   There's a heap of company in a star if you know how to get on speaking terms with it, and brooks tell stories, and the flowers are full of history, and birds are honest friends."

James M. Harbin, of English and Scotch descent, was born in Warren county, Tennessee, in 1823. On May 4, 1844, he started for California with a train of eleven wagons. Although he does not mention the name of the party with which he traveled, research established he was with the celebrated Stephen-Townsend-Murphy party. He tells of reaching the head of the Humboldt River where they "held-up." While searching for a pass through the mountains, they discovered what is now called Lake Tahoe, and the Truckee River. While searching, his supplies gave out. "I buckled my stomach to smaller compass and moved along." When they reached Summit Valley in September they found eighteen inches of snow on the ground and their supply of bacon was gone. "We killed an ox and had him roast, boiled and fried.

". . . At what is now Donner Lake we built a cabin and stored provisions. We weren't sure we could make our way down the mountain, so we planned to have a retreat open in case of need. Joe Foster and Dennis Martin were left in the cabin. They remained there until February and then went on ox-hide snowshoes down the Sierra. They succeeded in getting to Sutter's Fort.

". . . In the cabin we built as a retreat some members of the Donner Party afterwards perished. After leaving the two men at the lake the rest journeyed forward until we got to Yuba. There the snow became so deep, we left the wagons. Three families also remained. Aunt Mary Murphy was among the number in this camp. All the others resumed the march and we reached Sutter's Fort.

General Sutter provided them with mules and they went back to rescue those left at Yuba. "All of the party gathered at Sutter's before December, except the two men left at the lake. *Ours was the first emigrant train that ever got their wagons across the Sierra.*"

When Harbin arrived in California, he was about twenty-one years old, unmarried, and in a land still under Mexican rule. He tells of going on an exploring expedition down the coast to Los Angeles and San Diego. There he discovered three copper mines and hurried north to arrange for capital to work the mines, only to find the Bear Flag War in progress. Then came the war with Mexico. He joined the American forces and served under Commodore Stockton. He was wounded and taken prisoner. While he was in prison, his mother, father, and family arrived in California and settled in Napa County. When the war ended, he was released and received his honorable discharge from General Fremont at the Bell Building in Los Angeles, in April of 1847.

James Madison Harbin, Who, During His Twenty Years of Hermit Life in Mexico, Was Known Among the Natives as "King of the Mountains."

After his discharge, he returned north with 4,650 head of fine cattle and 700 horses. He bought the Thomas Hardy Mexican Land Grant. "It touched the Sacramento River and measured 17 miles in length. The site of Woodland is within the limits of the grant. I had more than that, but title to the rest of my ranch was derived directly from the United States."

From 1847 until 1858 he raised cattle. "I cleaned up $100,000 to $150,000 each year. Frequently a fat ox brought me $800. In 1858 my wealth aggregated $3 million. . . . About this time the tide turned and I began to be buffeted by fortune." He lost the ranch and holdings to friends named Jim Haggin and Lloyd Terris.

He mined in Virginia City and Gold Hill and soon made another fortune. He tried his hand at oil and lumber, too. He returned to Mexico to the mines he had located earlier in Durango, Vaca, St. Marcus, Socorra, and Cabrillo. Not having enough money "to get out the pay dirt," he called on Fred Warner, a Sacramento butcher with whom he had had cattle dealings. He told him about the mines and turned them over to him for four shares of stock. Soon the mines were paying $30,000 a month. In the meantime, he was away on another exploring trip. He returned to find that his trunk had been broken into and his four shares were gone. His friend Warner was willing to have his shares reissued but was over-ruled by the others. He made and lost several fortunes. His losses were brought about mostly by trusting and helping others. When he came down from the mountain it was George Hearst to whom he had loaned money to start a newspaper in 1865, who encouraged him to write his story for the paper, then being managed by his son, William Randolph Hearst.

ECHO LAKE - Euell Gray owned three-quarters of the lower lake property. It served as summer pasture for his large herds of cattle. Sixty horses were stabled there for riders and campers going into Desolation Valley. His small sons acted as guides, his wife, Nora Gray was appointed postmaster at the Lake's first post office. Mr. Gray sold the property to the government in 1934.

PHILO AND EUELL Y. GRAY
Members of the El Dorado Home Guard, 1902

"When he was young, he was the fastest runner in the county. He raced on the Krell Ranch, where they had a good race track. That's Cameron Park now. Some of the betting people used to bring in outside runners to try to beat Dad, but they never did. He never lost a race in his life."

Euell Gray served forty years in El Dorado County as a deputy sheriff. He was with Sheriffs Charlie Hand, Charlie Woods, George Smith and others. At the same time he was running 300 to 350 head of cattle. He wintered them at the homestead, Gray's Flat, and moved them to Echo Lake in the summer. In later years Gray bought property at Echo Lake, where he put in a store, a small hotel, and a boat concession. He kept about sixty head of horses, used for riding and packing parties into Desolation Valley.

James remembered how his mother started a post office at Echo Lake. "She was sworn in in 1926. Dad sold the lake property to the government in 1934 and we moved out in 1936. We all settled here except our sister Imogene. She married and lives in Concord, but the rest of us continued to enjoy living in El Dorado County. You know the old saying, 'what was good enough for Grandpa is good enough for me.' "

Today, Elbert Gray and his wife, Evelyn, who attended kindergarten together, live on the family homestead at Gray's Flat. Euell Gray, Jr., has retired and lives in Diamond Springs with his wife, Lorraine. Fifth-generation descendants of the Gray-Harbin pioneers are Nora Ann, Jamie, and Cathy Gray, children of James Wesley Gray and his wife, Mary Lou, who live on Coon Hollow Road, Placerville.

THE NIGHTINGALE FARM *consisted of a fine vineyard of muscat grapes, a large watermelon patch, every variety of vegetable, and many apple and peach trees. It was located four miles below Latrobe on the Sacramento and El Dorado county lines. Standing in the vineyard are James and Jane Nightingale, two of their sons, Thomas and Willard, and the wife of one of the sons. The picture was taken in 1896.*

STONEBRAKER HOUSE - *The Bryant family mountain home was built of lumber from the Bryant sawmill. The fireplace was constructed of rocks set on top of each other: no mortar was used to hold them. After 100 years, it is still standing. The Stonebraker house is located on the old Iron Mountain road (now Mormon Emigrant Trail) in the Sly Park area. "Stump Springs," an historical marker site, is also on the Bryant property.*

Related to Florence Nightingale

JAMES NIGHTINGALE was a native of Manchester, England, and a second cousin of Florence Nightingale, the "Angel of Mercy," who pioneered nursing in Britain and brought about hospital reform in that country.

JANE HEAPS NIGHTINGALE came to America with a group of young English girls interested in the Mormon migration. When they reached New Orleans and learned of the Mormon polygamy, Jane withdrew from the group.

Photos Foley and Pettey Collections

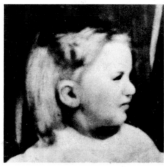

A tamarack tree, brought to California by Alice Nightingale in 1853, is still growing on the old Nightingale farm near Latrobe in El Dorado County. When the Nightingales arrived in California they went to the mines at Michigan Bar, bordering the Sacramento and El Dorado county lines. The family consisted of James Nightingale, his wife, Jane, and their children, Alice, eight years of age, Mary, five, Margaret, three, and an infant son named Will Lott. Loretta Nightingale Pettey and Doris Nightingale Foley, granddaughters of James and Jane, described the adventurous spirit of their ancestors, a spirit that brought them from England to the United States and then from Iowa, across the plains in an ox-drawn prairie schooner, to California.

James Nightingale was born in Bolton, Lancashire county, England in 1823. His grandfather, John Nightingale, and John's brother Pete, later knighted and called Sir Peter, were weavers in Manchester, England. John's son became the father of James, and Peter's daughter became the mother of Florence Nightingale, who pioneered nursing and brought about reforms in the hospitals of England. James was a second cousin to the "Angel of Mercy."

When he was a young boy, the family moved to Liverpool and lived at Standish Hall, the home of Miles Standish. It was part of the Nightingale estate, and the family claimed him as one of their ancestors. James had a great love for the sea. At the age of twelve he hid aboard a vessel in Liverpool. The captain, a friend of the family, notified his parents and somehow managed to keep him on board for the voyage. After that he followed the sea, joined the merchant marine and sailed around the world, often touching port in New York and New Orleans. His curiosity regarding the upper Mississippi overcame him and he shipped on a river steamer as first mate, delivering cotton to New Orleans. It was there he met Jane Heaps, his future wife.

Jane Heaps was born in Chorley, Lancashire county, England in 1824. After the death of her mother, her father arranged to have his business partner take over the guardianship of his children, Jane and Thomas. Unfortunately, after the father's death the partner confiscated all the money and property. He allowed Thomas to be adopted and placed Jane in an orphanage.

(Inset) LORETTA AMY NIGHTINGALE at age three

FLORENCE NIGHTINGALE BUNDOCK
daughter of Jane and James Nightingale

HERMAN L. BRYANT built and operated the Bryant sawmill near Sly Park in the early 1800's.

DORIS NIGHTINGALE
at age 8 years.

BRINGING LOGS to the Bryant sawmill on Stonebraker Grade in the Pleasant Valley-Sly Park area in 1897. The mill was owned and operated by Herman Leroy Bryant.

WILLARD NIGHTINGALE was born in Latrobe. He was the father of Doris Nightingale Foley.

MARGARET AND MAUDE McGUIRE, daughters of Alice Nightingale McGuire and cousins of Mrs. Loretta Nightingale Pettey of Camino.

ALICE NIGHTINGALE crossed the plains to reach California. She was an aunt to Mrs. Loretta Nightingale Pettey, resident of Camino, California.

MR. AND MRS. THOMAS NIGHTINGALE - The Reverend C.C. Pierce performed their marriage ceremony in Latrobe on June 22, 1898.

Photos Foley and Pettey Collections

As a young girl Jane worked in a factory. When a group of her young girl friends became interested in the Mormon movement to the United States, she joined them. When they arrived in New Orleans they learned of the Mormon polygamy and some withdrew, Jane among them. She found work in New Orleans and there met James Nightingale. They married in Nauvoo, Illinois in 1845 and lived on a farm in Lee County, Iowa, where their first three children were born.

Two burning desires to head west resulted in James' sending for members of his family to come from England to look after their Iowa farm while he and Jane went west. His first desire was to find the man or men responsible for the death of his brother, who had gone to Utah with a Mormon train. He was convinced that his brother had been murdered by a member of that group.

When they arrived in Utah they settled in Cottonwood, where they remained for almost one year. It was there that their fourth child, Will Lott, was born. However, said Mrs. Foley, "James had a John Bull temper, and in his attempt to find his brother's murderer he made many enemies. So many, in fact, that a friend, John Lott, advised him to take his family and get out before something serious happened. There were numerous massacres near Salt Lake and strong evidence that he was in danger, so with the help of friends they slipped away in the night and took the Donner Party route to California. There James hoped to fulfill his second desire . . . to find gold and acquire land."

In California he tried mining at Michigan Bar for a time, but he was convinced that a more substantial living could be made in farming. "He homesteaded land just above Michigan Bar," said Mrs. Foley. "He built all the buildings himself — the house, barn, blacksmith shop, and other outbuildings. He even built a picket fence around the house before he moved his family from Michigan Bar to the Latrobe homestead. I remember the door steps into the house were large flat stones. The ravine below was called Monkey Ravine because the slate rocks sticking above the ground resembled monkeys."

There were many Maidu Indians living in the area and Mrs. Pettey recalled one time when a plague of grasshoppers swarmed over the place, "even eating holes in the curtains in the house," she said. "The Indians dug tunnel-shaped holes in the ground all around the buildings and drove the grasshoppers in the holes with brush fans, chanting all the time. Then they sacked them and carried them up on a hill, where they built a fire and heated rocks.

"They baked the grasshoppers by laying a bed of hot rocks which they covered with leaves . . . then they put grasshoppers on top of the leaves, then another layer of leaves, rocks, and grasshoppers. They continued these layers of leaves, rocks, and grasshoppers until they were out of grasshoppers. When they were baked they'd store them away for the winter. They say they taste like shrimp, but I wouldn't know. I never ate any."

ON SKIS - *Laura and Stella Fowler with Willard Nightingale*

(Below) *THE HERMAN BRYANT HOME in Latrobe in the early 1900's. Home when the photographer called were, from left: Alida, daughter of Mrs. Bryant, center, daughter Grace, and an unidentified child.*

BRYANT'S SAWMILL, July 13, 1896 - (1) Rex Hallawell, (2) Helen Hallawell, (3) Eva Hallawell, (4) Myra Nightingale, (5) Bud Wayman, (6) Will Nightingale, (7) Ben Lynn, (8) Emerson Fowler, (9) Herman Bryant, (10) E.A. Fowler

MAKING ADOBE BRICK at Stonebraker. Herman Bryant, seated right, takes time out while Cullen Bryant (center) and Tom Nightingale (to his right) carry on with their work of making adobe bricks on the Bryant place at Stonebraker, located off Mormon Emigrant Trail east of Jenkinson Lake, Sly Park. On the right is Grace Bryant.

Mrs. Pettey delighted in telling, "My father, Thomas Nightingale, used to laugh when he told us about Mother's father, Grandpa Bryant. Dad said he had to go four miles through the fields to call on Mama (Frances Bryant). He had to visit her in the evening because he worked on the farm all day.

"When he got there, her father made sure some member of the family stayed in the parlor all the time he was there. Then, at nine o'clock sharp, Grandpa would appear in the doorway and say, 'It's time to go home now.' Dad said he had a terrible time trying to court Mother. He did succeed, though, and they were married by the Reverend C.C. Pierce in Latrobe in 1898."

About her maternal grandfather, Mrs. Pettey said, "Herman Leroy Bryant first came to California in 1864. After four years he returned to his home town, Great Valley, New York, where he married Charlotte L. Spencer. In 1870 she and his mother and a sister sailed around Cape Horn to San Francisco, and later came by stage to El Dorado County. Herman returned by wagon train, bringing all the household furnishings from New York."

The name Bryant became well known in El Dorado County as members of the family acquired homestead lands, raised cattle, and grew vegetables and fruit that they sold to neighbors and friends. They operated the Bryant Sawmill located off what is known as the Emigrant Trail. "It used to be the Iron Mountain road," said Mrs. Pettey.

"I remember my father, Thomas Nightingale, used to bring his cattle from our Latrobe farm to pasture every summer at the Stonebreaker place, beyond Sly Park. We called it 'Bryant's Retreat.' The old house still stands . . . it's over 100 years old. Another interesting thing . . . old Stump Springs was on the homestead. Most everyone has heard of Stump Springs. It was designated an historic landmark."

Mrs. Foley, daughter of Willard and Laura Nightingale, was only two weeks old when her parents moved to Camino. She was the first baby in the community. When the earthquake struck San Francisco in 1906, she said, they could see the flames from Camino. Her father carried her on his shoulders up to Danaher Mountain, where they watched the fires burning in San Francisco.

She remembered another fire, this one in Camino. "During a severe electrical storm, lightning struck George Rieber's barn. Mr. Rieber went into the barn to get his horses out. He managed to get them out, but they ran back into the burning barn and he lost them all. It was later learned that Mr. Rieber had buried his money in the barn and when he couldn't find it the next day, he killed himself.

"My folks moved away in 1909," she continued, "and when we returned in 1913 my father became the master mechanic of the Danaher Lumber Company. His uncle, Doctor Fryman, came to

CENTRAL PACIFIC RAILROAD, Nov.3, 1883 Willard Nightingale, age near 22 years, is the man with black bowler hat in center.

A GRANDCHILD gets a ride on an ox at the Bryant sawmill at Stonebraker.

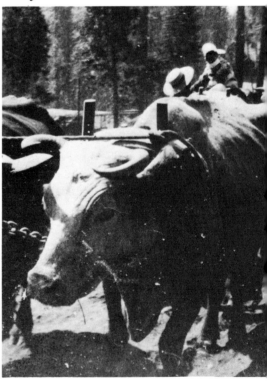

THE LATROBE SCHOOL in 1888 was attended by fifteen girls and thirteen boys. Among them were the children of the pioneer Bryant and Nightingale families.

CHILDREN of Herman and Charlotte Bryant who attended the Latrobe school are, clockwise: Alida, Cullen, Frances, Clarence, and Stanley Bryant, all born in El Dorado County.

Camino from Oakland and became the doctor for the Danaher Company. Father built a hospital and drug store for him in Camino. It was on a small scale, of course . . . a two-story building. When Dr. Fryman started practicing, a doctor in Placerville, Dr. Rantz, objected and there was a real feud between the doctors. Finally Dr. Fryman had to leave.

"When Dr. Fryman left, Father moved the family into the hospital and drugstore building. Later, Father was killed in a mill accident. After his death, Mother turned the hospital rooms into rental rooms and made a living that way.

"I remember the first time I saw my grandfather Nightingale. My parents took me to the farm at Christmas when I was about four years old. The whole family was there. They sat at a long table. Grandpa, being English and an old seaman, liked his hot whiskey toddies. He kept drinking them until he fell asleep at the table. His boys just picked him up and carried him to bed.

"They took me to a room to see my grandmother Jane, too. She was in bed and had been for five and a half years."

Discussing Grandma's five years in bed, family members later surmised that she had, one day, decided she had had enough and gone to bed and stayed there. She had experienced the trip across the plains with her infant son and three small daughters, known the fear of danger in Salt Lake, worked hard on the farm, and borne seven more children — a total of eleven. Since there was really nothing physically ailing her, they believed that she had decided that the only way to convince her family that she was tired was to go to bed . . . and that's what she did. She stayed in bed until she died in October of 1916 at the age of 92.

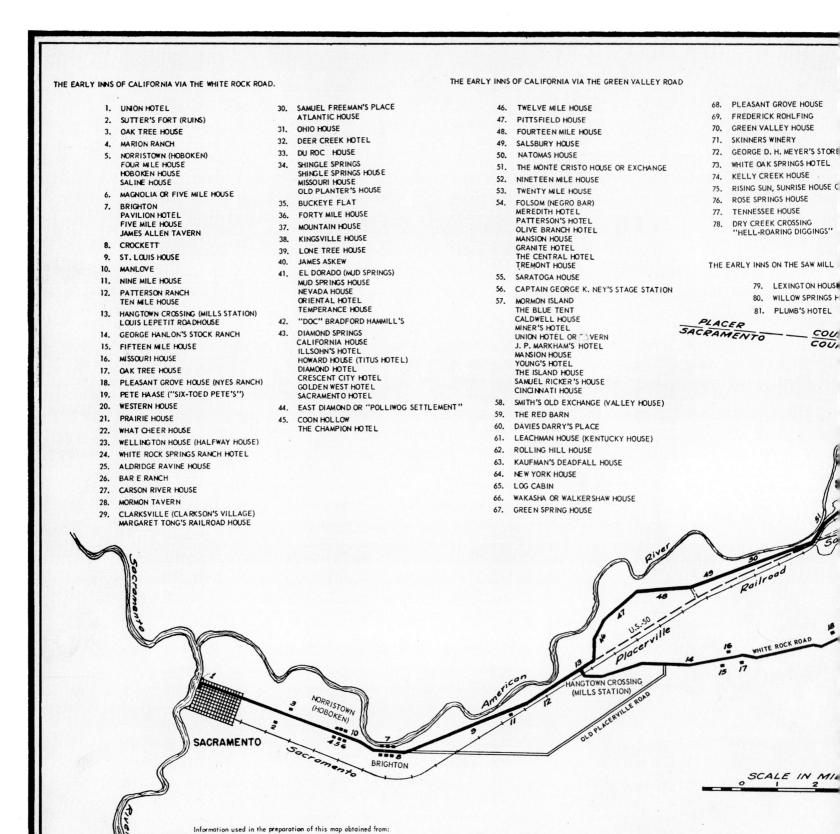

THE EARLY INNS OF CALIFORNIA VIA THE WHITE ROCK ROAD.

1. UNION HOTEL
2. SUTTER'S FORT (RUINS)
3. OAK TREE HOUSE
4. MARION RANCH
5. NORRISTOWN (HOBOKEN)
   FOUR MILE HOUSE
   HOBOKEN HOUSE
   SALINE HOUSE
6. MAGNOLIA OR FIVE MILE HOUSE
7. BRIGHTON
   PAVILION HOTEL
   FIVE MILE HOUSE
   JAMES ALLEN TAVERN
8. CROCKETT
9. ST. LOUIS HOUSE
10. MANLOVE
11. NINE MILE HOUSE
12. PATTERSON RANCH
    TEN MILE HOUSE
13. HANGTOWN CROSSING (MILLS STATION)
    LOUIS LEPETIT ROADHOUSE
14. GEORGE HANLON'S STOCK RANCH
15. FIFTEEN MILE HOUSE
16. MISSOURI HOUSE
17. OAK TREE HOUSE
18. PLEASANT GROVE HOUSE (NYES RANCH)
19. PETE HAASE ("SIX-TOED PETE'S")
20. WESTERN HOUSE
21. PRAIRIE HOUSE
22. WHAT CHEER HOUSE
23. WELLINGTON HOUSE (HALFWAY HOUSE)
24. WHITE ROCK SPRINGS RANCH HOTEL
25. ALDRIDGE RAVINE HOUSE
26. BAR E RANCH
27. CARSON RIVER HOUSE
28. MORMON TAVERN
29. CLARKSVILLE (CLARKSON'S VILLAGE)
    MARGARET TONG'S RAILROAD HOUSE

30. SAMUEL FREEMAN'S PLACE
    ATLANTIC HOUSE
31. OHIO HOUSE
32. DEER CREEK HOTEL
33. DU ROC HOUSE
34. SHINGLE SPRINGS
    SHINGLE SPRINGS HOUSE
    MISSOURI HOUSE
    OLD PLANTER'S HOUSE
35. BUCKEYE FLAT
36. FORTY MILE HOUSE
37. MOUNTAIN HOUSE
38. KINGSVILLE HOUSE
39. LONE TREE HOUSE
40. JAMES ASKEW
41. EL DORADO (MUD SPRINGS)
    MUD SPRINGS HOUSE
    NEVADA HOUSE
    ORIENTAL HOTEL
    TEMPERANCE HOUSE
42. "DOC" BRADFORD HAMMILL'S
43. DIAMOND SPRINGS
    CALIFORNIA HOUSE
    ILLSOHN'S HOTEL
    HOWARD HOUSE (TITUS HOTEL)
    DIAMOND HOTEL
    CRESCENT CITY HOTEL
    GOLDEN WEST HOTEL
    SACRAMENTO HOTEL
44. EAST DIAMOND OR "POLLIWOG SETTLEMENT"
45. COON HOLLOW
    THE CHAMPION HOTEL

THE EARLY INNS OF CALIFORNIA VIA THE GREEN VALLEY ROAD

46. TWELVE MILE HOUSE
47. PITTSFIELD HOUSE
48. FOURTEEN MILE HOUSE
49. SALSBURY HOUSE
50. NATOMAS HOUSE
51. THE MONTE CRISTO HOUSE OR EXCHANGE
52. NINETEEN MILE HOUSE
53. TWENTY MILE HOUSE
54. FOLSOM (NEGRO BAR)
    MEREDITH HOTEL
    PATTERSON'S HOTEL
    OLIVE BRANCH HOTEL
    MANSION HOUSE
    GRANITE HOTEL
    THE CENTRAL HOTEL
    TREMONT HOUSE
55. SARATOGA HOUSE
56. CAPTAIN GEORGE K. NEY'S STAGE STATION
57. MORMON ISLAND
    THE BLUE TENT
    CALDWELL HOUSE
    MINER'S HOTEL
    UNION HOTEL OR TAVERN
    J. P. MARKHAM'S HOTEL
    MANSION HOUSE
    YOUNG'S HOTEL
    THE ISLAND HOUSE
    SAMUEL RICKER'S HOUSE
    CINCINNATI HOUSE
58. SMITH'S OLD EXCHANGE (VALLEY HOUSE)
59. THE RED BARN
60. DAVIES DARRY'S PLACE
61. LEACHMAN HOUSE (KENTUCKY HOUSE)
62. ROLLING HILL HOUSE
63. KAUFMAN'S DEADFALL HOUSE
64. NEW YORK HOUSE
65. LOG CABIN
66. WAKASHA OR WALKER SHAW HOUSE
67. GREEN SPRING HOUSE

68. PLEASANT GROVE HOUSE
69. FREDERICK ROHLFING
70. GREEN VALLEY HOUSE
71. SKINNERS WINERY
72. GEORGE D. H. MEYER'S STORE
73. WHITE OAK SPRINGS HOTEL
74. KELLY CREEK HOUSE
75. RISING SUN, SUNRISE HOUSE
76. ROSE SPRINGS HOUSE
77. TENNESSEE HOUSE
78. DRY CREEK CROSSING
    "HELL-ROARING DIGGINGS"

THE EARLY INNS ON THE SAW MILL

79. LEXINGTON HOUSE
80. WILLOW SPRINGS HOUSE
81. PLUMB'S HOTEL

Information used in the preparation of this map obtained from:
Dept. of Interior - U.S. Geological Survey Maps.
Dept. of Interior - General Land Office Maps.
State of California Division of Highways.
Corps of Engineers, U.S. Army.

184

A number of pioneer families mentioned in "I remember" operated roadside stations and inns on the White Rock and Folsom roads between Sacramento and Placerville between the years 1849 and '59. In 1954, Ralph Herbert Cross published "The Early Inns of California" in which he included the above map. He spent seventeen years researching and writing what is considered to be the most thorough study of Gold Rush hostelries published.
The following inns are mentioned in "I remember": The Ohio House (31),

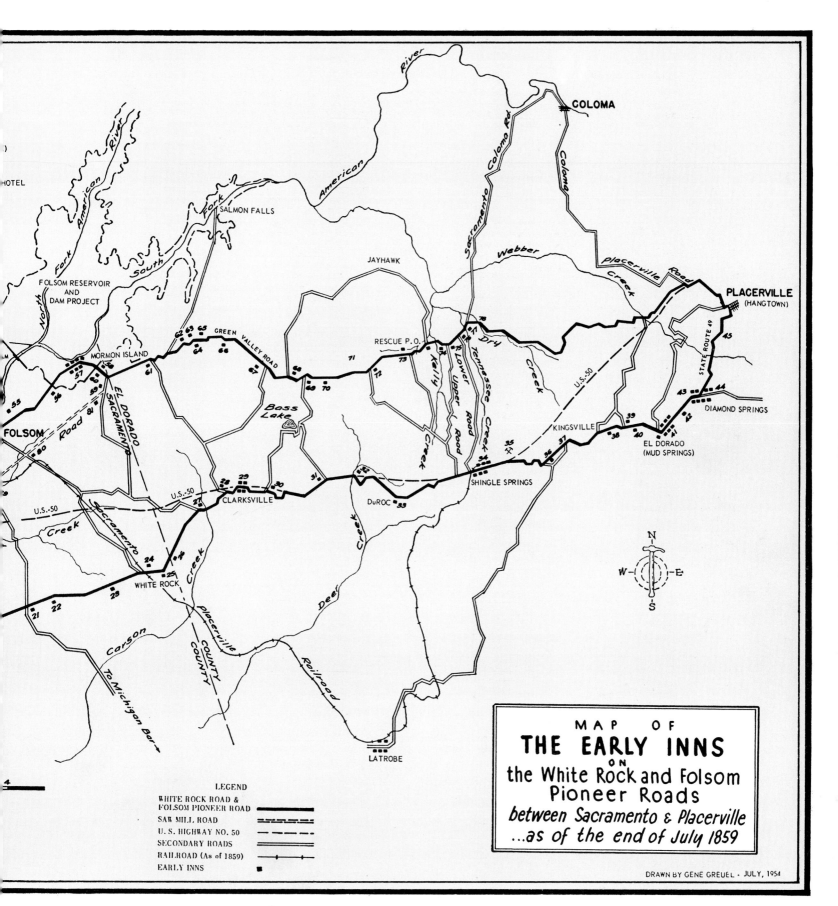

MAP OF
THE EARLY INNS
ON
the White Rock and Folsom
Pioneer Roads
between Sacramento & Placerville
...as of the end of July 1859

DRAWN BY GENE GREUEL · JULY, 1954

LEGEND
WHITE ROCK ROAD &
FOLSOM PIONEER ROAD
SAW MILL ROAD
U. S. HIGHWAY NO. 50
SECONDARY ROADS
RAILROAD (As of 1859)
EARLY INNS

Shingle Springs House (34), The Lone Tree House (39), The Diamond Hotel (43), Golden West Hotel (43), Natomas House (50), Leachman House (61), Rolling Hill House (62), New York House (64), Wakasha or Walkershaw House (66), George D. H. Meyer's Store (The Wing Store) (72), The Sunrise House (75), Plumb's Hotel (81). The Chamber of Commerce is grateful to Ralph Cross, Jr. of Oakland, California and to the heirs of the author Ralph H. Cross for granting permission to reproduce this map.

Early Days in Rescue

Ila Wing Brazil, daughter of Pearl and George Wing of Rescue, remembered names and places around Rescue, an area that played a great part in mining and farming in the early days of the county. Rescue boasted the first vineyard in the county, and Green Valley road was dotted with "mile houses," which provided the rest stops and overnight accommodations so necessary for the comfort of travelers in the Gold Rush era. "Louisa Pelton Wing was my father's mother," said Mrs. Brazil. "It was her father, Samuel B. Pelton, who built the Sunrise House in 1854." Mrs. Wing said the place had been called by several names, "Rising Sun House," "Sunrise," and "Pelton Hotel." Records show that it was built on the south side of Green Valley road, at the top of the hill between Kelly and Tennessee Creeks in the southeast angle of the junction of "upper road" to Gray's Flat and Shingle Springs (now Green Valley and Ponderosa roads). It was situated where it caught the first rays of the sun as it rose over the Sierra range to the east. Pelton named it the Sunrise House. "On both sides of the building, on the upstairs above the window, Grandfather built a sun. He had the rays of the sun coming out." It was considered one of the most popular roadhouses on the old wagon road and Pony Express route between Sacramento and Placerville. Pelton operated it until 1876 when he sold to John Carre, who opened a general store on the premises.

Mrs. Brazil mentioned the Engesser family and said, "As a child I spent many happy hours playing in their yard under a big fig tree." Their place is part of the Dorado Estates now.

Mrs. Brazil names many families she knew to be settlers in the area. "There was Louise Rust — she married John Fleming and they lived in the Pleasant Grove House, another old Pony Express stop on Green Valley road. That place now belongs to Mrs. Allen Dixon. Archie Fleming and his wife, the former Helen Treadman, live over on Deer Valley road. The Treadmans were early settlers, too. Mrs. Fleming's sister Julia married Charles Lorraine. They had a store just past Bass Lake on the Green Valley road. The place still stands.

"Mr. Lorraine was responsible for getting our first telephone line through here. That was about 1918 and it's still operating. It's called the Green Valley Telephone Company. They had 20 subscribers to start with and they still have 20. My mother was secretary-treasurer for the company for years. After her death I inherited the job. I do all the billing and keep the books for the GVTC."

GEORGE B. WING

JOSEPH WING, brother of John Wing who disappeared from his home in Rescue one day and was never heard from again.

(Inset) ILA WING BRAZIL

186

Photos from Brazil Collection

LOUISA PELTON WING - daughter of Samuel and Margaret Pelton who built Sunrise Wayside Station in 1854.

Photo courtesy Ralph Cross "The Early Inns of California"

SUNRISE HOUSE was one of many stage stops on the road from Sacramento to Placerville. Here travelers stopped overnight to rest and stable their horses. The two-story New England farmhouse was built by Samuel B. Pelton in 1854. Facing the east and located on the Green Valley road, it caught the first rays of the morning sun. Pelton erected signs at each side of the structure depicting a rising sun.

ONS AND DAUGHTERS of El Dorado County pioneers who lived in the escue area. Back row, from left: Bert Rust, Frederick Wulff, Leonard ing. Second row, from left: Aggie Bessell, Charlotte Wulff, James Wing. ated in front: Caroline Wulff and Lottie Wing.

A. S. BOSQUIT was an agent for Wells, Fargo & Co., railroad bookkeeper and telegraph operator at Shingle Springs when he married Miss Sarah C. Gray in 1873. When this picture was taken with his wife and sons (standing from left) Ernest, Elwin and (baby) Owen, he was Sheriff of El Dorado County.

Names of mines she recalled in the Rescue area were "Cedar Jack," "Red Raven," "Pyramid," "Dolores," "Jayhawk," "Rescue," and "Gray-Wing."

"My father, George Wing, was born at Gray's Flat in 1865. In later years he and his brother Leonard mined there on the Gray place. I don't know how successful they were, but it seems to me that father devoted most of his life to farming. He put in crops and he would go and work for fifty cents a day. He and his brother had a horse and wagon and hauled hay up to Georgetown.

"Grandfather Wing died when the children were small, so it was up to the boys to take care of their mother and help raise the family. There were six children. It was their mother, my grandmother, who had the old Brick House. She kept the drivers and other travelers overnight and fed them before they started out the next day. It was called Wing's Store. The family lived in the old Brick House that was built in 1854. After it burned in 1909, my father rebuilt. My husband, Arthur, and I came back in 1959 and we've done a little remodeling. I was born in this house and I guess this is where I'll die."

As a child Mrs. Brazil attended the Green Valley School for four years and later went to the Kenneth School, which at that time was located about a quarter mile beyond the Rescue post office. In 1962 Mrs. Brazil became postmaster of the Rescue post office, a position she still holds.

She regretted not having more family records, explaining they were lost in the fire in 1909. She did recall the grown-ups talking about the disappearance of John Wing, her father's father. As she remembered the story, he came into the house one day from the field, didn't say a word, took his gun from the gun rack, and was never seen again. When he didn't return at night, word was spread around and neighbors started searching for him. The sheriff was notified and the search spread throughout the area. They looked in old mine shafts and combed the woods, thinking he might have fallen and accidentally shot himself, but they found no sign of him.

It was many years later, after the family was grown, that a man came to the house one day when her father was out in the woods. The man asked her mother, Mrs. Wing, questions about who lived in the house and appeared to know the neighborhood very well. Never having seen her husband's father, she naturally could not say that the man was he. When George Wing returned home, his wife told him about the man and from what she could tell him, George Wing believed that man to be his father. Nothing more was ever heard of him. He never returned or made any attempt to contact the family again, if, indeed, the man was John Wing. So it still remains a mystery — what happened to John Wing? Where did he go and why did he leave home? For generations to come, descendants of the Wing family will no doubt be asking those same questions.

LEONARD WING
Brother of George Wing

EMMA, TILLIE AND LOTTIE WING
Daughters of Louisa Pelton Wing

DESTROYED BY FIRE in June 1909 - the hom
of the George Wing family on Green Valley roa
out of Rescue was rebuilt in December of that y

A GATHERING AT THE RSLS - Built in 1896, the Rose Spring Library Society was the general meeting place and social center for the Rescue community. El Dorado County, during that period, was noted for its many debating societies. It was here many of the most noted debates were held. Today, and since July 1, 1962, it has served as the Rescue Post Office, where Ila Brazil is the post-master. This picture was taken shortly after the building was completed. Present for the occasion were (on left side of picture front row - L to R) Mina Carpenter, Dora Arthur, Mary Fisher, Josie Cothrin, Tillie Wing, Lottie Wulff, Hulda Wise Wing, and Louisa Pelton Wing. (2nd row, from left) George Wallace, James Wing, George Wing, Leonard Wing, and Lottie Wing Sprague. (Back row from left) Arthur Fleming, Ben Fisk, Mr. Barter and Alex Skinner. (On right side front row L to R) Annie Smith Skinner, Julia Fleming Burston, Lizzie Fleming, (standing) Will Rust. (2nd row, from L) George Skinner and Chris Burston. (3rd row from L) Charles Holden, Gus Wulff. The little girl in the upstairs window is Pearl Wise, who later became Mrs. Ila Wing Brazil's mother.

RESCUE STORE - Only part of the original 1800 structure remained after Mrs. Weir remodeled the old building now operated by Bill and Jackie Freeman.

THE GEORGE WING FAMILY lived in this cabin while their new home was being built in 1909. Pictured are from left: John Crookes, Louisa Pelton Wing, George Wing, (child) Morley and Pearl Wing.

PLEASANT GROVE HOUSE was one of hundreds of way-stations from Sacramento to the mines in the Mother Lode. It became the first Pony Express Remount Station east of Folsom. Purchased by William Wallace Rust in 1864 and later operated by his son-in-law John Fleming. Today it is owned by Lillian Dixon.

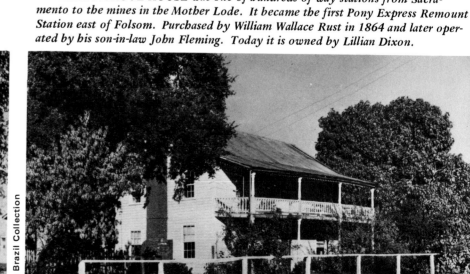

Photos from Brazil Collection

Grandma's Money Belt

Leo Swansborough was born in Pleasant Valley on March 1, 1888. When interviewed at his home on Panorama Drive, rural Placerville, February 18, 1975, he was looking forward to his 87th birthday. His mother died when he was three years old, leaving his father, George Swansborough, with three small sons to raise. One brother died when he was seven years old and the other was killed while working on a tunnel. "It was a big tunnel they were putting through on Big Creek for the Edison Electric Company," said Swansborough. "He'd been working just three hours and got caved on. It took three hours to dig him out. He's buried over in Pleasant Valley. He was twenty-four years old.

"Grandfather was English and Grandmother was Welsh," continued Mr. Swansborough. "I couldn't say what year they came to America, but I remember them talking about what a hard time they had. They came on a sailing boat . . . they were three months on the ocean. One of Grandmother's brothers was buried at sea. When they got here they settled in Pennsylvania. Grandfather was a miner and went to work in the coal mines at Pittsburgh. That's where my father was born, in Pittsburgh.

"When word of the gold discovery reached back there, Grandfather made a trip out here in 1851, and then went back for the family later. They came by boat around Cape Horn. They said when Grandma got here she was in bad shape. What she did . . . she put $3,000 in gold in a money belt and carried that around her waist the whole time . . . imagine. She was so bruised she couldn't even stand her clothes to touch her. They had four boys and three girls in the family. There was my dad George, Tom, Joe, Jim, and the three girls. Grandma raised them all by taking care of women having babies."

When they lived in Pleasant Valley, his father worked at the Davenport sawmill. He named the Davenport family as being one of the very early pioneer families and believed some of them still live in the Camino area. He was only six or seven years of age but he remembered that Pleasant Valley had a slaughterhouse operated by the Sweeney brothers, a dance hall, a post office, and a grocery store. There were a dozen or more homes along the road to Somerset and some on the creek going to Sly Park. It was in this area that his grandfather owned the Steadman place.

After his mother died, he lived with his grandmother, Anna Swansborough, at White Rock. He attended the Union school and when they moved to Placerville he went to the Placerville grammar school. "When I got to the seventh grade I quit and was on my own

P G & E EMPLOYEES identified are, from left: Dave Marks, Jim Price, Leo Swansborough, Adolph Martin, Joe Shepherd, Stephen......., Frank Ward, one of the Morey girls, Cecelia Morton, and Waldo Daniels. In back: Eddie Marchini and the "Boss" Joe Leonardi, on right.

MAIN STREET PLACERVILLE - The more thing

Photo William (Mike) DeNatly Collection

190

(Inset) LEO SWANSBOROUGH

John Winning Photo

LD CHINESE JOSS HOUSE - Mr. Swansborough members the church when it was attended regularly by the Chinese who lived in the Chinese quarters on Sacramento and Pacific streets. Built 1872, it was torn down in 1921 after being ndalized. Photo El Dorado County Historical Museum

ange, the more they remain the same.

from then on." He was eleven years old when he worked for the Crocker Brothers store, across the road from where Blair Lumber Yard is located today. "They had a big wood yard there at the store. I'd work ten, eleven, and sometimes fifteen hours a day cutting and hauling wood. When I was a kid I picked pears in Coloma. When I was sixteen I drove a six horse team for Rupley out of Sly Park, hauling lagging to the mines. I worked in livery stables . . . when the drummers (salesmen) come to town they'd rent a rig at the stable and I'd drive them around. I broke horses and punched cattle . . . I guess I've had more jobs than any man alive."

He said he rode cattle drives for many cattlemen in the county. "They'd take their cattle to the mountains in the spring . . . then round them up in the fall and bring them back down. I can remember many times when we went up with two hundred head and came back with five. Oh, yes . . . they'd steal, and steal, and steal. I won't mention any names, but they all did it. And there's another thing with the cattle. It was nothing to see five or six thousand head go right down Main Street through Placerville . . . sheep too. Forni had a lot of sheep. When that happened, nothing moved but the cattle or sheep.

"We lived across the street from the Crocker store, where Lutz has his used car lot. Then Dad got the idea he wanted a farm. I told him he didn't know any more about farming than a dog, but he and his brother bought a big farm out in Mosquito. It was 340 acres. They bought it from a man named Dickerson for $6,000, with sixty head of cattle and sheep. They didn't know anything about farming. That lasted about five years and Dad sold out to his brother. All that work and all he got was what he put into the thing in the first place."

Talking about his childhood, Swansborough said, "It's a wonder we weren't killed. When we lived in White Rock, I remember the Martin boys. They were hydraulicking there. We'd steal their gold. We got some nuggets . . . good size, too. We'd go up where the pipeline went down to the monitors and put rocks in the line and plug it up, then go down and take the gold out. Sometimes we'd turn the water off at the reservoir and take the gold out of the tailraces. We'd hide out and watch when they found out. Boy, they'd cuss us — we could hear them cussing. The more they cussed us, the more we stole. How old was I? Oh, that was when I was about six or seven. We couldn't take the gold home because Grandmother would find out. But around the Fourth of July we'd get some and spend it. We had to wait for holidays like that . . . we told her we panned it.

"And the poor Chinese people . . . we gave them fits. We'd tie their queues to hitching racks. They had hundreds of Chinese laying the tracks for the railroad to Camino. They'd march them up in the morning in single file, then bring them back at night. Well, we'd string a wire down low across the road there by Crocker's store, and when they'd come, they'd trip on that and a whole row of them would go down just like dominoes."

When asked at what point in his life he stopped his mischief-making and got serious about life, Swansborough answered, "I never did."

Hogans in Ringgold in 1850

Ina Butler Smith and her sister Laura Butler Van Vleck, descendants of the Phillip B. Hogan and Samuel Butler pioneer families, boast seven generations of the Hogan-Butler lineage who have resided in El Dorado County. "Great-grandfather Phillip Hogan made a trip to California in 1850. He liked what he saw and returned to Illinois for his family. In 1852 he and his wife, the former Jemima Gallahan of Dayton, Ohio, made the trek back across the plains to California."

The Hogans homesteaded in the Ringgold area, where through the years Hogan engaged in mining, milling, building, lime burning, and at one time operated a box factory. Later he devoted all his time to the farm that included an orchard of about 2500 fruit trees and a vineyard with 11,000 grape vines. They could not say exactly how many acres the Hogan Ranch encompassed, but Mrs. Smith said, "In those days every member of the family, regardless of age, could take up a homestead of 160 acres. If there were several children, you can see, quite a large acreage could be acquired."

Their mother was Cora Hogan, daughter of Charles and Clara Allen Hogan. Because the Hogan family moved around the county, Cora attended a number of schools. When they lived at Fort Jim, she had to walk four miles to attend the Pleasant Valley school. She later attended the schools at Sly Park and Coon Hollow. When they lived in their Placerville home on Cary Street, in back of the Ohio House on the corner of Sacramento and Main Streets, she went to the Placerville Academy.

In 1886 Cora married Nelson Butler. The wedding ceremony, performed by the Reverend C.C. Pierce, was held at Sportsman's Hall, the first and only Pony Express relay station on the overland Pony Express route from St. Joseph, Missouri, to Sacramento, California. Miss Hogan's parents were operating Sportsman's Hall as a resort hotel at the time, having leased it from the Blair family.

Mrs. Smith and Mrs. Van Vleck had little information about their grandfather, Samuel Butler. However, they had heard that he came to California with the group that left Salt Lake City, Utah, with the Neils Larsen wagon train in 1860. The Butlers settled in Larsen Valley on land adjoining the Larsens'.

They said that the Butlers raised cattle on the ranch and in the winter moved to their winter range in the Logtown area, three miles south of the town of El Dorado.

LAURA BU
about age 1

PHILLIP B.
HOGAN

JEMIMA
GALLAHAN
HOGAN

SAMUEL AND
HELENA BUTLER
*Grandparents of
Ina and Laura*

CORA HOGAN, age 8, and her brother George. They were born in Ringgold on the Hogan homestead.

MRS. CHARLES HOGAN
HARVEY ALLEN HOGAN

HARVEY S. ALLEN and his granddaughter Alice Hogan. Mr. Allen came to El Dorado County via plains in wagon train. He was a gunsmith in Placerville for many years. His daughter Clara married Charles Hogan.

Photos Ina Butler Smith Collection

COON HOLLOW SCHOOL - CLASS OF 1887
In the front row, from left, are Nettie Bamba, Ada Secombe, Vivian Weyman, Nettie Weyman, Beatrice Weyman, Alice Secombe, Eva Thomas, Harvey Hogan, Wm McIvery, Georgie Enner and Will Weyman. In the back row, from left, teacher Miss N. Merry, her sister Grace, Dillie Owen, Alice Hogan, George Hogan, Steve Alderson and Joseph Hocking.

Mrs. Van Vleck remembered that their family raised fruit and produce. "They received one cent a pound for beans and fifty cents for a lug of apples. They hauled their produce in horse-drawn wagons . . . and Mother told us that Father held the record for hauling the largest loads. It took four horses to pull the wagon with 267 boxes."

"We know Grandfather Butler was a Mormon, but we're not sure he was a 'real' Mormon," said Mrs. Smith. "He did have three wives, but not at the same time, and we know that he sired seventeen children. There was a son, Stephen, by his first wife, Samantha. Our records show that they married in 1832 in New York. She died in 1833. There were twelve children by his second wife, Hannah, between 1840 and 1856, and four children were born to his third wife, Helena. Our father, Nelson C. Butler, was the first child born of that marriage."

The sisters agreed that the Butler and Hogan families were very prolific and mentioned other local descendants, including their sister, Ethel Creed, and their brothers, Ray, Clyde, and Harry Butler.

Laura Butler married James Pearson in 1911. They moved to the old Western States Gas and Electric Company Camp 5, in 1913. It was there that three of their seven children were born. Mr. Pearson died in 1947 and Laura married George Van Vleck in 1951.

Four daughters were born to Ina Butler, two after her marriage to Roy Marshall, and two after her marriage to Nyron Smith. "Today," said Mrs. Smith, "I have ten grandchildren and two great-grandchildren, and all are interested in their family heritage."

John Blair Led the Way

While pioneers were pouring into California in 1856, James and John Blair were operating what was the first of many sawmills that were to make the Blair name synonymous with lumber in El Dorado County. During an interview with Mr. Gordon Blair, present owner and manager of Blair Brothers Lumber Company in Placerville, he talked about the migration of the Blair family from Scotland to America in 1850 and to California in 1854. His great-great-grandfather, Matthew Blair, was a weaver in the town of Paisley, Scotland, home of the celebrated Paisley shawls. He raised his family of six children by weaving in the famed Paisley manufacturing firms and instilled the principles of economy and industry in each of his children.

(Inset)
GORDON
BLAIR

Young John Blair was the first to leave Scotland for America, in 1848. He settled in Indiana, where he found employment and learned the cooper trade. Two years later, in 1850, his brothers Matthew and James sailed for America. Matthew was thirty years old and James was twenty-two. They settled in Ohio, across the Indiana state line.

The news of the great migration to California appealed to them. But not having sufficient funds for all to make the trip, they agreed, again, that John should go first. If he made good, James would follow. It was understood that whatever business John engaged in would be in the name of J&J Blair.

John made the trip, crossing the plains by mule train in 1852. In eighteen months enough money had been raised to allow James to make the trip. He traveled via New Orleans and Nicaragua, then proceeded to El Dorado County. By the time James arrived, John had purchased a tavern and hotel on the heavily traveled road from Placerville to Carson City. He catered to thousands of people and records show that five hundred head of horses and mules were fed and stalled at the popular way station called Sportsman's Hall. It was a relay station for the Pony Express and today is designated "State Historical Landmark #704".

In the meantime, having plenty of timberland, the Blairs started a sawmill. The original mill operation began in 1856 near the Five Mile House, five miles from Placerville. The mill operated by steam and cut eight to ten thousand feet of lumber a day. In 1860, the Blairs set up a second mill at Iowa Canyon. It was known as Elk Horn Sawmill and operated until 1870.

"It was about this time," said Mr. Blair, "that my great-grandfather, Matthew Blair, came into the picture. Leaving Ohio, he made the trip by sailing vessel with his wife and a son named Matthew. Upon his

JAMES BLAIR,
founder and owner of
J & J Blair Lumber Co.

MATTHEW BLAIR S[...]
killed in a sawdust pile
cave-in in 1867.

MISS JENNIE BLAIR,
daughter of Robert
and Abigail Blair.

ROBERT BLAIR,
father of Jennie, Rob-
ert J., Jessie, and John[...]

194

COMBELLACK - Men's furnishing store was established by William Combellack, a native of Cornwall, England, who first settled in Oakland, California in 1853. He came to Placerville in 1884 with his wife Mary Ellen Dunston Combellack. Their children William "Bert," Frederick, Ella, Fern and Hazel were born and raised in El Dorado county. "Bert" married Jessie Blair, daughter of Robert and Abigail Blair. Their sons Allen and Robert took over the store in 1956. (William Combellack Sr. is seen on left.)

Photo Combellack Collection

Photo Combellack Collection

BLAIR LUMBER YARD AND STORE was located on the corner of Cedar Ravine and Main streets, Placerville, where the Inter-County Title Company is today (1976). Identified are (1) Frank Philips, (2) Pete Watt, (3) Robert Blair, (4) John Blair. Note sign on store: Highest prices paid for all kinds of hides and furs.

Photos at left Jennie Blair and Gordon Blair Collections

In 1890, this ox-drawn log truck arrived at Blair's Sly Park Sawmill with a load of logs. The Sly Park Mill was operated by J. B. Blair, son of James Blair. Photo William "Mike" De Natly

arrival he took over the operation of the mills. It was at the Elk Horn mill that he was killed in 1867. He was working alone, shiving sawdust. Water had washed a channel fifteen feet deep through the bank of sawdust and while he was working there, it caved in on him. He was found the next day with his dog lying over him, with strands of his hair protruding from the sawdust."

Other Blair mills and approximate dates of their operation were the South Long Canyon mill, 1870 to 1880, the North Long Canyon, from 1880 to 1890, the Sly Park mill, 1890 to 1908, the Plumb Creek, 1908 to 1910. In 1911 they started the Fresh Pond mill; it operated one year. Long Canyon mill operated from 1913 to 1925. A great percentage of the lumber cut from 1920 through 1925 was sold to the Western States Power Company for flume lumber. That company is now PG&E.

A sawmill without timber is like a gold mine without gold, so the Blairs obtained timber holdings in the Pacific area, three miles north of Pacific House. That meant building a road and spanning the American River with a bridge, which was done in 1926. The Pacific House mill was built in 1927 and was operated by Walter, Arthur J., Albert W., and Matthew E. Blair, Jr. In 1958 the mill and timber holdings were sold to Michigan-California Lumber Company.

Mr. Blair said that the first mills used powered carriages operated by wooden gears called rack and pinion. Cable and pulley drive carriages were used in the early 1880's. From 1901 to 1902 his grandfather, Matthew Blair, Sr., cut lumber by contract for the El Dorado Deep Gravel Mining Company. "This," said Blair, "was at the Ditch Camp mill located at Silver Fork, thirty miles east of Placerville. Lumber from this mill was transported by flume approximately fourteen miles to the Pollock Pines area."

The first logging was done by oxen and skid roads. Logs were also transported on log trucks which were built of heavy timber and used large wooden wheels with steel rims. These were drawn by oxen and horses. Wherever the terrain was too steep for these log trucks to travel, chutes were built and logs were slid down hills to a point close to the mill. Logs were all dry decked, mainly because of an inadequate supply of water to have a pond.

After the sale of the Blair holdings in 1958, Arthur and Gordon Blair continued in the retail lumber and building supply business. In 1970 Arthur Blair retired. Today, 1976, Gordon Blair continues to operate the Blair Brothers Lumber Company, the business that was started 120 years ago during the Gold Rush.

El Dorado Vineyards

Ramona Sweeney Bacoccini, daughter of William and Bertha Hocking Sweeney, was born in 1904 at her grandparents' ranch home on Sweeney Road, off Happy Valley Road, east of Somerset. Her father was born in Coloma and her mother in Grass Valley, where they married in 1902. Her father was employed as a boss in logging camps in the Shasta and Redding areas; he died when she was three years old. She was raised on the Sweeney ranch and attended the local schools. Her husband, Peter Bacoccini, was born in Sacramento. When interviewed at their home on Coon Hollow Road in Placerville, they talked about El Dorado County as they remembered it when they were children.

Mr. Bacoccini said, "When I was a little boy, I worked with my dad on the Pierroz ranch. That was when we first moved up here from Sacramento in 1903, after our home and ten-acre farm were left under twenty feet of sand. The river broke about five hundred yards above us and flooded everything we had. We didn't save a thing, it was that sudden."

He said that they worked for the Pierroz dairies for seven years and eight months. "Pierroz had the first dairy down there. It was right below the nursery and mortuary (Pierroz and Cold Springs Roads). All that land used to belong to the Freighter ranch. It was a big place and at that time it was all planted in grapes. There was a big still out there on the Marco Varozza ranch on Cold Springs Road, just past the Middletown cemetery. They had a 600-gallon capacity still and shipped brandy back east.

"They raised tons and tons of grapes years ago. That's how the railroad got in here from Shingle . . . because of the grapes raised here and down around Shingle. Every place up here had grapes. There were so many it didn't pay to pick them. We got five dollars a ton. That was back in 1917, '18.

"The county then was mostly farming; they raised pears and grapes. Everybody had five or six cows and made their own cheese to sell. My mama used to make a lot of cheese, and we sold a lot of milk.

BERT SWEENEY, noted jerkline driver transporting a 14,000 pound solid cast iron piece to the Eureka Slate Mine near Kelsey. He was a teamster all his life, hauling logs and lumber from Silver Lake, Sly Park and Camp Creek areas where the Blairs, Bryants and Snow brothers operated sawmills. He hauled logs to Diamond and Shingle Springs, and lagging and shoring posts to the Union Mine. He used four- and six-horse teams with two wagons. In most of his heavy hauling he used the jerkline team. Old-timers remember him as "the greatest jerkline man in the west."

IDA AND MICHAEL SWEENEY, grandparents of Ramona Sweeney Bacoccini of Coon Hollow, rural Placerville. The picture was taken on their wedding day. They came to El Dorado county in 1854 and settled on land on the north fork of the Cosumnes river south of Happy Valley road. Today, Sweeney road runs between Happy Valley road and Coles Station, east of Somerset. Photo Bacoccini Collection

(Inset) RAMONA SWEENEY - 1906 - was photographed by Mattie Flower in a field of Shasta daisies that grew in abundance in the meadow that is now inundated by the water of Jenkinson Lake, Sly Park.

piece solid cast iron.
Wt 14000 lbs

Photo Euell Gray, Jr. Collection

*1897 - BRIDGE DEDICATION and picnic
at Camp Creek bridge located between
Pleasant Valley and Somerset.*

Photo Bacoccini Collection

"We were running the big dairy then, milking sixty-five cows, and didn't buy a bit of hay; we'd cut hay on all these hills, way down to where that meadow is at the bowling alley. All the hills across from the cemetery were in grain; Father used to mow it. Yes, there were twenty-three dairies running here and we couldn't keep enough milk . . . there were more people here then. Look at all the mines that were running then — the Pacific, the Sherman, the Epley, the Larkin, and other mines over around Kelsey. We had to have the milk out by six in the morning, because the men went to work at seven. We delivered it by horse and wagon. We kids would jump up on the wagon with a gallon can and pour out a quart into their containers."

Mr. Bacoccini said that his family came to America from Italy in the 1800's. His father, Peter Bacoccini, served six years in the Italian army, for which he received $100 a year. "He served two years for each of his two brothers and two years for himself. That's how he got the money to come to America. He was a lieutenant when he got out."

Mr. Bacoccini said that he was driving a truck out of Plum Creek for the Beach mill, and hauling lumber for Pearson and Brumalt, when he met Ramona Sweeney. She was eighteen years old and employed at the Ivy House, where he stayed when he came in to town. They were married in 1923 at Carson City. They had two daughters, Eleanor Bacoccini Skiles of Placerville and Marjorie Bacoccini Barrett of Rancho Cordova, and two sons, Richard Bacoccini of El Dorado and Elbern Bacoccini of Michigan. They now have eleven grandchildren and thirteen great-grandchildren.

Photos Ethel Tidd Collection

THE TEMPERANCE HOTEL in Lotus in 1892. Mrs. James Turnbeaugh (seated in doorway) holding her infant daughter Irma. Others in the picture are (from left) Edna and Hattie Turnbeaugh, Albert Roberts, and Martha Turnbeaugh, seated in front of her father James Turnbeaugh.

THE TEMPERANCE HOTEL IN 1916, improved by James Turnbeaugh (right), his mother, Martha Gray and his wife Charlotte. (front row from left) Ray Lawyer, his sister Ethel, Clarence Turnbeaugh, and a friend named Marjorie Hall. In the back row (from left) Jim and Martha Turnbeaugh.

BALDERSTONS' was located east of Virner, on the Wentworth Springs road leading to Uncle Tom's Cabin, Loon Lake and the Desolation Valley area. The two-story home appears to have been constructed of poles, and was the home of Allen Balderston, son of John Balderston, Irma Lawyer's uncle. The smaller building on the left housed the store. The place was known as Balderston Station.

Photo Amy Drysdale Collection

Irma Lawyer Remembers

RAYMOND LAWYER -
*Supervisor of El Dorado
County Fourth District*

Irma Lawyer was born in the town of Lotus, near Coloma, in 1892. She had passed her eighty-second birthday when she was interviewed in May, 1975, at her home in Lotus. Her parents, James and Charlotte Balderston Turnbeaugh, owned and operated the Temperance Hotel on the town's main street. "I don't know why they called it the 'Temperance,'" said Mrs. Lawyer, "I saw more whiskey poured there than you can imagine." The first interview with Mrs. Lawyer took place at Uncle Tom's Cabin in the fall of 1974. Her son, Raymond Lawyer, an El Dorado County Supervisor from the Fourth District, was also present. Every spring for fifty-three years Mrs. Lawyer has left her home in Lotus to go to Uncle Tom's in the mountains, where she and her husband, Archie, went to live after their marriage in 1912. Their first home was on Pollack Creek, near Uncle Tom's, which was owned at the time by Charles Schultz. When he moved, she and her husband bought the property.

Located twenty-seven miles east of Georgetown on the Wentworth Springs road, Uncle Tom's Cabin is above the 5000 foot elevation in timber country where winters are often severe. It is said to have been named after a black man who lived there, mining and trapping in the early mining days. Mrs. Lawyer said that, as far as she knew, no one ever knew the man's real name. White trappers started moving into the area, many seeking Tom's help in trapping and getting their hides out, and after a period of time the name became established.

When the Lawyers moved to Uncle Tom's, they continued to operate it as a roadhouse. Cattlemen, teamsters, and tourists stopped on their way to Wentworth Springs, Desolation Valley, and Lake Tahoe. To accommodate the cattlemen there were corrals and a barn at no charge. If they stayed overnight they either slept outdoors or in one of the cabins. "The food," said Mr. Lawyer, "was put on the table, family style . . . all you could eat for fifty cents. It was not unusual for them to charge their meals when they came up in the spring and again when they went below in the fall, but they didn't pay up until the next spring when they returned. It did present a hardship of sorts, but we made out all right.

"A lot of the Lawyer family time was spent in the dray business, hauling hides from the area to the tannery for rawhide . . . and then there were the tourists. Many came by horse and wagon from the

RMA LAWYER *standing in front of the
emperance Hotel in Lotus, 1975.*

Dick Stanfield Photo

199

Photo Joe Cola Collection

valley. They stayed two and three weeks at a time, both at Uncle Tom's and Wentworth Springs." As Mrs. Lawyer and her son reminisced they recalled names of many early families and activities in the area. "You take John and Frank McCullock," said Mrs. Lawyer. "They drove their cattle in here and then took them across into Grizzly Flat and Long Canyon ... they'd pack in. At times they'd drive 350 head down across the Rubicon River. And Charles Swift rented grazing land here for his 500 goats. Swift was the father of Rupert Swift of Latrobe. Then there were the Scalarei brothers. They were uncles of Rose and Joe Leonardi, and Phil and Sheldon Leonardi. They all lived in Lotus."

She said they were always there in early spring to take care of the men who arrived to repair the flume boxes. She mentioned a George DeBour ... or DeVore. "He owned the ditch that ran about eight miles from Uncle Tom's to the South Fork of the Rubicon. The men always boarded with me ... and Archie packed food in for the PG&E survey crews that were surveying up here. They were working the river from Lower Hell Hole down to Volcanoville." Mr. Lawyer told of a road from Georgetown Divide to Onion Valley, below Uncle Tom's, a distance of about four miles, that was built by hand with nothing more than a shovel and wheelbarrow. "Gil Hanson and Alec Leonardi completed ninety percent of that work alone. Alec was a brother to Joe Leonardi of Placerville.

"Lumbering operations brought logging crews into the area and that helped the Lawyers," he continued. "Of course the loggers in those days were more or less 'Buck-type' men ... they weren't so much married ... They just had themselves to take care of and they'd come over to Uncle Tom's on the weekends ... and some way or other there happened to be a couple of slot machines, and a lot of beer and good food. It turned out to be quite profitable for the Lawyer family."

They laughed as they recalled an incident that happened back in the mid-20's when Irma made a speedy exit from the building with a slot machine. She said, "The boys came up and told me the sheriff was coming ... oh, that scared me half to death. I grabbed the slot machine and ran out with it." Asked where she took it, she replied, "Out back." To this her son said, "Why don't you tell her the truth, Ma? Tell her you hid it in the outhouse." Mrs. Lawyer said she can laugh at it now but will always remember how frightened she was at the time. She explained that it was only "the boys". They had tied red rags over their car headlights and driven in, causing quite a commotion in front of the place. Another time "the boys" hid her slot machines on the roof and she didn't find them for days. Playing jokes at Irma's expense seemed to be half the fun of stopping at Uncle Tom's Cabin.

UNCLE TOM'S CABIN is located 27 miles east It has stood for more than 100 years. It is repe early years. White trappers brought their hides the years went by the place became known as has spent 53 years living and operating a touris

ETHEL AND RAYMOND LAWYER of Lotus. Children of Archie and Irma Lawyer. Today, April, 1975, Ethel is Mrs. Clarence Tidd and lives on Mosquito road in Placerville, Raymond is serving his third term as El Dorado County Supervisor, and lives with his wife Marie and their children Ethel and Archie in their home on Marshall road, Coloma.   Photos Ethel Tidd Collection

...orgetown on the Wentworth Springs road. ...bat a black man lived and trapped there in the ...for him. They called him Uncle Tom, and as ...Tom's Cabin. Irma Lawyer (shown center) ...to here during the summer months.

RAY LAWYER in 1936 - after securing his Bachelor of Science Degree in Forestry at Oregon State College.

Raymond Lawyer died unexpectedly June 19, 1976 before he could see the completion of his favorite project, the El Dorado County Government Center.

In more serious moments they talked about their family. In 1850, a young man named Jay Lawyer left St. Joseph, Missouri, with a wagon train headed for California. He stopped for a while in Nevada Territory before coming to El Dorado County in 1852. He is said to have mined for a time before settling on a ranch near Kelsey.

"In later years," said Mr. Lawyer, "he was in business with a man named Bingham. They had a dry goods store at American Flat. The people trusted Grandfather and often left their gold with him at the store for safekeeping. The sad part is, Grandfather had a habit of drinking too much at times. Then one time a man left his gold . . . Grandpa must have had too much to drink because months later, when the man came for his gold, Grandpa couldn't remember where he put it. They say he searched every place he had ever hid gold but he couldn't find it. This went on for some time, and then one day they found his body. He had committed suicide. They say he worried so over not remembering, and because he believed people would think he stole the gold, he just killed himself. The worst part is that soon after his death they found the gold - supposedly right where he hid it."

After the first snowfall at Uncle Tom's Cabin, Mrs. Lawyer returned to her home in Lotus. There, during a second interview, she talked about her family and told of many incidents that reflect a way of life in what was once a crowded mining town.

The Temperance Hotel was run by her grandparents in the mining days. In 1888 it passed to her parents, James and Charlotte Turnbeaugh, and when her mother died it was left to her brother who gave it to Irma. "Mother raised seven children here. We were all born in this house and we all went to the Lotus school down the road. Our father went there too, and so did my children, Raymond and Ethel. Three generations of our family went to school there. My daughter Ethel was born here. Raymond was born on the Lawyer Ranch near Kelsey."

Referring to her pioneer heritage, she said that her father's family, the Turnbeaughs, came to El Dorado County from Quincy, Illinois, via Cape Horn in the early 1850's. Her mother's name was Balderston before her marriage. The Balderstons were natives of England. They migrated to America and stayed for a time in Illinois before traveling west by wagon train. They spent a short time in Nevada and arrived in El Dorado County in the early 1850's.

"The town of Lotus, as I remember it, had two saloons, two grocery stores, a blacksmith shop, several residences on Main Street, and, of course, the school down the road. There were a number of wineries here . . . the Chinaman's Winery in Coloma, the Othic Winery, the Rassmussen Winery, the Honn Winery, the Imo Winery, and the English Winery . . . there were wonderful vineyards all around here.

COLOMA 1885 - Points of interest identified are the Melvin Gallagher home, barn and packing house in the foreground on the right. The home on the left side of the road is the Thole home. Across the bridge on Main Street is the Community Hall (right). At the extreme left is the Coloma Schoolhouse and Edwin Markham home. In the center of the picture can be seen the Wagner family farm and orchard. Other homes in the area are those of Fred Thomas and Wm. Bake

LOTUS SCHOOL about 1898. Pictured are from left: front row, David Grother, George Grother, Ernest Coonrod, an unidentified boy, George Wagner, Herbert Wagner, Walter Wagner, Helen Gallagher, Alice Turnbeaugh, Dick Gallagher, Lorena Wagner, Allan Gallagher, and their teacher Alice Parker. In back row from left: an unidentified boy, Amelia Leonardi, Herbert Coonrod, Alice Uhlenkamp, Irma Turnbeaugh and Anna Bassi. The two students in back were unidentified.

Photos Ethel Tidd Collection

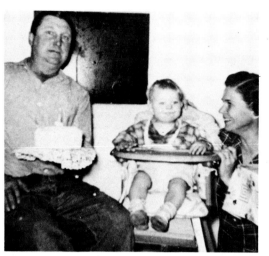

A SPECIAL OCCASION - Ray, Archie and Marie Lawyer on Archie's first birthday, 1955.

THE EMANUEL CHURCH in Coloma was the first Protestant Church in the mining era. It was founded January 4, 1854 by Right Rev. William J. Kipp, D.D. Bishop of the Episcopal Diocese of California.

We kids used to pick grapes from morning 'til night. All this country was covered with fruit then, apples and pears. Vince Norris had a big apple orchard here. He used to pack his apples in boxes. I would go with him in his spring wagon and open the gates for him while he went all around selling his boxes of apples . . . around Shingle Springs and into the farm basin. Yes, this was all fruit through here then.

"Mother said the tenants at the hotel were miners, teamsters, and people going to and coming from the mountains up Pilot Hill and Georgetown way. They'd stop overnight and on Sunday she served a Sunday dinner. James Marshall who discovered gold was a close friend of Grandma Gray. He visited her a lot. She was my father's mother. Father knew Marshall, too.

"Coloma was a good sized town then . . . I remember a lot of families that lived there. You know, when you're a kid you remember. I knew the Thomases, the Smiths, the Stearn's, the Mitchells, the Elgys and Kanes, and Schultz, the Gallaghers and Howells . . . I remember them all . . . Edgar DeLory and the Papinis . . . there is only one girl left now, Virginia. She comes up every summer to run their resort, the Mount Pleasant Resort. I can remember the Chinese taking gold out of the Papini place even then. Then there were the Monroes and the Burgess boys."

She recalled the time John Wagner, who owned a store, almost drowned when the bridge crossing the creek went down. "He was returning from Shingle Springs with his four-horse team freight wagon loaded with supplies for the store. The horses and all went down the creek. And then down by Greenwood Creek, that's three or four miles down on the way to Pilot Hill, Levi Darrington was moving cattle and he was in the wagon with the supplies for the drive when Greenwood Creek bridge went down with him. The river and creeks around here were bad when they were high."

She remembered the days when there were tramps in the county. "Men would come to the back door of the hotel and ask for something to eat. Mama always had a big wood pile out back and she'd tell them to go cut up a few pieces of wood while she got them something. She always fed them . . . she never let anyone go away hungry."

When asked how she met her husband, Archie, she said, "Well, I had a boy friend in Sacramento and he was up to see me. We were out on the front porch and Archie Lawyer and Henry Bacchi rode up. Henry said, 'Irma, don't you want to go for a ride with Lawyer?' I said, 'Sure,' so Henry helped me up on his horse and away Archie and I went. When we got back, this boy from Sacramento said, 'Well . . . I thought I had picked a peach but I guess I got a lemon.' That was the last I ever saw of him." Asked if she had any other romances, she said slowly and with a smile, "Oh, yes, lots of them."

THIS PLAQUE IS DEDICATED TO THE MEMORY OF
RAYMOND E. LAWYER
SUPERVISOR 4TH DISTRICT EL DORADO COUNTY
WHO WAS INSTRUMENTAL IN THE PLANNING OF THIS
GOVERNMENT COMPLEX. THE STONE IN THESE WALLS
CAME FROM THE 100 YEAR OLD WALLS ON HIS PROPERTY
AT PILOT HILL. HIS UNTIMELY DEATH PREVENTED
HIS PARTICIPATION IN THESE DEDICATION CEREMONIES.
1976

204

John Winning Photos

205

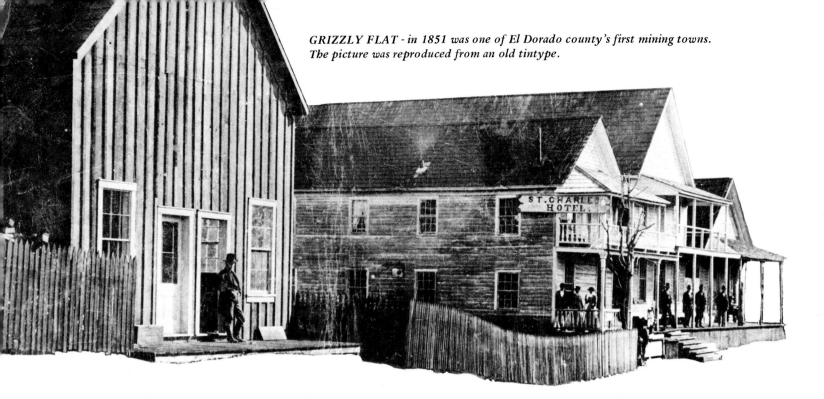

GRIZZLY FLAT - in 1851 was one of El Dorado county's first mining towns. The picture was reproduced from an old tintype.

Father Mined at Grizzly

Cora Voss Myer was born in Grizzly Flat in 1886. She remembers Grizzly Flat as a busy mining town. Her father, William Voss, was a miner and worked for the Mt. Pleasant mine, where he was superintendent of the Gravel mine for years. She explained that the Mt. Pleasant was a company mine which included the Gravel and Eagle King mines. Mrs. Myer, the daughter of Josephine and William Voss, was 89 years of age when interviewed on May 27, 1975 at the home of her daughter, Lorene Myer Mitchell, on Pleasant Valley Road, east of Diamond Springs. She said she could not tell much about her grandparents because she never knew them, and because her mother did not talk much about family. "Well, maybe she did, but you know, when you're little you don't pay any attention to grownup talk." She also explained that her grandmother had died when her mother was only four years old, so her mother barely remembered her.

Mrs. Myer said that she and her brother, Willie, attended the Grizzly Flat school and added, "They had sixty scholars and one teacher. The teacher taught all grades but didn't get paid very much. I heard they got $60 a month. I know that's all Sarah Darlington got. Sarah Darlington was the sister of the Mr. Darlington who has that old farm at the bottom of Texas Hill on Cedar Ravine Road."

THE DIAMOND HOTEL when Anton and Katherine Myer owned and operated the hostelry. Those identified in the picture are, from left: Louis Myer (on horse), Jerry O'Leary, William Voss, (an unidentified man), Anton Myer, Katherine Myer, and (an unidentified woman, employee at the hotel). Picture taken in 1920.

The Darlington two-story ranch house burned in 1976. The barn, more than 100 years old, is being torn down by the El Dorado County Historical Museum. Its hewn timbers, square nails, and other metal attachments will be salvaged and preserved.

206

(Inset) CORA AND WILLIE VOSS of Grizzly Flat

ANTON AND KATHERINE MYER

Photos Cora Myer Collection

Mrs. Myer couldn't recall exactly how large the town of Grizzly Flat was when she lived there, but she did remember: "There were two dance halls; sometimes there would be a dance in both halls on the same night. All they did was stand out in the street and yell, 'Dance tonight at So and So's,' and they had a crowd. The children, too — we all danced when we were tots. My childhood friend, Georgia Nail, and I used to dress up and go to the dances. I remember we'd put vanilla flavoring on for perfume. Georgia and I used to have good times. Her mother was real strict . . . one thing I always remembered . . . she told me that when she was naughty she had to go out and cut the switch she was to be punished with. We'd get into mischief, but we weren't really bad, just mischievous. There was one thing we did that we shouldn't have . . . when we got tired at the dances, we'd go out and sneak back of the house of a cranky old lady that lived there, and we'd throw rocks on her roof to scare her. We didn't mean any harm. One day we heard her son tell a man that he had his gun loaded, and if he caught anyone throwing rocks at his house, he was going to shoot. Well, we didn't do that anymore.

"Georgia and I had lots of good times together. I always felt sad for Georgia. She never had a father — he was drowned at Bucks Bar before she was born. He drowned in December and she was born in June. The water was high and he was warned, but he didn't heed the warning. You see, it was December and he wanted to get things for Christmas and all. I remember hearing them tell about it . . . that her father bought baby clothes that were to be for Georgia and afterwards they found all these little baby clothes floating down the river. Georgia was a strong girl and she wasn't afraid of anything. She had to do all the chores and chop wood. They had a daily stage at that time. It wouldn't get in until nine o'clock at night so she'd have to be there to get the mail, and that's when we almost always got into mischief. Her last name was Nail. She had a sister Hattie; I think there was eight years difference in their ages. Her mother didn't marry again until eight years after Georgia's father drowned. She married John Smith, but then she took sick and died on the operating table. When she died, Mr. Smith had the Nail place, but he had it put back in Georgia's name but she didn't take it. He was a good man. He lived on Oak Hill and he had two brothers, Andrew and Frank. They were real old-timers and well known around here.

"A man named Hoskins owned the store and just about everything else at Grizzly Flat. He used to haul logs by oxen right down past our house. The roads were always deep with dust and when they came down, the dust just rolled in as they went by.

"We lived at Caldor for a while, too, before it burned. I used to walk from Caldor to Grizzly. Then there was the time my brother Willie shot himself . . . it was an accident. He was out looking after the cattle over at Capps Crossing, he had his gun with him and somehow he set his gun down, but his hand was over the muzzle and it went off and shot his fingers off . . . on both hands. It was awful in those days . . . no doctors . . . if you could get one he had to come out by horse and buggy and that took hours. Well, Willie's wife, Maggie, wrapped his hands as best she could, got him on the one and only horse there, and headed the horse for Grizzly, to our home. When he got there, Dad got Dr. Reckers to come up and he took him to Placerville to the Sanatorium. Poor Maggie, she walked with their three little ones from Capps Crossing to Grizzly through the night to get to our house.

"Another terrible thing happened there. Some men got into an argument in a saloon there on Main Street and they went out into the street and one was stabbed. His name was Ed Stafford. I saw him under the trees where he died. They didn't find the man who killed him for a long time. They had a trial and all, and he got out of it . . . said it was 'self defense'."

The incident she remembered occurred shortly after she married Anton Myer in 1904. Mr. Myer was a miner and worked in the mines all his life. Three of the couple's four children, George, Alfred, and Leslie, were born in Grizzly Flat. Their daughter, Lorene, was born in Diamond Springs where Mr. Myer's parents, Kate and Anton Myer, owned and operated the Diamond Hotel. She mentioned the many times she had visited the hotel, the room she had slept in, and the meals served by the Myers.

"I know that living in those years was a lot different than now. I think they managed better than we do today . . . most every family had a vegetable bin. They grew their vegetables and put them in this bin . . . carrots, rutabagas . . . everything they grew they put in the bin, covered them with dirt, and that's the way they stored them for the winter. And if they didn't make their own butter, they bought it by the keg. They always bought enough flour and beans to last through the winter . . . and that's the way they lived . . . not like today. You couldn't run to a store and buy a can of this or that. Besides, you couldn't get out most of the time because of the roads. Yes, it was a lot different, I would say."

Photo Cora Myer Collection

GRIZZLY FLAT SCHOOL in 1896 - Sixty children were enrolled in the one-room school with one teacher teaching all grades. Cora Voss was ten years old when this picture was taken. She identified all she could remember, left to right, front row: Willie Martin, John M......, (two small girl visitors unidentified), Artie Hanson, Clarence Berry, Ira McDonald, Theresa Bonham, Marvel Edner, Flossy McDona.., Lizzie Lyon and Elvira McDonald. In the second row, left to right: Eugene Martin, Ned Morey, Irving McAfee, Willie Bonham, Charles Martin, Herbie Me..more, Harvey Wentz, Bert Edner, C.. l Myer, Willie Voss, Frank Martin and Euge.. Martin. In the third row, left to right: Gracie Martin, Louie Berry, Nellie Martin, Lloyd Fisher, Maude Odlin, Willie Henson, Lucy Martin and Marian Odlin. In the back row, from left: the teacher Mr. C. E. Peters, Edgar Odlin, Lizzie Kefer, Emma Kefer, Mary Kefer, Sadie Bonham, Elva Odlin, Hattie Nail, Alice Berry, Minnie Lyon, Georgia Nail, May Morey, Cora Voss, and Walter McAfee. The gentleman in back of McAfee was Mrs. Cora Voss's father, William Voss.

MURDER INVESTIGATION - The boxes in the road were placed there by the sheriff of El Dorado County while investigating the fatal stabbing of Stafford that occurred in the saloon across the street from the Joe Lyon store.

ANTON MYER FAMILY - Identified are, in the back row, from left: Anton Myer, Jr., Nellie Myer (Webster), Emil and Carl Myer. In the middle row, from left: Louie, Mary Myer (Stafford), Rose Myer (Perry), and Alice Myer (Simpson). In front: Katherine and Anton Myer. Child is Louie Stafford.

WHAT SPECIAL EVENT brought the gentlemen of Grizzly Flat together to be photographed has long been forgotten but Georgia Leoni, in 1975, remembered them to be (back row from left) Ed Stafford, Francis Meyers, A. A. McDonald and John Juckes. (Center row from left) Charles Edner, Frank McAfee and Albert Meyers. (Front row from left) Will Stafford, C. E. Peters and Joseph Meyers.

Photos Georgia Leoni Collection

209

Leoni Meadows

Georgia Nail Leoni was born June 1, 1885 in Grizzly Flat at the home of Mr. and Mrs. Frank McAfee, where her mother was living following the death of her husband. George Nail had drowned in the Cosumnes River in December of 1884. Mr. Nail was returning from the town of El Dorado, where he had taken his wife and young daughter, Hattie, to stay with relatives, away from the snow and the severe winter weather of the Grizzly Flat area. There had been heavy rains and the Cosumnes was running high. When he attempted to cross the river at Buck's Bar on the return trip home, he, the team, and the wagon were swept away in the raging waters. His body was found two weeks later. Georgia, born six months later, never knew her father.

She attended the Grizzly Flat school and in 1910 she married Stephen Leoni, son of Stefano and Tresa Leoni, natives of Switzerland who came to California in the 1860's. In 1868, the Leonis homesteaded land in the vicinity of Grizzly Flat and through the years developed their 1040-acre ranch into a landmark known today as Leoni Meadows. They raised cattle and garden produce, much of which was shipped as far away as San Francisco. One year there was a friendly feud among the neighbors and a considerable wager was made as to who could grow the largest cabbage. Leoni produced a 60-pound cabbage, ending the dispute and collecting the wager.

When interviewed on April 15, 1975, Georgia Leoni was living at the Hill Top Manor Guest Home in Placerville. During our visit she referred to many of the old photographs she had saved through the years, and laughed at the style of clothing worn in earlier days. She talked about friends who were members of the Three Forks Grange and spoke about the many good times she had at the Grange Hall in Fairplay. "There are not too many living now," said the 90-year-old Mrs. Leoni, and added that she looked forward to visits from her friends.

(Inset) GEORGIA LEONI

MT. PLEASANT MINERS - George W. Nail (circled in upper right) drowned in the Cosumnes River at Buck's Bar in December of 1884. He was the father of Georgia Nail Leoni who was born June 1, 1885 at the home of her uncle Frank McAfee.

Photos Georgia Leoni Collection

210

Photo Georgia Leoni Collection

STEFANO AND TRESA LEONI (seated) came to California in 1860. In 1868 they homesteaded land in the vicinity of Grizzly Flat. They farmed and raised cattle and established what today (1975) is known as Leoni Meadows. This photograph was taken in September of 1910, the day their son, Stephen (right) married Miss Georgia Nail (center). Their older son, Herman (left) was the best man at the wedding.

Lucile Watters Recalls

THE FAIRCHILD FAMILY, 1895 - Mahlon Dickerson Fairchild (center) arrived in San Francisco in 1849. He pioneered in mining, newspaper publishing and business enterprises throughout the Mother Lode. Identified with him in the picture are, from left: Bertha Ellen, Julia Deborah, Mary E. Milam Fairchild, Mahlon D. Jr., Mahlon D. Sr., William F., Emma Elizabeth and Mary Caroline.

In 1840, when Mahlon Dickerson Fairchild was thirteen years of age, he was an apprentice on his father's newspaper in New York. On March 15, 1849, he left New York with his father on the steamer "Crescent City" for Chagres. From there they went by native boat through the Isthmus of Panama. On May 9th they boarded the whaling ship "Sylph" for San Francisco and the mining fields of El Dorado County. This and other information about the pioneer Fairchild family was contributed by Lucile Marjorie Watters, granddaughter of Mahlon D. Fairchild.

In 1852, he returned to New York with his father, who remained there two more years, but Mahlon returned immediately to California with his two brothers, Oscar and Theodore. There the three became involved in hydraulic mining. In 1859, they were publishing the semi-weekly *Observer* in Placerville. Mahlon D. Fairchild married Mary Emma Milam in 1865, and in 1869 they moved to Nevada, where he took up hydraulic mining at Treasure Hill, went into the lumber business, and ran the *Silver Bend Reporter* at Belmont, Nevada.

Miss Watters said, "After his marriage, my grandfather continued his mining activities in White Pine, Austin, Treasure City, and other towns in Nevada, practically all of which have become ghost towns. From Nevada, my grandparents moved to Georgetown, in El Dorado County, and here they lived for about twelve years. My grandfather engaged in hydraulic mining at Mount Gregory, which was a few miles above Georgetown.

Miss Watters remembered one story in which her grandmother, Mary Emma Milam, played an important part. It happened when the Milam family was crossing the plains in their ox-drawn covered wagon. They were part of a 35-family wagon train leaving Illinois for California in 1852. Her grandmother was fourteen years old and her brother, Gerald, who delighted in teasing his sister, was sixteen. An incident that could have resulted in serious trouble with Indians was brought about by Gerald's teasing.

"The trip had been a hard one, so it was decided they would camp for a time. Early one morning a young Indian came to the encampment. He was friendly and stayed only a short time before riding off in the direction of Gerald and his sister, who were some distance from the rest of the party. Gerald, being in one of his teasing moods, gestured and pointed to his sister, saying, 'Wouldn't she make a fine squaw?' The Indian, thinking Gerald had given him the girl, started to

FRANK HA. WATTERS - father of Lucile Watters

BERTHA E. FAIRCHILD WATTERS - mother of Lucile Watters

(Inset) LUCILE WATTERS

FRANKIE PLUMADO FAIRCHILD was the daughter of El Dorado county pioneers Mr. and Mrs. Frank Plumado. She was born at Reservoir Hill December 11, 1861. She attended the public schools and the Conklin Academy in Placerville. She married William Fairchild in 1885. She became well-known in the state for her courageous stands on matters of California history, especially the preservation of early landmarks.

JOHN LIMPINSEL, Placerville grocer, was a tenant in the second building erected by W. F. Fairchild shortly after 1911. The first Fairchild building, located at 465 Main street, is said to have been built with the money Mr. Fairchild obtained from gold he found when excavating the building site. The two Fairchild buildings on Main street remain as evidence of the Fairchild contribution to the improvement and growth of the mining town of Placerville.

take her with him. They both tried to explain it was all a joke, but the Indian became insistent. When the situation started to get completely out of hand, the Indian no doubt realized that if they were overheard, the commotion would bring a number of men, so he left peacefully.

"The two terrified youngsters rushed to the covered wagon and told their parents what had happened. Their mother quickly had her daughter change into some of Gerald's clothes and gave her a boy's haircut. Then, appearing as a boy, Mary climbed down from the family wagon, and stayed outside for a brief time where she could be seen working along with the men and boys. A hiding place was hastily prepared in one of the wagons and she was then hidden away.

"As soon as they could get the wagon train ready, they started off. After two days of hard travel, the Indian reappeared, accompanied by a number of his tribesmen. The Indians demanded the girl that the young Indian now considered his own. They told the Indians she was killed in an accident, and, after much explaining, finally convinced them she was dead. Nevertheless, the Indians followed the wagon train for several days. After they departed, Grandma stayed in hiding for about two weeks.

"Before the wagon train arrived in Utah Territory, Grandma's father became desperately ill and showed no signs of improvement by the time they arrived there. The other members of the party continued on to California, and the family remained behind in Utah in an attempt to nurse Great-grandfather back to health, but it was too late. He lived only a short time. Great-grandmother and the children, stranded in Mormon country and unable to make the trip to California by themselves, had to settle there for a time."

Mary married a Mr. Brassfield while living there and had two children. Before her second child was born, her husband, who, like herself, was not a Mormon, was shot and killed as they were about to leave for California. After her son's birth, Mary obtained the protection of the United States troops and left Utah Territory for Nevada. In 1865, she married Mahlon D. Fairchild.

On January 24, 1898, the *Mountain Democrat* published a Souvenir Edition commemorating the fiftieth anniversary of the gold discovery. A section devoted to "Prominent Persons and Places" included a description of William Francis Fairchild, son of Mahlon D. Fairchild. "W.F. Fairchild is one of Placerville's self-made men. He was born in Salt Lake City and came to California when four years of age. His business education has been obtained in active commerce of life. He worked 10 years for Dr. B.F. Shepherd of Georgetown, he studied pharmacy and in 1885 bought out the City Drug store, upon the corner of Coloma and Main Streets, in Placerville, in the brick block which was erected over the stump of the tree used by the Vigilantes in '49. He subsequently studied medicine under Drs. Dryer and Wrenn, simply to be a more complete master of his profession. In 1883 he married Miss F.A. Plumado . . . who was to become a leader in womens' clubs, and a well known author of historical articles."

Photo Yohalem Collection

213

Joe Rupley, Stage Driver

When big Joe Rupley headed his team down Main Street in Placerville yelling, "All aboard for Rupley ranch," the sound of his booming voice, the beating of horses' hoofs, and the clatter of the big wagon wheels brought all ranch hands, who had come to town with him, flying out of the doors of stores, saloons, or "wherever" to get aboard when Rupley made his swing around the Bell Tower heading back to the ranch. They knew that if they didn't make it, they would be left behind and would have to walk to the ranch, some five miles from town. This and other stories were told when fifteen descendants of John W. and Jane Rupley met at the home of Francis and Phyllis Rupley Snyder in Pleasant Valley, where they spent an afternoon reminiscing. Seven of those present were Rupleys by birth, the others by marriage.

John Wesley Rupley, his wife, Jane McNeil Rupley, and their sons, Theodore, Wesley, and Jacob, left Marion, Ohio, in September of 1849. They traveled in ox-drawn wagons with a train that included 150 miners walking to get to California and, hopefully, gold. Their son Theodore walked the distance while his brother Jacob drove one of the ox teams. They were one year following the Oregon Trail and arrived in California just prior to its becoming a state on September 9, 1850, thereby making John Wesley Rupley eligible to be recognized as a territorial pioneer in California history.

The 1849 trip was not the last for the Rupleys. They went back to Ohio and returned to California in 1852, again by wagon train, bringing with them fig trees, shrubs, and seeds for their new home. They traveled through Modoc County, where they bought horses from the Indians. With a stud named Shocklee and a mare named Tunesee, the Rupleys started breeding their own horses. Mrs. Rupley, a native of Oklahoma, was one-half Cherokee Indian and one-half Scotch descent. Before long, other settlers were calling upon her to act as interpreter in their negotiations with the Indians in the area.

In time the Rupley family grew. A daughter, Columbia, and three sons, William, George, and Joseph, were born at the ranch.

Mabel Rupley Ranier, a granddaughter of John Wesley and Jane Rupley, and a daughter of William and Mary Rupley, was nearing her 82nd birthday on the day of the interview, and those present looked to her for information about the earlier generations of Rupleys.

She said that she had been born in her grandmother's home on the Rupley homestead, located in the vicinity of Merryman's Corner.

JOHN WESLEY RUPLEY - A descendant of Jaco[b] Rupley, who came to America in 1743 to escape religious persecution in Russia. The Rupleys settl[ed] in Pennsylvania.

JANE McNEIL RUPLEY, wife of John Wesley Rupley, was a native of Oklahoma. Of Cherokee and Scotch descent, she was seven feet tall, weighe[d] four hundred pounds, and spoke seven languages and Indian dialects.

INDIAN HATTIE told the Rupleys about trouble between the white men and the Indians when she was a little girl. One day her mother hid her in the woods and told her not to move. She came back the next day and said the white men had driven off the Indians. The Indians started back to Carson Valley, but there was a storm...in the spring they were found frozen to death. They say that is how Desolation Valley got its name.

214

GRACE E.
FARNSWORTH
Sister of Clarinda
Farnsworth
Jerrett

Photo
Phyllis Snyder
Collection

JOSEPH RUPLEY (seated) with his three sons
(from left): Elmer O., Fred A., and Charles J.

CLARA
JERRETT
RUPLEY
Wife of
Charles Rupley
and mother of
Phyllis Rupley
Snyder

EMMA
MEYERS
AND LAVINA
OLSEN, who
became Mrs.
Amelio Celio
and Mrs. Joseph
Rupley respectively,
at a double wedding
at the Meyers Hotel
in Camino.

The ranch property started at Merryman's and followed the Newtown road east for more than a mile, on the north side of the road. She remembered her mother saying that after she married in 1880, when they lived on the ranch, the place resembled an Indian reservation. Every year, nearly one thousand Digger Indians camped on the ranch and surrounding foothills. Phyllis Snyder said that it was a tradition in the Rupley family to "let the Indians live." She pointed out that their immigrant ancestor, Jacob Rupley, who arrived in Philadelphia in 1743, had refused all pressure from local authorities and neighbors to order the Indians from his vast Pennsylvania land holdings.

Mrs. Ranier continued by telling the group about the day the old home burned. "My grandfather was about a mile away cutting wood. I heard George hollering for help and saw the smoke, so I ran to the house. I took Ruth, Joseph's invalid wife, out of her wheel chair and set her down in the corral. Then I put the babies, Genevieve and Little Joe, in the wheel chair. George and I got them away from the fire."

She remembered walking five miles to go to school at Smith Flat. "It was two and a half miles there and the same back. Papa didn't send me to school until I was nine years old. My brother Albert and I always had work to do before school and then again when we got home. We didn't have any time to play in those days.

"When I got older I went to dances. I liked to dance. At first we went in the horse and buggy but later I had my horse and I rode horseback to the dances . . . most of them were held at Smith Flat, Buck's Bar, or Diamond Springs. We'd dance from nine o'clock at night 'til three or four in the morning. It was always daylight when we got home."

She remembered the toll road at the end of the property. "It went to Lake Tahoe and on to Carson Valley. The one to Carson went right by Grandfather's old home. They didn't have a toll gate until Mr. Wiley came there. If I remember rightly, they charged two and a half dollars for a horse and five dollars for a wagon. And they served breakfast for two and a half and dinner for five. It was a lot of money in those days but, you see, they didn't pay in money, they paid with gold dust mostly, and they measured it by the amount you could pick up between your thumb and your forefinger. With Grandmother Jane, it was a good pinch."

When asked about John Wesley and Jane Rupley's children, who perpetuated the Rupley name in the West, she named them one by one. She said, "Theodore devoted his life to mining. The mining claims he made on the farm he turned over to his father. Then he went to Nevada, to Genoa, and to Mexico; he mined all over the country. He finally married and came back to El Dorado County and lived across from where the Carriage Room is now. Wesley never married. He died when he was very young. He got over-heated trying to get some stock into the corral and drank cold water and died. He was the first member of the family to be buried on the ranch. After that, Grandmother moved up to the toll road.

215

"Nobody knows what happened to Jacob. He fought with my father William over a violin. He threw Father's violin in the fire and burned it. They had a terrible fight and Jacob threatened to kill Father. He took a shot at him and just grazed his head, then Jake (Jacob) took off. They didn't hear of him until years later when a woman wrote, saying that he had died. She could have been his wife, I don't know. That was down in San Bernardino.

"William, my father, stayed on the ranch. There were four children. Mary Maude, my sister, died when she was twelve from drinking well water. She turned yellow as gold. They said it was yellow jaundice then but now they call it hepatitis. She was buried on the ranch by the big rock."

George was on the ranch early but went to Mill Valley. Their daughter, Columbia, was born on the ranch. She married twice. "Her first husband, Mr. Beck, died, leaving her with a child, Violet Mae Beck, now dead and buried in the Rupley cemetery. She later married Bert Holliday, who was a blacksmith at Grizzly Flat. They had three children, a son, John and twins, Herbert and Venita Mae. Venita grew up and married Guy Wentworth and was known as Nettie Wentworth.

"Joseph was a fine stage driver. Before there were any trains he used to drive stage from Sacramento to Carson City. They changed horses every twenty miles. He married four different times. His first wife was a local girl, Charles Olsen's daughter, Lavina. Lavina and Joseph, and Emma Meyers and Armenio J. Celio were married in a big double wedding at Meyer's Hotel. Lavina and Joe had sons, Charles, Joseph, Frederick, and Elmer. His second wife was Dora Bell Henwood. They were married July 23, 1890, by the Reverend C.C. Peirce. She left him and he married Mary Parr. I guess he met her over in Nevada. I heard them talk about it . . . she didn't live around here. She took a liking to someone working on the ranch, a man from Grizzly Flat, so she up and left Joe and went to Eureka with him. We heard from her once, that was when the man she ran off with was killed. A train ran over him.

"Then he married Ruth Kyser. She was his last wife. He and Ruth had four children. The first two died and are buried on the ranch by the big rock. The two that lived were Genevieve and Joe. They called him Little Joe. Ruth died and before their father Joseph died he made arrangements for them to go to the Mooseheart school in Illinois." During the conversation it was pointed out that Genevieve and Little Joe have visited the family here several times.

Albert Rupley, Jr., a grandson of Joseph Rupley, and son of Fay Cannon, remembered hearing his uncles Charley and John, and his father tell stories about his grandfather. "When they went hunting or fishing I used to go with them. I remember them saying he'd come through Placerville with four horses . . . run them as fast as they could go around the Tower. There'd be a cloud of dust in the summer and a sheet of mud when it rained. And, on election day . . . years ago they paid the stage companies to haul men to town to vote. This one time,

TESTING THE STANLEY STEAMERS - When pro
carriages Joe Rupley reluctantly turned to the new
steamers were tried out...the salesmen are easily ide
on the test trip to Lake Taboe, about 1907. Friend
left: John B. Rupley, Elmer O. Rupley, Hazel Rupl
Sacramento, Mr. Malone, Joseph Rupley, Albert Ru
from Sacramento, Clara W. Rupley, wife of Charles
Burgess, who drove the stage for Rupley, Charles Bu
mother of Clara Jerrett Rupley.

RUPLEY BROTHERS John and Albert Rupley, in
to baul mine lagging out to pasture and bought a n
pieces. The men standing on the tractor wheel wer
not identified.

Photo Theodore Rupley Collection

*nanded the farewell to horse-drawn stage
of transportation, the automobile. Two
ecause they wore the popular auto dusters
nily members who made the trip are, from
•ife of Elmer, Rube Levi, auto dealer from
•arles J. Rupley, Mr. Arnold, a salesman
•heel. In the back seat, left to right: Todd
•rville music teacher, and Clarinda Jerrett,*

Joe went to Pino Grande to get a load of voters. On the way down, there were nine passengers and nine bottles of whiskey. With the brakes off and the horses flying, he made about two turns and the stage turned over. It threw everybody out, but they were all so drunk nobody got hurt except Grandpa. He had a big black eye.

They laughed as they told how people called Joe Rupley the busiest man in El Dorado County, saying, "If he owed you money and he met you on the street, he'd say, 'Hello there. Say, I owe you some money, don't I? Well, you know, I've got it right here in my pocket but I'm too busy to give it to you today.' And down the street he'd go."

It was true. Joe Rupley was a busy man and so were his sons who grew up to work with him. They operated seven or eight stage lines in the county, they mined, raised cattle, bought timber land and logged, operated saw mills, and hauled freight. Then the time came when the family noted a change in Grandpa Rupley. He didn't "tear into" new challenges, he didn't joke as much, and he didn't laugh as much.

His grandchildren said it was because of the automobile. When bids for stage lines in the county were opened in 1909 or 1910, Joe Rupley lost out to Al Richardson of Lake Tahoe, who operated a stage line with Pierce Arrow automobiles at the Lake. Rupley faced up to the inevitable and purchased two Stanley Steamers and a White Steamer, but that did not get him the contract. "He wasn't ready in time, and he never got over it," said Albert. "But he insisted, to the very last, that he drove the last horse and buggy and the first Stanley Steamer over the summit." Joseph Rupley died in 1920.

*ut the eight- and ten-horse teams they had used
•actor. The load being hauled carried 9000
•ied as Rupley brothers. The other men were*

Photo Fay R. Cannon Collection

217

The Girl Next Door

Fay Cannon, a Rupley by marriage, told the story of the pioneer Jones family. She said that her grandfather, Fleming Jones, was born in 1850, before his parents, Minerva and Napoleon Jones, came to El Dorado County from Wisconsin in 1851. Her father, William Albian Jones (called Al), was born on the Jones ranch on Newtown Road. He married Emma Kern, who was born in Placerville on Cedar Ravine Road. They moved to Smith Flat, where Fay was born.

"It was just a few years back that they dismantled the old Smith Flat school and hauled it away. My mother and father went there. My husband, A.J. Rupley, and our two children, Albert Joseph and Mary Jane, went there, too, but it's gone now. I went to the old grammar school up on the hill back of the Episcopal Church on Coloma Street. It's gone, too.

"I was three years old when my parents moved to Placerville from Smith Flat. When I was ten, we moved to Colusa, where my father managed a butcher shop and cold storage place. When I was fifteen, Mother and Father divorced and I came back to Placerville to live with my father and grandparents on the Jones homestead, across the road from the Rupley homestead."

She said her grandparents, Fleming and Florence Jones, pioneered at Audrain Lake near Lake Tahoe where they dairied in the summer, selling butter and beef to shops in Placerville. After leaving Lake Audrain they moved to the Silver Creek area, now called Crystal Basin. They built their dwelling, a horse barn, hay barn, milk house, and corral out of peeled logs. "The old milk house was still standing when we were up there last. The middle fork of Silver Creek is still called 'Jones' Silver' on the map."

When she talked about Placerville, Mrs. Cannon said, "The sidewalks were just planks, two planks side by side, and the crossings were in about the same place they are today. In the middle of town you could almost jump across, it was so narrow. Then there's the old Inch Building where George Duffey has been for so many years. There used to be a telephone office in there. And I remember the O'Donnell residence. They had a beautiful garden and lovely home right there in the heart of town. Then there were the saloons. I think we counted twenty-seven at one time, right on Main Street. When we were coming home from school there would be fights, the pianos going — you never heard such noise. Many a time we'd pass just when they would pitch a drunk out on the sidewalk. It was some town."

When asked about mining and mines, she said she had two mines, The Lone Star and the Hazel Creek, a mine that during 1947 and 1948 produced $2 million. In 1965 the Mountain Copper Company explored the mine but said it was not a big enough operation for them.

MR. AND MRS. WILLIAM ALBIAN JONES - The groom was the son of Fleming Jones, his bride Miss Emma Kern of Cedar Ravine, Placerville. They married in November of 1892.

AUDRAIN LAKE in the mountains near Tahoe where Fleming and Florence built their home, a barn, milk house and corral out of peeled logs in 1869. Only the milk house remains.

218

Photos Fay R. Cannon Collection

AL JONES, son of Fleming Jones (left) is pictured with the butcher, Mr. Walch and a family friend Will Koletzke in front of one of two butcher shops opened in Placerville by Fleming Jones. Picture taken about 1895.

ROBERT
LAUREN JONES
Son of
Fleming Jones

"They left the mine in beautiful shape," said Mrs. Cannon. "Then one Saturday night eight young men from Pollock Pines went up there and blew everything up — the mine, trucks, houses, everything. There was nothing left. It came out in the investigation that they stole some powder and fuse from the Timm mine over in Kelsey and took it to the Hazel Creek. We didn't even know the young men. It was proved that the eight were guilty, but nothing was ever done to them. They said they did it for kicks.

"There is one story Grandfather used to tell about a man named Mr. Parrot who owned a butcher shop in town. Grandfather had beautiful cattle, so he asked Mr. Parrot if he would buy beef from him and Parrot said "No." Grandfather asked him several times, but he always said "No." So one day Grandfather got in touch with a friend in Sacramento, one he had known when he had his butcher shop down there. He asked him to send him the best butcher he could find in Sacramento and he did. The man's name was Walch. He was a great butcher and sausage maker. Grandfather started a butcher shop and before long Mr. Parrot was out of business. Grandfather did so much business that he opened a second shop. He also had his slaughterhouse on the ranch and had wagon delivery routes around town.

"Another story I like . . . Grandfather liked to gamble. He had an interest in a bar at Grizzly Flat. In those days there was a lot of gambling going on. He came home one night with a great amount of money, put it down in front of Grandma, and said, "There, go build your new house." Grandmother was always afraid the old home was going to catch fire and burn. Every time she heard a crackling sound she'd run outside looking for a fire. In 1883 she built her new home of all clear lumber, not a knot in any of it. She had it built on the homestead where the first house was. It's ninety-three years old now and my son Albert Rupley, Jr., and his wife, Aileen, live there. We joke about it being the house that was built with gambling money."

As Fay Cannon talked, a girl-next-door romance came to light. She lived on her grandfather's homestead on Newtown Road, and Albert Rupley lived on his grandfather's homestead right across the road. In 1918 they were married.

"In 1929, Albert built the house I live in now. Being in the lumber business, he naturally wanted to build with lumber. The Rupleys were Pennsylvania Dutch, so I thought it would be nice to have a Dutch Colonial house. We built it on the site of the old Rupley home that burned. If you look out the window, you can see the old Jones home, where my son and his wife live.

"I lost my husband, Albert, in 1950, when he was struck by a car at Pollock Pines. He was sixty years old then, but he was as active in his business as he had been in earlier years. He had the A.J. Rupley Forest Products, logging operations, sawmills working all over. His death was a terrible shock to us and, of course, brought a great change in my life."

In 1970, Fay Rupley married Dale F. Cannon of Burbank, and they now divide their time between Placerville and Burbank.

BUILT WITH GAMBLING MONEY in 1883 the Jones home still stands on Newtown road and is occupied by the grandson of the man who gambled and won and built the home for his wife. It has stood for 93 years and is visible from Highway 50 in the Merryman valley.

Veerkamps Arrive in '52

Inez Veerkamp, daughter of Mia and Louis P. Veerkamp, was born in El Dorado County, where she has lived all her life. When interviewed at her home in Placerville, she recalled stories told by her father. However, she preferred to rely on P. Sioli's book, "History of El Dorado County," published in 1883, to provide information about her grandparents and great-grandparents. Her grandfather, Francis Joseph Arnold Veerkamp, was twelve years of age when he came to America from Hanover, Germany, with his parents, Bartholomew and Louisa Oelcker Veerkamp.

They first settled in Montgomery County, Ohio. In 1836 they moved to Lincoln County, Missouri. On April 11, 1852, Francis, his wife Louisa Tobener Veerkamp, and their year-old son, Henry, left by wagon train for California. He was thirty years old then and his wife was twenty-seven. They arrived in Hangtown on September 11, 1852. They stayed a short time in Uniontown, now Lotus, before settling at Granite Hill, now Gold Hill.

She said, "Grandfather didn't come out here to mine. He was a farmer and his interest was in agriculture." The original Veerkamp farm consisted of about 200 acres. Then in 1873 he bought 160 acres of the original Charles M. Graner land that Edward Schnell had purchased earlier, in 1869, when he started the Wakamatsu Tea and Silk Farm.

Francis "Frank" and Louisa Veerkamp had ten children. With the exception of Henry, all were born on the farm. By 1883 Veerkamp had established himself as one of the county's most successful farmers. He engaged in general farming and fruit growing. It was estimated he had about 20,000 vines and fruit trees. He was exceptionally successful in the sale of his produce. "I remember Father talking about the difficult times they had getting over Echo Summit. Grandfather hauled by horses, mules, and wagons then. That would have been in 1860. The road was nothing but a dirt trail over the summit. They made overnight stops at Kyburz, Pacific House, and Strawberry. The stopping places would be crowded with animals, wagons, and people . . . some going east with loaded wagons and others going west empty. He took his produce to Auburn, too, where it was shipped to San Francisco by railroad. During the midsummer months when the fruit was mature, he had his wagons delivering all around the county, and in the fall they took the dried fruit over the mountain to Carson Valley, Genoa, and Virginia City. I believe he even made trips to Bodie."

MEMBERS OF THE VEERKAMP FAMILY - Francis and Louisa Veerkamp are shown with six of their ten children. The four sons standing are, from left: Egbert, Francis J. (Frank), Berthold and William. Seated on right is Henry, their oldest son, and young Louis P., their youngest child. The picture was taken about 1895.

GOLD HILL SCHOOL - CLASS OF 1915-16 - The first six girls in the back row are, from left: Louise Enos, Irma Brandon, Florence Brandon, Frances Veerkamp, Gertrude Sweeney and Florence Veerkamp. The ten girl students in the third row are, from left: Etta Rogers, Ada Veerkamp, Dorothy Veerkamp, Elvira Marchini, Mary Sweeney, Elsie Veerkamp, Eugenia Marchini, Mabel Isaacson, Inez Veerkamp, Merna Anable, and teacher, James P. Brown. The eight boys in the second row are Clinton Veerkamp, Walter Daley, Arthur Isaacson, Roy Isaacson, Merton Anable, twin brother of Merna Anable, Raymond Johnson, James Sweeney, John Johnson, twin brother of Raymond Johnson. In the front row, from left are: Norbert Akin, Donald Veerkamp, Elwin Veerkamp, Leo Akin, Ernest Veerkamp and Maurice Veerkamp.

220

Photos Inez Veerkamp Collection

She said her mother's maiden name was Mai Amelia Bergantz. She was born in Nevada and was the oldest of thirteen children. When she expressed a wish to become a teacher, her family "saved and scraped together" enough money to send her up to the Stockton Business College. There she studied and returned to El Dorado County to take the county teacher's examination. "She began teaching in 1893," said Miss Veerkamp. "She taught at the Cold Springs school, the Newtown, Willow, and Gold Hill schools. Some of her younger sisters and brothers were her pupils. We used to laugh about her teaching all those kids for seven years and then getting married and raising eight of her own."

Inez and her sisters, Gladys and Ada, became teachers. Gladys taught for ten years, Ada for thirty-six and Inez for forty-one years . . . all in the El Dorado County schools. Counting the seven years that their mother taught, the Veerkamps devoted ninety-four years to teaching and earned the reputation of being the finest teachers in the county.

Today, Inez, who never married, is retired. Clinton is the father of three sons and continues to farm. Maurice, who has four sons, is retired. Elwin, the father of four, is engaged in farming and the cattle business. Ada, who married Martin Rose, is now a widow and has two boys. Gladys and her husband, Leo Akin, live on Gold Hill Road. Malcolm, father of two boys and one girl, remains in the dairy business on the old homestead. Muriel Veerkamp married Lee Roy Brown. She is a widow with three sons and makes her home in Placerville.

"We are the third generation," said Miss Veerkamp. "Now the children are the fourth, and there is every indication that the fifth generation of Veerkamps is on the way." She spoke of the family's interest in music. She remembered that she was ten years old when their parents bought a piano. Every Saturday they traveled with their father by horse and wagon into Placerville to take piano lessons. Later, when a Mrs. Pinther moved to Coloma from San Francisco, they took lessons from her. "She had another name," said Miss Veerkamp, "because she had a son named Rudolph Kunich. She finally married Henry Kane, a son of a pioneer family."

When asked about the Japanese who had started a tea and silk farm colony on land later bought by her grandfather, she said she knew very little about the history of the group. "I remember Father telling us when we were kids, he knew where the cocoonery was built, so they got that far along. They tried to grow the tea and mulberry trees, but they didn't do too well.

"Many news stories have played up the idea that Okei lived in the Veerkamp home for years. They came here in 1869 and she died in 1871, so it couldn't have been for such a long period of time that she lived with them. I used to hear my father and uncle talk about Matsunosuke . . . he worked for Grandpa. Dad always said he was a wonderful gardener. He lived until 1909. He's buried in the Coloma cemetery, but it's an unmarked grave."

222

WHEN FIVE JAPANESE DIGNITARIES visited the grave of Okei on March 17, 1966, the author covered the story for the Mountain Democrat and took this picture. Placing flowers at the grave is Ichiro Matsudaira, son of the former ambassador to the United States and chairman of the board of directors of the Bank of Tokyo Limited, Japan. Accompanying him on the pilgrimage were, from left: Zozo Ishimatsu, of San Jose, Soichi Nakatani, Sacramento, Dr. Terry T. Hayashi, of San Francisco and James Otagiri, of Tokyo, Japan. Placerville has chosen Warabi, Japan as its Sister City, and annual visits are now exchanged between the cities. A duplicate headstone of Okei's grave is enshrined on a park hillside outside Wakamatsu, Japan.

GOLD HILL SCHOOL, 1898 - On November 6, 1897, a cyclone struck Gold Hill, destroying the Gold Hill school house. Books and shake shingles were found as far away as Pleasant Valley. A report in the Mountain Democrat states that the school piano was left standing on the floor of the school; the rest of the building was blown away. The cyclone also destroyed Crawfords' barn, and moved their house off its foundation. It blew Lou Veerkamp's fruit house over. The teacher in the picture is Mai Bergantz, who later became Mrs. Louis Veerkamp. The girls are Maude Veerkamp and Cora Anable. Robert Veerkamp is seated.

Photo Inez Veerkamp Collection

The Story of the Wakamatsu Tea and Silk Farm of Gold Hill

On a hill overlooking the gold discovery town of Coloma is the grave of Okei San, a young Japanese girl who came to America with the first contingent of Japanese who, under the leadership of Edward Schnell, planned to establish a Japanese colony in America. They arrived at Gold Hill about June 8, 1869, bringing with them thousands of three-year-old mulberry trees, large quantities of bamboo roots, tea seeds, wax tree stock, grape seedlings and other seeds from their native land. Schnell had purchased 160 acres of land from Charles M. Graner, adjacent to the Veerkamp farm. It was the start of the Wakamatsu Tea and Silk Farm of Gold Hill. All went well for a time and there was every indication that the farm would be a success. Then the scarcity of irrigation water, lack of funds, and failure of financial assistance to come from Japan as promised doomed the pioneer project in less than two years. Schnell left the colony with his Japanese wife and two children, promising to get funds and return. He never did. The settlers sold their valuables while waiting for Schnell. When they realized he was not going to return, some returned to Japan and others left the settlement to find employment elsewhere. Only Matsunosuke Sakurai and Okei San remained. The Veerkamp family employed Matsunosuke to work on their farm, and Okei became a housemaid. It is said she frequently climbed up the hill to watch the setting sun and gaze in the direction of her homeland. Okei died in 1871 at the age of nineteen.

— John Winning Photo

Betty Yohalem Photo

A Day to Remember

Being in the right place at the right time resulted in getting an interview that was totally unexpected. While Mr. Henry Morey, of Placerville, was being interviewed, he received a telephone call from a long-time friend, Mr. Rhoads Grimshaw, of Auburn. Mr. Grimshaw, at the age of 83, was the nation's oldest licensed helicopter pilot. He had just landed his 'copter' at the Placerville airport and invited Henry and his wife Anita to "fly down to Sam's with me for some apple pie." Instead, Mr. Morey drove to the airport and brought Mr. Grimshaw to the Morey home, where he joined in the interview. "After all," said Mr. Morey, "Grimshaw's grandfather, William Daylor, was one of the three men who founded this town."

Prior to Mr. Grimshaw's telephone call, Mr. Morey had said that his grandfather, Henry Sylvester Morey, was a shipbuilder by trade. He and his wife, Ellen Maria Snow Morey, traveled west from Maine by wagon train in the early 1860's.

They came directly to El Dorado County and settled in Placerville, where he started a flour mill. "When the mill burned, he took over a foundry on Main and Canal Street," said Henry Morey. "They made anything and everything that was made of iron, such as stamp mills and stoves. He made the rims for the wheels on Studebaker's wheelbarrows. Our father later worked with Grandfather in the foundry, where they turned out lots of work for Pino Grande and the Southern Pacific Railway.

The Moreys had three children, Frank Henry, Arthur S., and a daughter, Lillian. All were born in Placerville and attended local schools. Frank H. Morey married Maude Ruoff Stone of Amador county. Their three children, Henry, Evalyn, and Dorothy, were born in Placerville and, like their father, attended school there. Today, Henry is married to the former Anita Derham of Oakland, California. They have one daughter, Dorothy Burnett of Placerville. Evalyn married Mr. Norman Chamberlain. They make their home in Placerville and have one son, Daniel Morey Chamberlain. Dorothy Morey married Alex A. Flink and lives in Mexico.

When Mr. Grimshaw arrived, the conversation turned to stories about the old Morey Foundry and Mr. Grimshaw's relatives. At one point, when Morey talked about a Victory Ball Mill (stamp mill) built

RHOADS GRIMSHAW - The oldest licensed helicopter pilot in the United States. This picture was taken in 1973 when he was 83 years of age.

Photo Grimshaw Family Collection

(Inset) HENRY MOREY - at age three years

224

HENRY S. and
ELLEN MARIA
MOREY at home
in Placerville.

EVALYN and
HENRY MOREY
at ages eight and
three.

DOROTHY MOREY

MAUDE
RUOFF STONE
of Plymouth
became Mrs.
Henry F. Morey.

HENRY FRANKLIN
MOREY

Photos Morey Family Collection

at the Morey Foundry, Grimshaw said, "I don't know if you'd re-member, Henry, but I bought a stamp mill that your folks made and sold to a company that was mining chrome at Rattlesnake Bar on the American River. I bought it from the Noble Electric Steel Company when they stopped mining chrome in 1918, and, do you know, some junk dealer went down there and blew it to pieces and hauled it away before I got possession of it. I still have the bill-of-sale at home."

There were other mills built at the Morey Foundry. "One," said Morey, "was a five-stamp mill made for the Crystal Mine at Omo Ranch. The mine manager was an Englishman and they operated with English capital. One time his daughter came from England with friends and was showing them around the mine. She walked into the shaft, fell in a hole and was killed. The owner said he wanted no more of consolidated mining and went right back to England. They owed quite a bill at the foundry, so they told Grandfather to take every-thing, mine and all . . . they just wanted to get away. That's how our family got the patent to the Crystal Mine.

"Some miners, when they couldn't make a go of it, would skip town and not pay their bills. It wasn't just the foundry that lost but all the other stores in town that gave them credit." Morey continued, "Then there were the others. They were taking out lots of gold but wouldn't pay their bills. There was one up in Georgetown. Dad said that every two or three months, when the foundry needed its money to keep going, Grandfather loaded the men in a truck and brought them down with a shotgun . . . usually. That was the only way he could get paid."

He laughed as he recalled, "There was this mine over in Pleasant Valley. They owed a big bill. Grandfather got word they had cleaned up and were skipping out, so he met them at the Diamond Springs-Pleasant Valley crossroads with a shotgun . . . that was one that didn't get away." The family ended up with five patented mines in the county . . . through sheriff's sales or non-payment of debts for ma-chinery and supplies."

"I still own two mines," said Grimshaw, "the Pyramid, located nine miles from here at Rescue, and one in the Ophir district, near Auburn. You know, I did my first mining when I was about seven or eight years old . . . right on the Cosumnes River. I made about four bits a day . . . now that's fifty cents. It was rough in the summer when the water was low, but I did that for three summers. I usually made between $100 and $150 in the summer before I had to go back to school on my grandmother's ranch at Michigan Bar."

Encouraged by Mr. Morey, Mr. Grimshaw continued to tell other stories about his family.

"My great-uncle, Sebastian Keyser, came west with John Sutter in 1839. He helped start Sutter's Fort and he owned one-half of Johnson Ranch on the Bear River. My great-grandfather, Thomas Rhoads, and two of his sons, Daniel and John, were working at the sawmill when Marshall found the gold there.

225

Photos Morey Family Collection

THE FOUNDRY was first started by Mr. H. L. Hinds.in 1856. Henry Sylvester Morey leased it from Hinds about 1863 and later purchased the plant and property. It was located where the Vreeken Shell station is today (1975). Men identified by Henry Morey are from left: Jules Besse, Fred Allen, Bill Vivian, Al Radenmark and Frank Morey.

EXTERIOR VIEW OF FOUNDRY - Here H. S. Morey and his son Frank turned out patterns and built mills for the mines, supplied Michigan Cal and Caldor with castings for train wheels, built the engines used on Pino Grande cable, and cast the rims used for the Studebaker wheelbarrows.

FOUNDRY OWNER AND CREW - from left: Henry Sylvester Morey, Jules Besse, Fred Allen, Frank Morey, George Green and Gideon Jeffrey.

GOLD DREDGING on the COSUMNES - Rhoads Grimshaw on the Barkley Ranch in the 1940's. The gold closing order shut the operation down. To keep the dredge from being carried away by high waters, it was tied off by cable to rocks and trees.

THE RHOADS SCHOOL HOUSE, built in 1873 by members of the Rhoads family.

Photos Grimshaw Family Collection

"My folks, that is the Thomas Rhoads' side, left St. Joseph, Missouri, to come to California on April 5, 1846. They took the Oregon Trail route as far as Fort Hall, Idaho, then turned back into Wells, Nevada, and down the Humboldt River. They arrived in Fort Sutter on October 5, 1846, six months to the day from when they started.

"My folks were part of the Donner Party . . . no, I should say the Donner Party was part of my folks' wagon train. The first word of what had happened to the Donner Party was received at Johnson Ranch when W.H. Eddy strayed into the ranch-house to ask for help. Daniel and John Rhoads were with the first relief group to go to the help of the stranded emigrants. It was John Rhoads who carried little Naomi Pike out of the mountains to Sutter's in 1847.

"My grandfather, William Daylor, who founded Dry Diggins — you call it Placerville now — had a partner named Jared Sheldon. They worked for Sutter at the Fort. In 1842 they went out on their own and got a Mexican land grant and started with cattle. They had 25,000 acres. The size of a grant was determined by the amount of land encompassed within the area covered by a man, on horseback, riding from sunup 'til sundown, returning to his starting point. The Daylor-Sheldon grant ran five miles in one direction and eighteen in the other. You see, they had studied the land they wanted long before they headed out, so when the day came they knew just what they were after. It was said they probably changed horses along the run, but they got their land.

"Daylor married Sarah Rhoads in 1842 and Jared Sheldon married Sarah's sister, Catherine Rhoads. Daylor later became my grandfather. I was born on that Mexican land grant on December 18, 1890. My grandmother was the first white woman married in Sutter's Fort. Her picture, a very rare China painted picture, is hanging in Sutter's Fort." When Mrs. Rhoads found it too lonesome, living in the middle of 25,000 acres, he said, they sold land for ten cents an acre so she would have neighbors. Much of the land was taken over by squatters. Later, when children came along, they built a school house on the Jackson road. The building is still standing today on the Jackson road at Sloughhouse. When they could not get a teacher, Judge Grimshaw taught. William Robinson Grimshaw was the first judge in Northern California.

"Daniel and John Rhoads were working at the sawmill with Marshall when he found that gold and, like every other man there, they quit. They hurried back to the ranch to get tools and provisions to go prospecting. That's when Daylor, Sheldon, and a partner named Perry McCoon joined them and they headed for Coloma. On the way, they stopped at Weber Creek where that old railroad trestle was between Diamond Springs and Placerville; they took out $17,000 the first week. When one of their horses got away, they sent a Mexican

SARAH RHOADS DAYLOR

vaquero after it. He returned telling them he found the horse at a creek where gold was lying on the bed-rock (Hangtown Creek), so they went there to see.

"They were the first to work the place they named Dry Diggins. When they found it wasn't as rich as Weber, they turned it over to some people from Tennessee and returned to Weber. That's where my grandmother, Sarah Rhoads, panned out $5,000 worth of gold with a knife, spoon, and dish pan. She sent some back to England and had a watch made. The watch is still in the family . . . a cousin of mine has it."

Norma B. Ricketts, of Sacramento, California, wrote in the preface of her story, "Thomas and Elizabeth Rhoades," "It is hard to imagine that any family could be associated with more events which were part of early America than the Rhoades family . . . Readers will notice different spellings of the name . . . most of the Utah side of the family used 'Rhoades' while the California branches spelled it 'Rhoads'."

EPILOGUE

Rhoads Grimshaw died on December 21, 1974, while flying in a heavy fog near his Auburn home. His helicopter crashed after striking the top of an oak tree. He had circled his home, as he usually did, to let Mrs. Grimshaw know he was home. She said, "I went out and looked up, but the fog was so bad I couldn't see him. Then, the next thing, I got the telephone call."

Months after his death his widow fulfilled his promise of giving pictures and documented materials to complete his story. When doing so, she also told about the young Rhoads Grimshaw, a chapter of his life that has not been recorded in any of the many publications about his family.

"I know he must have told you about mining on the Cosumnes when he was six or seven years old . . . he always found a way to make money," said Mrs. Grimshaw. "He started early. The family had prunes on the ranch and when the pickers finished, he'd crawl on his hands and knees and gather all the prunes that had fallen. He took the sacks that his father had cast aside because of some small defect. He'd mend them and use them to sack his prunes. His folks said he made his own prune pit and lye. They didn't know he was doing this until the buyers came one time and he showed them his sacks of prunes and asked them what they would pay for them. They paid him $100 and from that day on his folks never spent any money on him. He made his own.

"He kept books when he was six years old. In the attic of their home one time we found his report cards, all A's, and records that he had

CAR AGAINST PLANE - *Rhoads Grimshaw accepted the challenge. It was a featured attraction at the California State Fair in 1913. Judges favored the plane...Grimshaw insisted he won. Earlier that same year Grimshaw was declared the winner in a grueling 42 hour round trip car run from Sacramento to Lake Tahoe. He drove a stripped 1909 20 horse-power Ford he had rebuilt himself. Only two other cars completed the drive which took them over snow covered roads from Phillip's Station on to the Lake.*

THE OREGON TRAIL ROUTE - *Rhoads Grimshaw, whose grandparents came to California in 1864 via the Oregon Trail, flew his helicopter over the route "every foot of the road" in August of 1973. He set down in the ruts still there where thousands of emigrant wagons had traveled.*

"JUST FOR A LARK" the 83-year-old pilot dropped in to visit a distant cousin, Judge Hanley of Lake Tahoe. He is pictured landing on Judge Hanley's pier. Grimshaw was flying planes before WWI.

Photos Grimshaw Family Collection

kept from the time he was six. His parents didn't realize they had a very brilliant child. He could make anything. He'd go to the dumps and find old clocks, anything that had a metal or mechanical part. He made little mechanical toys and boats that actually ran on water. He made automatic fishing reels before they ever had them . . . he sold his at Lake Tahoe and he made an air rifle long before the "Daisy" rifle came out. He never patented any of the things he made."

She spoke of his interest in automobiles. . . "He had his first car when he was fourteen years old. I remember when we first started keeping company, he was besieged with girls, and I told him it was because he had one of only six automobiles in Sacramento at the time."

In 1913 Grimshaw was the first to complete and win the Sacramento to Lake Tahoe car drive. One newspaper account said, "The first car to reach Lake Tahoe for the Sacramento Star Trophy was a 20-horse power Ford, driven by its owner, Rhoads Grimshaw, a young resident of Sacramento." The article told of his encounter with snow after reaching Phillip's Station and of his passing three other cars stalled and one buried in a ten-foot snow drift.

"He wouldn't give up on anything. If he set his mind to a thing, he did it. He was the same way with this search and rescue work he did. Shortly after he got his helicopter, they asked him to help, and he did. He knew all the country, the mountains and canyons, and I'm sure he was a great help to the Sheriff's department." From a collection of more than twenty letters and resolutions commending him for his help, one read: "Congratulations upon an achievement which proves that you can indeed 'teach an old dog new tricks'. Your example in earning a helicopter pilot's license teaches the rest of us that, regardless of age, we should not retire to the rocking chair but should continue to expand our abilities." Signed, Harold 'Bizz' Johnson.

Another read: "It gives me great pleasure to join the people of Auburn and Placer County in commending you for your unselfish contribution to Search and Rescue operations in our state . . . a tradition in your family, I am told, dating back to the rescue of the Donner Party in 1847. I send my warmest best wishes." Signed, President Richard Nixon.

Note: William Daylor founded Dry Diggins in 1848. His grandson, Rhoads Grimshaw flew into town one day in 1974 to visit his friends, an event that resulted in his recording for El Dorado county historical archives, the last interview he was to give about his illustrious pioneer family. His tape recording made with Henry Morey is on file at the El Dorado County Chamber of Commerce along with those of others interviewed for this publication.

Wubbena and Dixon Families

Mrs. Audrey Dixon Brown, when interviewed at her home in Sacramento, talked about both her maternal and paternal grandparents. Her grandfather, Gerget Mensen Wubbena, may not have been the first seaman to jump ship at Yerba Buena, but he could have been the youngest. He was born in Hanover, Germany, on November 22, 1822. During this period, every boy was pressed into service at the age of fourteen. When Gerget's turn came, he was "impressed" into the shipping service as a cabin boy. Unfortunately, he did not like the job and in 1837, at age fifteen, he jumped ship and hid in the sand dunes around Mission Dolores.

Mrs. Brown, whose mother was a Wubbena, said, "I was unable to substantiate what he did or how he survived until 1850. I learned through the California Historical Society and Bancroft Library that he worked for Vallejo. However, the records list him as Gerget Mensen, indicating that he probably had dropped the name Wubbena for fear someone would recognize the name and pick him up. From the Maritime Service in Honolulu I found that he was on a Holland ship in the East Indies when he no doubt heard about the discovery of gold in California.

"In 1850 Grandfather came back to California and homesteaded land. In 1853, he bought a squatter's right title to an adjacent piece of property. In 1854 he married Kristina Louisa Fritz, a native of Germany. They were married in "The Little Church Around the Corner" in New York. Records show he shipped out as a first mate, working his way back to California by way of Cape Horn. He brought his wife with him and settled in the town of Washington, in Nevada County; it's on the old back road from Nevada City to Emigrant Gap.

"Because he didn't have enough money to build and buy all the things they needed for the homestead, he went to work and drove stage for a while. Then came the smallpox epidemic in 1855, and Grandmother, who had had smallpox, nursed the pioneers and miners in that area. The miners in Washington presented her with a belt buckle made of gold from the mines there.

"When they settled in El Dorado County, he changed his land from brush-covered hills to the finest vineyards in the country. He had 15,000 grapevines. In late 1878 he went back to Europe. Carefully avoiding Germany, he went to France and brought a special kind of grape vine back with him. He had his own distillery and the place was known as the McDowell Hill Ranch, located about a mile and a half from what was then termed Nigger Hill. It's under Folsom Lake now.

(Inset) AUDREY DIXON BROWN

MR. AND MRS. FRED DIXON taken in 1897 or 1898. Mrs. Dixon was Emma Wubbena. They were married June 1896.

JAMES DIXON drives a stage coach in the Placerville Armistice Day Parade 1923.

Photos Audrey Dixon Brown Collection

"My mother, Emma Franc Wubbena, was one of seven children born on the ranch. Her brother, Charles Wubbena, was a butcher in Auburn. Nicholas and William both worked on the ranch. Rosena married Thomas Rust and there was another sister named Angelina whom everyone called Lena Wubbena.

"I remember my mother saying she walked four miles to school. That was before they had a bridge over the Middle Fork of the American River at Mormon Island. There was a rowboat that used to take them back and forth to school. When the river was too high they didn't go to school. Mother said there were two schools, the Mormon Island School and Negro Hill School. I have some of the textbooks my uncle had when he went there."

Her paternal grandfather was Henry G. Dixon, born on December 12, 1822, in Glasgow, Scotland. He married Miss Hannah Pickerskill of Yorkshire, England. They had two sons, William and Robert, both born in Waukesha, Wisconsin.

"Because we have no records to substantiate, we don't know when or why they left Wisconsin. However we do know they came down the Mississippi River on a flatboat as far as New Orleans. From there they went by boat to the Isthmus of Panama. Grandmother rode a mule across the Isthmus, holding one small son in her arms while the other rode in back of her. We don't know how they reached El Dorado County, but we have notes left by Grandmother telling where each one of the children was born.

"Their son, James Dixon, was the first white child born at Lake Tahoe. Charles Dixon was born October 18, 1864, George was born in Sacramento County on the Hagin Grant on March 29, 1866, James Dixon was born in Log Cabin #2 at Lake Tahoe on October 27, 1867, and Elizabeth was born April 27, 1869 at Log Cabin #2. So we know the family lived at Lake Tahoe in the very early days of California. The property referred to by the Lake Tahoe Historical Society as Marker #11 is land that my grandparents owned and sold to Charlie Sibeck.

"My father, Fred Dixon, was born at Middletown, just outside of Placerville, on May 18, 1871. He often told us that they were poor and that he was twelve years old when he was driving team. He drove a team of six horses over the summit when he was thirteen . . . so that would have been about 1884. He went alone and slept under the wagon . . . not only for warmth but because he always felt a little more secure close to the wagon wheel. When he was eighteen, he worked at Marble Valley for Mr. S.H. Cowell, or Henry Cowell, the head of the Cowell Company. It was Cowell and Davis. They started originally contracting cement work in Santa Cruz. He later bought the old property at Marble Valley. It had a rather poor grade marble that was used to make dust for putting in paint. That's what they are mining there today. I remember when they had two kilns and remnants of another one run by Taylor down on Deer Creek.

231

Photos Audrey Dixon Brown Collection

THE DIXON LIME KILN located in Marble Valley, south of the present highway 50 in the vicinity of Clarksville. Fred Dixon was 19 years old when he took over the management of the kiln, then owned by Cowell and Davis Company. "Lime was a poor grade of marble. They made dust for putting in paint. That's what they are mining there today (1975). Another kiln was operated by the Taylors down on Deer Creek. The lime was burned by Chinese labor using eight to twenty men during the summer months, giving work to many." Fred Dixon is left. Standing beside the horse, wearing long white apron, is Al Wing. On wagon is Robert Craig. Others could not be identified.

THE WUBBENA HOME was built on land homesteaded in 1850 by Gerget Mensen Wubbena. He did not build until after he had purchased a squatter's right title to an adjoining 160 acres. He turned the land from brush-covered hills to one of the finest vineyards in the county. He had 15,000 vines. In 1878 he went to France and brought back a special wine grape. He had his own distillery. The place was known as McDowell Ranch. Today it is under the water of Folsom Lake. Mrs. Brown could not identify the members of the family.

"Mr. Ernest Cowell was to be my godfather. In April of 1906 he took us to San Francisco and we stayed at the Union Square Hotel. I was baptized on Sunday. On Wednesday morning we were in the hotel when the earthquake hit. My father, along with everybody else, ran down the stairs to see what it was. Fires were breaking out all over. He went down to the Cowell Lime Company there and got one of the drays they used to roll barrels on. He could find only one horse. He took Mother, my sister and me, and some other people and we went to Mr. Cowell's home on Jackson Street. I vaguely remember riding out on the dray . . . everybody yelling and screaming. The next day they thought the fire was going to cross Van Ness and get into the area where we were. I have no conception of how we got there . . . but we went to Golden Gate Park and we were put up along with Mrs. Cowell and the Chinese houseboy . . . she had two or three helping her. We were in tents and my most vivid memory is of the soldiers marching back and forth, patroling the tents. We didn't see them . . . just their feet going by. We were out there for four or five days. Then father was able to get us across the Bay and we moved into a house in Oakland. That was before the days of Lake Merritt. The people who owned it moved out because they were afraid. They practically gave the house away just to get rid of it. My folks kept that home for a number of years."

Talking about her life in El Dorado County, she said that she was Queen of California at the Panama Exposition in 1915. She enjoyed horseback riding, and the Cowells were noted for their racehorses. "Whenever they had a horse that for some reason couldn't be used on the track anymore, he ended up as a saddle horse for me. Father was noted for having the best blooded stock in the county.

"Once I was riding a very spirited horse and Dr. Herman Davis, from Sacramento, had a new automobile, a roadster with the top down. My horse was not accustomed to automobiles. I think it was the first one he ever saw, and Dr. Davis was not an adept driver. He hadn't driven his car much. He'd only bought it the day before. My horse started plowing around and Dr. Davis, instead of stopping and letting me handle my horse, decided that if he blew the horn it would frighten the horse enough to get him away. Instead, the horse started to buck and ended up with his front feet in the back of the roadster. Another time, when I was eight or nine years old, we'd been over to Live Oak to visit Grandmother Dixon at the Clayborn home. It was fifteen or sixteen miles across the field, where El Dorado Hills is now. We noticed a fire had started up and the north wind was blowing. I was riding a flighty mare, not too well broken for riding. My sister, who was a polio victim, was riding in the surrey with Mother and Dad and Aunt Elizabeth. Dad had his hands full trying to outrace the fire and I wasn't strong enough to hold my horse. William Barton, for whom Barton Memorial Hospital was named, was in the area and saw what was happening. He caught up with me, turned my horse, and brought me out of the path of the fire."

JAMES DIXON was the first white child born at Lake Tahoe. He was the son of Henry G. and Hannah Pickerskill Dixon. He was born in Log Cabin No. 2 on the California side of the lake on October 27, 1867. This picture was taken about 1938.

Photo Yohalem Collection

James Wilson Marshall

The subject is one that could be carried on for a lifetime. But the limitation of space and time demand that the last chapter of "I remember" be written. I can think of no ending more fitting than one that would remind us of the man whose accidental discovery of gold at Coloma was responsible for bringing the subjects in this book to California. James Wilson Marshall was a man who should have become wealthy but died in poverty. Much has been written about his discovery and the impact it had on the nation and the world. Writers and historians will no doubt continue to pry into his life, some writing with reverence, others vilifying his character because of his weakness. Marshall was disliked and ridiculed by some of his fellow El Doradoans, but he had many friends.

An article paying tribute to Marshall was written by Miss Margaret Kelley, a school teacher and daughter of Mr. and Mrs. Patrick Kelley, neighbors of Marshall in the town of Kelsey. The *Mountain Democrat,* in its Seventy-Fifth Anniversary Souvenir Review Edition of January 6, 1928, printed Miss Kelley's tribute. Clarence E. Barker, publisher, and George C. Reeder, special editor of the Anniversary Edition, prefaced the story by calling it a valuable contribution to history.

Miss Kelley says, in part, "Having read so many misstatements about the great pioneer, even at this late day, I feel that in duty I should be remiss, did I not take up pen in defense of him I knew so well.

"I would have others know James W. Marshall as I knew him, during the last 15 years of his life, seeing him almost daily about his work in the old mining town of Kelsey, either in his mines, or doing carpenter work in his shop, or in the neighborhood. The sound of his anvil was always heard at some period of the day, as he shaped a piece of iron, or sharpened tools for mining purposes, in the old shop which is still standing.

"I would have the younger generation know the great pioneer as a citizen of the community, interested in the school and school children, patronizing school benefit balls, and attending school exhibitions; the first to applaud our youthful efforts, and unstinted in his praise always.

"I would have you see him as he walked, with great dignity, side by side with Rev. C.C. Peirce, to attend gospel services at the old Kelsey school house, where that pioneer preacher appeared once a month.

"I would have you see him visiting the neighbors, who were ill, for whom he had gathered medicinal herbs, whose virtue he knew so well and applying the same as tea or poultices; or using, or lending his galvanic battery for those who suffered from rheumatism, away back in the seventies, when that instrument was a new thing in healing.

"I would have you see him as I have seen him when he entered the house where the Angel of Death had visited. I would have you see James W. Marshall, the man benevolent, charitable to those in need, honest, so honest that dishonesty enraged him; courageously truthful; slightly embittered by remembered bitternesses; yet a man of sentiment, with an unforgettable regard for friends of the past, and an unmeasurable love for the neighbors among whom he lived and died.

"He had all of the distinctive qualities of the frontiersman, the warrior, the explorer, and the discoverer, and in some sense their frailties, as well.

"He drank, and sometimes too much, as many, many other pioneers did, as many, many others do, who were not pioneers."

James Wilson Marshall was one of the county's early pioneers, one who brought California to the attention of the world.

The real greatness of our El Dorado County pioneers lay in what they did. They came from all corners of the world, hopeful of fortune but determined to remain when the dream faded. The roots of the present lie deep in the past, and nothing in the past is dead to him who cares to know how the present comes to be what it is.

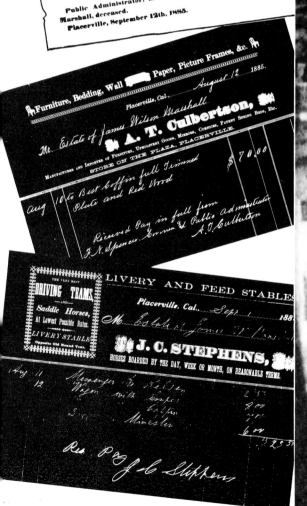

Photo Yohalem Collection

Acknowledgments

Preparing a book for publication, especially when it is your first, can be an exciting and frightening experience. Conducting interviews with the people whose stories fill the pages of this book was an experience I will remember always. I thank them for the gracious manner in which they received me into their homes and for their generous contributions of treasured family photographs and documents they entrusted to me.

I am especially grateful to Jacqueline Branch, El Dorado County Chamber of Commerce manager, for the confidence she placed in me to carry out her idea. She is to be commended for her foresight in originating this Bicentennial project for the County.

My gratitude is extended to the two successive boards of directors of the El Dorado County Chamber of Commerce, under the presidencies of Jack Tammi and Edwin Mathews, for their approval and to the El Dorado County Supervisors William V. D. Johnson, W. P. "Dub" Walker, Franklin K. "Budd" Lane, Thomas Stewart, Raymond Lawyer and his successor Floyd Kutter for their unanimous endorsement and support.

An enormous debt of gratitude is felt toward Wm. A. Steward, a personal friend. His professional expertise is responsible for the unique composition of this book. He donated an infinite amount of time and energy to the project as well as donating the space and production facilities of his business to put the book together. I am and will be forever grateful to him, his wife Anne, his daughter Barbara Hillmer and his son Alan for their encouragement and help in this effort.

I especially thank John Winning for his masterful technique in the revitalization of the old photographs reproduced for the book, and for the many trips he made over back-country roads just to capture some additional picture to add beauty and authenticity to a landmark mentioned in the book.

El Dorado County's beloved artist, George Mathis, generously contributed the covered wagon drawing for the book jacket and John Steward created the unusual posterization of an old photo for the end papers, each donating his artistry to the book.

That "I remember..." can be considered a community effort is realized by the number of individuals and organizations who contributed their time, talent and knowledge in many ways.

Invaluable guidance was given by Robert Greenwood of Talisman Press, Georgetown, publisher of "James Marshall" by Theressa Gay, "The Governors of California," "The California Gold Discovery" and many others. His years of experience and his sharing of information kept me on course.

Larry Belanger, editor and publisher of the Mountain Democrat, volunteered his time in the initial editing of the stories.

The volunteer women of the County Chamber of Commerce, the "Ambassadors," purchased the cassette recorder used to conduct the interviews, and members Evelyn Stanfield and Boots Leslie helped by transcribing a number of the tapes. Other volunteers who transcribed were Beverly Anderson and Mrs. James Anderson.

Kristine Rosenlof contributed innumerable hours of volunteer time when she transcribed 20 of the initial tapes.

Although the book is one of stories of individuals, some research and information for development was needed. To that end the following organizations played a great part for which I am most thankful.

James Sweeney, County Recorder, was most helpful in pointing out documents long stored in the archives of his department. Especially appreciated are those pertaining to the Emancipation Act.

The Lake Tahoe Historical Society, president Pat Amundson and Library Committee chairman Del Laine were generous in permitting use of their files when I visited the Lake area.

236

THIS WAS THE HOME OF ARTHUR J. AND DRUSY DHALLIN
The Drusy mine in the Indian Diggings area was named after his wife by Mr. Dhallin.

John Winning Photo

Gus Till, area manager of Marshall Gold Discovery State Park and park secretary, Carol Caldwell contributed pictures, diaries, and park history which were greatly appreciated.

Bruce Robinson, curator of the El Dorado County Historical Museum, was most helpful and Beverly Cola, museum committee chairman, devoted innumerable hours searching through the museum files for old pictures and documents. Her exceptional knowledge of El Dorado County history and its pioneer families was most helpful. To both I extend my sincere thanks.

Others who contributed were the El Dorado County Historical Society and the Heritage Association. County Librarian Alice Stjernquist and especially Bonnie J. Battaglia of the Georgetown Branch Library were helpful in securing the old files of the Georgetown Gazette and the picture of the first school in Georgetown.

The El Dorado County Friends of the Library made available outstanding tapes recorded by them in 1959 thru 1961. Copies of the tapes were presented to the Chamber of Commerce by President Daisey Miller. Their program of recording was suggested by former county Librarian Edith Gantt and was carried out by Claire Rosier Freeman, Isadene Raffetto Murry, and Charles Clifton at a time when Normadene Carpenter was president. It continued through the years with recordings made by Isadene Murray, Lizanne Barker, assisted by Harriet Smith, Dorothy Belanger, Barbara Berry and Holly Elliott. It is an important contribution to the county and while they did not fit within the format of "I remember...", the tapes will prove invaluable to historians in the future.

Individuals who also assisted in research and preparation were Betty Durrett, Berna Applegate, Charlotte Horvath and Mildred Gallion.

Special mention should go to Betty Smith and Beverly Cola, assisted by Betty Laarveld, Beverly Anderson, Billie Sue Wilson, and L'Marie Sanders, who compiled the index. To all who volunteered I am sincerely grateful.

Betty Yohalem

Index

Jinkerson House, Indian Diggings   John Winning photo

End papers - "Sunday Morning at the American Hotel - Georgetown, 1891."
A posterization by John M. Steward of a photograph from the Drysdale collection.